# Remarkable Women

Insight Publishing
Sevierville, Tennessee

# *Remarkable Women*



Published by Insight Publishing Company
P.O. Box 4189
Sevierville, Tennessee 37864

10 9 8 7 6 5 4 3 2

*Printed in Canada*

ISBN: 1-932863-34-6

## Table Of Contents

## A Message From The Publisher

If you poll a thousand people and ask them who had the most dramatic impact on their lives, 950 will tell you it was their mother. If you can get a married man to really open up about who motivates them, supports them, and gives them purpose for living, the vast majority will tell you it's their wives. Ask any Dad with one or more daughters and they will confess to being totally smitten by their little girls, regardless of how old they are. If you study history with a keen eye, you'll see how civilizations have advanced in no small part because of the courage, spirit, passion, vision, and brilliance of women. They are, without a doubt, simply remarkable.

Insight Publishing is proud to present a unique collection of remarkable women in this fascinating book. They will be quick to say, however, that *they* are not remarkable at all. In fact, many were reluctant to be in our book because they were afraid some would accuse them of being boastful or proud. To be honest, we asked each of these professional women to share their expertise and to highlight the impact other women have had on their lives and careers. We were delighted with the results!

As you read their frank and insightful interviews, you will find a treasure chest of information and inspiration that will help your business, your relationships, and your life in general. All of us at Insight Publishing are proud to know these remarkable women.

**Interviews conducted by:**

David E. Wright

President, International Speakers Network

# *Chapter One*

## Marcie Shepard

### THE INTERVIEW

**David E. Wright (Wright)**

Today we are talking to Marcie Shepard. Marcie is not your usual climb-the-ladder-to-success career story. In fact, she spent the first 20 years of her life being career-confused. On her 42$^{nd}$ birthday, she realized she was half-way through her career and still hadn't figured out what to be when she grew up. Her birthday wish that year translated into a birthday commitment to discover work that she loved. Marcie, welcome to *Remarkable Women!*

**Marcie Shepard (Shepard)**

Thank you, David.

**Wright**

Many people say you have had a remarkable career. Why do you think they say that?

**Shepard**

I think it's because I experienced such a dramatic transformation in my career. I went from 20 years of being career-confused to being career-clear for the past 14. It certainly did not happen overnight and it evolved along the way, but bottom line, I feel like my work-life now is somewhat of a miracle compared to what it used to be. Being totally career-clear impacts almost every other part of your life.

**Wright**

Totally career-clear... Exactly what does that mean?

**Shepard**

It means that you love your work. I love everything about my work. I love my clients, my seminar participants, my topics, my products and my revenues. It means that I love my marketing life style, my training schedule, which gives me 12 weeks off every year, and my travel logistics, which keep me within a 30-mile radius of my home. It means that I love my worker-style—that of being self-employed. I love it all and wake up every day grateful for what I have accomplished and thrilled to be looking ahead to more.

**Wright**

Wow, that is remarkable. So let's start at the beginning. How did you become career-clear?

**Shepard**

First and foremost, I made a commitment to becoming career-clear. On my 42nd birthday I committed to doing whatever it took in terms of time, money, and effort to figure out what I was supposed to be when I grew up. I came across a poem on commitment by W.N. Murray and read it over and over again. By continually re-reading it, I went from hoping it was true to believing it was true. It kept me persevering on my quest.

Next I became clear on one thing at a time. I became clear on the right role, the right topics, the right audience, the right clients, and the right marketing life style for me. In retrospect, I can say that becoming career-clear is like putting together a jigsaw puzzle. It takes a lot of pieces but once you have enough in place, you begin to see the picture.

**Wright**

How did you achieve all that clarity?

**Shepard**

In a variety of ways. I first had to discover the right role for me. I did this by paying attention to my inner body language when I saw people working. For example, I attended a public seminar and listened to the seminar leader describe what it was like to be a national seminar leader. The thought of travel, of teaching adults, of being self-employed—I could hardly contain myself every time I thought about it!

I attended a week-long retreat and at the end watched the woman in charge of putting the retreat together receive all kinds of accolades. I was so envious of her I could feel it in my bones. I analyzed my reaction and realized that I did not want to be a conference planner, but I did love the thought of public recognition. Another insight into who I was and the type of role that might be right for me.

During this time, I also read books on how to discover your "right work." One of them by Richard Bolles, *What Color Is Your Parachute*, suggested three steps: 1) Become God-centered; 2) Become self-aware; 3) Become other-focused. Deepak Chopra's book, *Seven Spiritual Laws of Success*, suggested asking two questions: "What are my gifts" and "Who shall I serve." I thought I wanted to be a speaker/seminar leader, but I didn't know if my "gifts" were the "right gifts" for that type of job. So I went to a career counselor and completed a series of assessments. They all indicated that I had the "right gifts" (the right personality style, the right interests, etc.) to become a speaker/seminar leader. Another piece to the puzzle.

**Wright**

Very interesting. What else?

**Shepard**

Prior to turning age 42 I had experienced a mid-life crisis. Out of a need to survive and to start creating a life that would satisfy me, I began reading self-help books and listening to motivational tapes. These books and tapes helped me become crystal clear in terms of the topics I was really interested in: Overcoming a crisis; Re-building Self-Esteem; Creating A Life That Suited You. I knew what I liked to learn and therefore I became clear on what I would like to teach.

The next question was, "Who did I want to teach?" I knew the answer was adults, but which ones? The answer came when the universe stepped in and offered me the opportunity of a lay-off. This was back in the early 1990's when thousands of people were being laid off. The lay-off was the kick-in-the-pants I needed to start my own speaking/training business. And the "who to teach" became very clear. My compassion became my compass. I wanted to help people who were being laid-off learn how to "turn their trauma into a triumph."

I spent the next few years focused on serving the unemployed through both keynote speaking at conferences and through offering half-day seminars. I acquired these opportunities through volunteer work, something I had devoted a significant part of my life to. I gave numerous pro bono speeches and from them eventually got paid speaking/training jobs. Over time, and through trial and error, I realized that I preferred seminar leading to keynote speaking because I enjoyed "playing with the audience" as opposed to being in the spotlight. Once I discovered this, I had another piece to fit into the puzzle!

**Wright**

This is exciting Marcie! It sounds as though you were well on your way.

**Shepard**

You're right David. At this point I had achieved clarity on my right role, my right topics, my right audience, and my right marketing technique. What was left was finding the right client. Although I loved serving the unemployed, I knew I would never make a lot of money at it. Since part of my "ideal job" involved earning significant pay, I had to determine where I could make the kind of money I wanted. Once again, through my network formed from volunteerism, I gained entrée into some major corporations in CT and began earning revenues that made my heart sing.

It's been a wonderful journey. My career now is better that I had ever imagined.

Discovering my right work has been the single most important thing I've ever done. It has enabled me to work with hundreds of unemployed people going through their transitions. I've been able to help career-confused people become clearer about their right work. I've been able to work with thousands of corporate employees in expanding their personal and professional development. And it has all been a labor of love.

Now my next step will be to help entrepreneurs gain clarity on the right marketing life style for them.

**Wright**

Why entrepreneurs and why marketing?

**Shepard**

Once again, my compassion has been my compass. Over the years I have watched many entrepreneurs make the heart-breaking decision to give up their business. They failed not because they weren't good at what they did. They failed because they hadn't found a marketing technique that they loved.

**Wright**

Can you share with us a little bit about this new business?

**Shepard**

I'd be happy to. An associate and I have put together a website which offers entrepreneurs audios and guidebooks on numerous marketing techniques. For example: 1) "A Day in the Life of a *Search Engine Positioning* Marketing Life Style"; or 2) "A Day in the Life of a *Volunteerism* Marketing Life Style"; or 3) "A Day in the Life of a *Written Newsletter* Marketing Life Style" or 4)"A Day in the Life of an *Endorsement Campaign* Marketing Life Style."

Once you have listened to enough of these to decide which marketing life style is right for you, you then can buy the "How To" material, which offers a multitude of ideas/steps to successful implementation of the technique.

**Wright**

Wow, that sounds like it is going to be incredibly helpful to entrepreneurs!

**Shepard**

We hope so David. My associate and I want to prevent other entrepreneurs from making some of the same mistakes we made. We both tried a variety of marketing techniques that worked well for others but did not work well for us. Through trial and error we finally came upon the technique that was right for us, but it took a long time. We want to shorten the marketing learning curve for entrepreneurs in the speaking/training/consulting business.

**Wright**

Marcie, I think you and your associate will be making a great contribution. Is there anything else you would like to share with our readers?

**Shepard**

To summarize David, creating a career that's right for you requires a great deal of clarity. Clarity in terms of who you are, your strengths, your weaknesses, your preferences, your dislikes. Some of the ways to achieve this clarity include: Making a commitment to achieve clarity, looking for role models, paying attention to your inner body language, reading career-focused books, going to a career counselor, completing assessments, allowing your compassion to become your compass, avoiding "paralysis by analysis" by starting it—even if you are not being paid and even if you are doing it imperfectly at first. The main point is that the more in alignment your work is with who you truly are, the more satisfaction you will derive from it.

Some people are fortunate in that they know at a very young age exactly what they want to be when they grow up. Others of us have to work at figuring it out. But trust me when I say it is worth every minute of it. Once you have discovered work that you love, you will be different from most. You'll be waking up on Monday mornings saying, "Thank God It's Monday"... and it won't be because you just had a terrible weekend! It will be because you have found work that brings out the best in you.

**Wright**

I have read so many books on the subject of work habits and what people think about work And I hate to use percentages, but I've seen them across the board from 87 to 93... you know all kinds of percentages for people who get up every morning and drive to the place they don't want to be. That would be like going to hell every morning, wouldn't it?

**Shepard**

Yes it would. The good news is we don't have to do that. If you take the time to find out who you are and then match yourself up with the right work, your entire life is different. Not just your work life, your entire life, because you get absolutely energized by your work as opposed to coming home on Friday night and barely making it to the couch.

**Wright**

What an exciting conversation!

**Shepard**

Thank you, David.

**Wright**

You've taught me a lot today. I'm going to go to my mental blackboard and write "clarity" a hundred times.

**Shepard**

And remember, David, there's this amazing phenomenon about truly committing to something. The description by W.N. Murray about the Scottish Himalayan Expedition describes it best.

*Until one is committed there is hesitancy, the chance to draw back, always ineffectiveness. Concerning all acts of initiative (and creation) there is one elementary truth, the ignorance of which kills countless ideas and splendid plans: That the moment one definitely commits oneself, then Providence moves too. All sorts of things occur to help one that would otherwise never have occurred. A whole stream of events issues from the decision, raising in one's favor all manner of unforeseen incidents and meetings and material assistance, which no man could have dreamt would have come his way. I have learned a deep respect for one of Goethe's couplets: "Whatever you can do, or dream you can…begin it. Boldness has genius, power and magic in it."*

**Wright**

Wow! Today we have been talking to Marcie Shepard. She's not the usual climb-the-ladder-to-success story as we will define in a lot of the chapters in this book. But I'm going to listen to her and try some of this "do what you love to do." I can't imagine how that would feel. Thank you so much Marcie, for taking so much time out of your day to be with us on Remarkable Women.

**Shepard**

It was my pleasure David. Thank you.

## About The Author

Marcie Shepard began her training company in 1991. Since that time she has led seminars for well over 12,000 people in the United States, England, and Australia. Within her second year of business, Marcie was named one of ten entrepreneurial success stories by the CT Small Business Development Center. During her work with Fred Pryor Seminars, she earned the title of "International Specialist." She was invited to deliver a presentation at the National Convention of the National Speakers Association in 1994 and 2004. She is founder of "T.G.I.M." (Thank God It's Monday)!

**Marcie Shepard**

Marcie Shepard Seminars

PO Box 288

Collinsville, Connecticut 06022

Phone: 860.693.8646

Email: marcieshepard@sbcglobal.net

www.marcieshepard.com

www.hoorayenterprises.com

# *Chapter Two*

## PATRICIA FRIPP

### THE INTERVIEW

**David E. Wright (Wright)**

Today we are talking to Patricia Fripp. Patricia has won every award and designation given by the National Speakers Association, including their Hall of Fame award. She was the first woman to hold the office of President in the over 4,000 member national association. *Meetings and Convention Magazine* called her one of the 10 most electrifying speakers in North America. Patricia is a keynote speaker and sales trainer for Fortune 500 companies and associations worldwide. Patricia is a speech coach for executives and celebrity speakers. She is the author of *Get What You Want* and *MAKE IT So You Don't Have To FAKE IT*, and the co-author of *Speaking Secrets of the Masters* and *Insights Into Excellence*. All of this is not bad for a young woman who became a hair stylist at 15 and arrived at the U.S. at 20 with little money and to contacts. Patricia Fripp, welcome to *Conversations with Women on Success and Leadership*.

**Patricia Fripp (Fripp)**

Good morning.

**Wright**

Meetings and Conventions Magazine calls you one of the most electrifying speakers in North America. What made you decide to enter the highly competitive field of public speaking and training?

**Fripp**

First of all, I have to tell you that that quote was a few years ago, but like every great line it can keep going forever. I believe that was actually in 1989 that they said that, but I would like to think it's still true! I entered the highly competitive world of public speaking, like so many other people, because it was very natural. I was traveling nationwide for a hair product company doing seminars for stylists. I was speaking in my local community to promote business to Rotary clubs, Kiwanis clubs. People started asking, "What would you charge to say that to my group?" Then when someone said, "You must go to the National Speakers Association Convention," which I did in 1977, that's when I realized this is what I can do when I grow up. In other words, I had entered the hair styling field at 15. When I went to the National Speakers Association at age 32 I was still loving hair dressing. I had my own salon I was building, I traveled nationwide doing hair styling shows, I had my hairstyles in magazines. I was doing well. I realized, though, when my lease was up when I was 40, I will have spent 25 years behind a hair styling chair, done everything that there is to do in hair styling as it was, and I didn't want to be an old hair stylist.

So I realized speaking might be something I could transition into. One of the most sensible things that I did was understand that this is a long-term goal and that I shouldn't quit my day job now, which I couldn't, I had a 10-year lease. Rather, I should use the next few years to use speaking to help build my business to the point that it didn't need my income so I could really devote my time to speaking. And that's what I did. It was a gradual thing.

When I became President of the National Speakers Association in 1984, which was actually a year ahead of the schedule, I sold my salon to one of my staff and went on the speaking circuit as it were. Over the years, how I make my living today, is very different than how I made my living in the first early years when *Meetings and Conventions Magazine* said I was one of the 10 most electrifying speakers in North America. Then I was primarily a keynote speaker. Now, although I still keynote conventions of 2,000 people, most of my work is actually with smaller groups. In fact, often I get the same fee to speak to 2,000 people as to talk to eight, ten, or twenty people in the boardroom doing sales presentation coaching.

**Wright**

Having booked speakers for 15 years, male speakers seem to outnumber female speakers by a wide margin. In your experience, has it been harder to make it as a female speaker?

**Fripp**

In the early days, when I first joined NSA, from 1977 to 1982, the speakers bureaus, for example, Mike Frank—who was the gentleman who basically discovered me and really helped me in the early days—would say to people (and this was true of all bureaus), "Would you consider a woman?" And sometimes the answer was no. Then it got to the point it was such an advantage because people were saying, "We want a speaker. We have to have a woman because we're now getting so many dynamic women." I used to say to people, "Look, I don't care if you don't hire me, but how dare you hire a male speaker when you've got 2,000 women in the audience? There are good women speakers." I would hear tales.

I remember speaking to one group, this particular group had been meeting for 79 years, and this was going back to the early '80's. There were 37 people at the head table if you can believe that. The guy said to me, "Not only are you the first woman who has addressed this group in like 87 years, you're the first woman who's ever sat at the head table." And there were 37 people up there! Those were interesting times and it was to your advantage. I remember one group was considering me or Ty Boyd. I said, "Why did you pick me?" They said, "Because of your gender." In that case, he said, "This is a male dominated industry, but we at least have to prove that we're modern thinking. So both your or Ty's message would be perfectly good. We know you'd both do a great job. We just need it to come from a female perspective." So you see, then it got to be an advantage. Even now, believe it or not in 2003, very often I'm the first female speaker. Less and less, but now it's more of an evening thing. And I think if you look at the National Speakers Association, you're probably going to find the membership is about 50/50. Admittedly, there are more established men, but that's true in any industry. However, you have some women speakers who are as successful, or more, than their male counterparts.

**Wright**

It seems that success has as many definitions as people who define it, not to mention the fact that success has personal meanings as well. How do you define success?

**Fripp**

For me personally I would say success is having the ability to control your own life.

**Wright**

So independence then?

**Fripp**

Absolutely, independence. I couldn't have said it better. Independence. When you work for yourself, and my entire life ever since I was 20 years old, I have worked 100% on commission or I've been in business for myself, creating any money that I or my little company spends, I have to make, and you look at it differently. I personally find a lot of security in that. Even with the economy down, I've never been as busy, so that's another part of flexibility. Bottom line, to me success is, well it's nice to be able to buy what you want, but it's really the ability to say, "I appreciate your inviting, but I have no interest in going there that time of the year," or "I really don't find a close enough connection to your audience that I choose to accept."

**Wright**

So more than money then, it's being your own boss.

**Fripp**

It's independence, feeling like you're in control.

**Wright**

I'd like to read a direct quote from you. "It never ceases to amaze me that intelligent, well-educated, and ambitious individuals frequently overlook the number one skill that is guaranteed to position them ahead of the crowd, namely the ability to speak eloquently in public." So why do people who want to get ahead not go to speech coaches?

**Fripp**

People that want to get ahead don't necessarily have to go to high-priced speech coaches. There are lots of ways to be a more effective speaker. For example, in 1975 one of my friends who was successful—a guy I had met in a self-improvement seminar—said, "You've got to go to Dale Carnegie class." Well, I love Dale Carnegie. I took the sales class, the speaking class, the management class. Then he said, "You'd better go to Toastmasters to keep practicing." Toastmasters is the least expensive way that you can practice on a regular basis in front of a supportive environment. I think everybody, absolutely everybody, should do something. People don't do it because, one, they're nervous to start with. So you are when you're skiing or driving a car or sitting down at a computer screen when you've never turned one on. Everything is scary to start with. That's part of it. We don't want to look like idiots and I guess a lot of people think they're going to look or feel foolish. Also, it's not a priority. A lot of people think, "Well, I'm good enough" and people say, "This is all right for you to say the importance of speaking, but I'm not a paid professional speaker. I don't speak in public." Another of my quotes is, "Outside the privacy of your own home all speaking is public speaking." There is no such thing as private speaking! Even if you are one on one networking, even if you are walking down the hall and step into the elevator and you meet the Chairman of the Board of your company, you've go to the 13th floor to say something that makes him or her remember you long-term that can be at your advantage, so that's public speaking.

**Wright**

Before I got into the business of helping and booking speakers 15 years ago, I had no idea that there was such a thing as a speech coach. Of course, I knew that Hollywood had coaches, but I didn't know the general public did. For example, if I were a car salesman starting out that's the first thing I would do. I would spend money in learning how to communicate. It's the difference between going to a health club and having a personal trainer.

**Fripp**

Yes. A lot of people contact me and I say, "You're not ready for me. Go through the different stages." For example, I always say to my clients or people who come to my website that I can help you no matter how much you've got to invest. If you have absolutely no money I've got hundreds of free articles, about the first 50 are on speaking.

You can even listen to some of my tapes over the internet free if you can't afford to buy them." Then we have tapes, CDs, books, speaking classes. There are lots of ways you can do it. There are lots of community colleges that have very inexpensive speech coaching. The secret is, with speaking as with using your computer skills, you don't take one class and think, "I've done it." It's an ongoing process your entire career to keep improving.

**Wright**

By the way, I do think that your website is one of the most generous that I have ever seen in any industry. You really do have a lot of free things in there. I hope that our readers will go to that site. It's Fripp.com. Some of those stories in there and Frippisms were really, really great.

**Fripp**

Oh good. I've been in business, as you know, for many years. I have good relationships with bureaus, I have past clients. I've got one client who buys me five days every year, who first booked me in 1986. So I've been around a long time with a lot of good backbone of clients and relationships with bureaus, etc. I get more legitimate leads from my website than any other marketing put together. It is not just put up a website and they will come. It is an ongoing, consistent, relentless strategy. It's one thing to go to Google to look for someone. It's another thing to go to Google and just look for a subject area. It takes time, money and energy to get to the top of Google.

**Wright**

Just how important are powerful presentations and speaking skills to business leaders and corporate executives?

**Fripp**

First of all, let's look at you as a new person in a company. You want to make your mark, your ambition. Speaking skills are so important because, one, you have to have confidence to introduce yourself in the cafeteria or when you're meeting people who are important to the company. Two, if you're in meetings it's very important to, if you have great ideas, have the confidence and the ability to share them well. Three, it is very important that you have the confidence or the skills to volunteer to run a meeting or do something like that which shows you're in charge. It's a great opportunity to, perhaps, get involved with your company programs as far as the United Way or something like this. All these things help position you. Then if you have to give a report to the management of your firm, for example, it's very important that people remember you and remember you positively and how you present your ideas—clearly and concisely. I always say to my speaking schools, "Welcome to Fripp world—the world of clear, concise communication where professional, powerful, persuasive sales presentations are the norm." That doesn't happen when you just get up and wing it. You think ahead of time. You think what is the best way, how can I say it in less words, how should I stand, how should I look, what should I wear, how is my eye contact. It's sort of getting off the subject, but I compare the sales presentation or a business presentation to a theatrical performance so we look at everything that is important in theatrics.

For example, Michael Caine said, "Rehearsal is the work. Performance is the relaxation." Rehearse. Jerry Seinfeld says, "I'll take an hour taking an eight word sentence and making it five because it will be more impactful." So edit your remarks down. The idea and comedy of the punch word at the end of the sentence. We analyze what salespeople or what people important to their boss say and make sure the most important word is at the end of the sentence. For example, one of the things that people do to step on their punch word is to add "today" at the end of the sentence. I'm very excited to present my report "today." No, report is the important word. If you must say "today," which you don't need to, but rather "today I will present to you," you will hear the results of my report.

So we literally analyze sentences one at a time to get in the habit of putting the important words first. Alan Alda said, "It's the stuff between the lines that make a good performance." In other words, pause occasionally! If you say something important, let people remember. So, one, it's important helping you on your career. Next, if you are going to a convention to run a trade show, that is whether you are speaking to people sitting next to you, whether you're networking in the hall, whether you're running the trade show, it's all public speaking. It's all public speaking. Then, if you are in sales and going out giving presentations or making a sales presentation, you have to be compelling. You have to be interesting.

**Wright**

You have stated that a company's biggest challenge in recruiting, retraining, and motivating is its most valuable asset, employees. You use a phrase I've never heard before, "Act as if their name were on the door—employees." Could you explain what you mean?

**Fripp**

Every company that you ever talk to will say for the most part their biggest challenge is getting and retaining the best employees. If we look at the employee's standpoint I would say the future belongs to the competent. However, we need to be more multi-faceted in our competence. We have to be charismatic communicators who are technically competent, have exceptionally good people skills, good work habits, an abundance of healthy energy. And I always tell people, "I don't tell you how to live your life, but it's very difficult to be a dynamic success if you don't feel well." Lastly, it doesn't hurt if you look good. Whether we like it or not we are judged on how we look. You might not like it, but you better get over it. It's a trueism. My mother, who was a very wise woman, always said, "Patricia, of course it's the inner you that counts, but you have to dress up and look good so you can attract people so they can find out how nice you are, how competent you are, and how valuable you can be to them." So that's the background from the employees.

We know in today's environment you're probably not going to stay around and get a gold watch, but everyone has to make a contribution to the company and the company has to make a contribution to them. I always say to audiences, "You are living in yesterday's world if you want to be employed. That is yesterday's world's thinking. We need to be employable and it takes different skills to be employable now than it has in the past, and it will take different skills to be employable in the future than it does now. A lot of these skills we don't know what they are. You just have to make an education out of every single day." Now, acting as if your name were on the door is making a decision as if you owned the company.

In my seminar and talks I give lots of funny little examples, but a couple of quick specific. My brother and I wanted to get into a movie house to see a movie. It was basically 10 minutes after it started and it was the last show of the day. I said, "We want two tickets. We know we're late. We don't care; we want to get in." The woman said, "You can't. We closed the drawer." I said, "Well put in the money in the morning." "No," she said, "not once we've closed up." So I go to someone else and say, "Look we want to get in. Let us in free, put the money in the drawer tomorrow or keep the money yourself." He was honest, but he wasn't empowered and he called the manager. We said, "Put the money in the drawer tomorrow. Let us in free." I mean, there were other people in the movie house. They weren't keeping it open just for us. She said, "No, not once people are late." As I walked out I said, "It's very obvious none of you here own this business because I always thought the number one key point in business is if people want to give you money, you take it." In that case they weren't working for the customer. They weren't working for the movie house. They were working for a paycheck. If we only work for a paycheck we're not going to be very valuable.

So you see, you make your decisions in dealing with customers as if it were your business. You have the ability, through your speaking skills and energy and appearance and involvement, to stand out. If there's a layoff, who's going to be laid off? Is it you acting like your name is on the door, who the Chairman of the Board actually knows who you are, or someone who's just going through the day? It makes you more employable.

**Wright**

Do you really think that today's employees can be motivated? Is it possible to expect and get loyalty?

**Fripp**

Yes, but you certainly have to understand that different generations are motivated different ways. I'm certainly not an expert. There's a young man called Everett Chester who talks about the Y generation and certainly, different generations are motivated different ways, but yes, we are motivated. What an employer has to do is find the best available talent and then put them in an environment where they are more likely to be motivated.

**Wright**

And be a good role model?

**Fripp**

I would say it isn't what you say you believe; it's what you model, encourage, reward, and let happen.

**Wright**

Leadership is another term that many find difficult to define. How do you define it, or to put it another way, what does a great leader look like?

**Fripp**

A great leader doesn't necessarily look one way. However, my favorite leadership quote is from General Eisenhower who said, "Leadership is the ability to decide what has to be done and then get people to want to do it." Again, especially if the business environment or your industry is challenging, to be an effective leader you have to be a charismatic communicator. I grew up hearing tales of Winston Churchill getting on the radio and would get people to fight in the streets just with his words. That was a leader.

**Wright**

You often work with entrepreneurs. They seem to be a different breed of businessperson in that they don't seem to have any problem with self-promotion.

**Fripp**

I wouldn't agree there. The successful ones learn how to be effective self-promoters. For example, I just landed—through my website—a very, very big account. The woman said, "One, you give away more information than everybody else." They couldn't believe that. Secondly, other people they were considering were quoting me. So why get a copycat when you can get the expert? Then the next thing she said was, "You're such a shameless self-promoter and that's exactly what we want our salespeople to be." Yes I am, but I'm a shameless self-promoter based on top of having something that people want to buy, I mean there is substance. I'm a shameless self-promoter; however, I know very clearly people don't care what we say about ourselves. They only care what flesh and blood characters like them say about us. All my bold claims are backed up with hundreds of references, whether it's speech coaching clients, speech coaching school, sales clients, audience members, or meeting planners. How many thousands of people can be wrong?

**Wright**

What are your plans for the future. In other words, what would make Patricia Fripp the most satisfied, happy, and fulfilled in her personal and business life?

**Fripp**

The most exciting thing for me actually is the feeling of competence. I grew up in England at a time when people didn't expect much of girls. My brother is one of these kids who was top of the class and has become an internationally acclaimed guitarist and musician, as well as being a great thinker. So, of course, growing up I thought well, I'm not as smart as other people; I better work harder. I got in the habit as a young person of working very hard, harder than everybody else. How I became a good speaker is exactly how I became a good hair stylist. I had good teachers, I practiced more than everybody else, and what got me to a whole new level was when I started teaching other people. One thing I say when people have been through a speaking school is, "Next thing you do is go find someone and teach them what you think I just told you, then you'll understand it." Now, and it boggles my mind, I sit either across the table from a client I'm coaching or with a sales team of sophisticated salespeople selling sophisticated solutions to other companies' sophisticated problem, and I'm telling them how to do it.

I think one very important thing is never forget where you came from. Any way you look at it, I'm a hairdresser who made good. When people say to me, "Where did you get your degree in behavioral psychology? Where did you get your MBA in Business," I always say, "Twenty-four years behind a hairstyling chair." The difference between me and most hairstylists is I took advantage of opportunity. Literally, as a very young person, I said, "What made you the best salesperson in your company? What did your little company do that a big company wanted to pay you millions of dollars?" Such an education. Part of building your career is just taking advantage of the opportunities. Every time you are somewhere are you going to be remembered? Patricia Fripp's basic networking philosophy: No point going anywhere that people don't remember you were there. Then, if anyone has a conversation with you, are they going to remember it? For example, the key to connection is conversation. The secret of conversation is to ask questions. The quality of the information you receive depends on the quality of those questions.

**Wright**

You made the point a while ago that it doesn't hurt to look good. It also doesn't hurt to have a great British accent!

**Fripp**

Thank you, thank you, thank you. For example, when you walk in to deal with a CEO or a very high-level Vice-President in a very large successful company, you need to know he knows I've got a custom-made suit on. I always remember one of my friends a few years ago, always very well-dressed and a very successful businessman, he was buying a new suit. He said to the salesman, "I've got to be honest. I can't tell the difference between the $1,400 suit and the $1,800 suit." The salesman said, "Sir, not many people can, but the people you want to impress know the difference." You can say that's a great salesperson, and it obviously is. However, people who are outrageously successful who are used to certain things feel comfortable when there is a connection. Whether it's only me, whether it's my self-confidence, or whether it's theirs. I like to say, "You might be brand new in sales and buy one good suit and five different shirts and ties. It's better to have one and look good because you don't want to look like you've never sold anything of what you're selling. They don't want to be your first client. Maybe you've just joined a successful company and you're new, but look like you've made plenty of sales."

**Wright**

What a great conversation. I really appreciate you taking all this time with me this morning to talk about success and leadership. I know how busy you are and I really want you to know how much I appreciate it.

**Fripp**

Well, certainly. Thank you .

**Wright**

Today we have been talking to Patricia Fripp. We have also found out why today that she has won every award and designation given by the National Speakers Association. Thank you so much for being with us. Before I leave I want to re-emphasize that at www.fripp.com you will get more information than most website I have ever visited. Thank you so much, Patricia.

## About The Author

Meetings and Conventions magazine calls Patricia Fripp, CSP, CPAE, "...one of the most electrifying speakers in North America." Award-winning and internationally-acclaimed professional speaker Patricia Fripp... her client list includes top corporations and associations, Fortune 100 companies and associations worldwide. Her high-content, high-performance, user-friendly delivery brings unanimous raves!

**Patricia Fripp**

527 Hugo Street

San Francisco, California 94122

Toll Free Nationwide: 800.634.3035

Fax: 415.753.0914

Email: PFripp@Fripp.com

www.fripp.com

# Chapter Three

## Doris Lee McCoy, Ph.D.

### THE INTERVIEW

**David E. Wright (Wright)**

Dr. Doris Lee McCoy is an author, a speaker, a consultant, and a psychologist. She also has television experience as a TV personality, and as a moderator/producer of three TV series—the last one was "The Changing Woman." She has been a professor for many years, and is a member of the Explorer's Club, which sounds very interesting. Finally, she has her own foundation, the American Spirit Foundation. Doris, welcome to *Remarkable Women.*

**Doris Lee McCoy (McCoy)**

Thank you, David. It's a privilege to speak with you and your readers.

**Wright**

Doris, let's talk about the books you've written. The *Magazine, Radio, and Television Interview Report* labeled you as an "American original." Why did they call you that?"

**McCoy**

I guess it was because I went on an unusual journey that most people do not take. I did it because I was concerned about the state of affairs in America. Many of our values seem to be slipping away. Our younger people don't seem to have the respect that we knew when we were growing up.

After my last book, *MEGATRAITS: 12 Traits of Successful People*, I realized that America had some major problems. Although our country is still the leader, we have a reservoir of power and strength that is starting to spring a few leaks. It was because of that I have carried my patriotism a little bit further than most people. So I decided to go around the country and find out whether our leaders were positive or negative about what was going on in our country. The question I asked them all was, "Where will America be in the next twenty years?"

As people mature, they want to leave a positive heritage to their children, grandchildren, and all the children of the world. When I started out I had no idea which leaders I would be able to meet. I was unknown to most of them. So the first question I asked myself was, would they even give me an interview? I was just a concerned woman from California who wanted to get insights from America's leaders. I learned very quickly that I had to pitch my request in six to eight seconds.

As a result, I was able to interview 100 well-known people like President George W. Bush, Senator Hilary Clinton, Colin Powell, Steve Forbes, Sandra Day O'Connor, Barbara and George H. Bush, Rudolph Giuliani, Senator Jay Rockefeller, and quite a few other interesting people who are making decisions for all of us. I wanted to do this for the average American who wouldn't have the opportunity to speak directly with these people.

**Wright**

How were you able to talk with all these well-known people, particularly since most of them didn't even know you?

**McCoy**

When you believe you are living out your God-given purpose in life somehow you are provided with opportunities. So then you can jump in and do it, or you can just ignore it. I obviously jumped in. Getting a few of the interviews required some ingenuity and creativity. For example, I was in Philadelphia on a business trip and I noticed Colin

Powell in the elevator. I didn't know where he was going, but I jumped right in. In about six seconds I made the pitch to request the interview. Of course he was not going to stop and do it right there, but at least I knew the secretary to go through that would enable me to get my request to his desk.

I stood in the rain for about two and a half hours outside of Beijing, China, to get my interview with the First Lady, Hillary Clinton. I painted out graffiti on a wall in Germantown, Pennsylvania in order to interview George H. and Barbara Bush. At one point, Barbara said, with a slight grin, to the former President, "If you don't work harder on painting that wall, they might fire us."

I had some very interesting experiences just getting to these people. I was attending an event at Xernona Clayton's Trumpet Awards at Turner Broadcasting, where she presents awards each year to the most outstanding African Americans in the United States. I had written to get an interview with Richard Parsons, the chairman of Time Warner, who was to be honored. I received a very polite "no," which I'm sure meant my letter went into the waste paper basket.

In Atlanta at TBS I was up near the stage after Richard had given his talk. We were asked to take hands to show a sign of solidarity, which we did. He happened to come by and take my hand. I was thrilled, because now I could tell him how much I appreciated his comments in his acceptance speech, and I also had the opportunity to ask him personally about the possibility of doing an interview. He said, "Just write a letter to me at my office." I replied, "I did, but I hear that you threw my letter away." Then he said very nicely, "Well, that's before I had a chance to meet you." Since then he has become a good friend. I often read about him in the newspaper, and send him congratulatory notes. He often is kind enough to respond. So it's interesting how one gets to meet these people.

**Wright**

I may call the *Magazine, Radio, and Television Interview Report* and tell them to change the *An American Original* title to *Gutsy Lady*. Did you get some strong opinions from these famous people?

**McCoy**

Yes. That's a good question, because many of the people that I have interviewed have confronted life's difficulties with solutions to those problems. They are passionate about these concerns. Through their actions, they have often made those strong statements.

Dr. Mimi Silbert believes that we can retrain people who have been incarcerated, drug addicted, and who often are homeless, and turn them into productive members of society. I doubted that at first, but later saw that she has been able to do just that through the Delancey Street Foundation.

Betty Flood Morrow, founder of the Women's Press Club of New York State, says, "Good news is hard to come by. People don't like to report it. It's not exciting and it doesn't sell newspapers or television."

Dr. Sylvia Earle, Advisor Deep Ocean Engineering, is very adamant about our treatment of the oceans. She is known by *TIME* magazine as "Her Deepness" and has gone to great depths under the sea. She warned, "It isn't just that birds are beautiful, that fish are good for our diet, or that clear water is aesthetically pleasing. It is that this is vital to our future. It's the future of all humankind, the food we eat and the natural food chain."

Patricia Schroder, President and CEO of The Association of American Publishers, spoke with me about her hopes for the future and her frustrations with today's technology. She said, "There are many days where I feel that technology is working on me and not for me. There is a great possibility that we can get that flipped around so that I'm not getting skimmed in me e-mail and I'm not getting 3,000 phone calls at home wanting to sell me vinyl siding. Where is the technology that can shut out what I don't want?"

Supreme Court Justice Sandra Day O'Connor said, "We see more and more a difficult environment for young people to get jobs—jobs that are interesting over the long pull and will be productive economically."

Delores Jordan, President of the James Jordan Foundation, and Author, lost her husband in a very unfortunate shooting accident. I asked her how she was able to put her anger behind her. She said, "I feel bitterness and hatred, but how does that help?" So with her foundation she has been out promoting better parenting, "Because the two kids that shot my husband did not have that support system."

Dr. Bettie Youngs, a well-known author, points out that some people are like "tasteberries," an Asian fruit that puts a sweet taste in your mouth. Some people that we pass by during the day can give us a special "tasteberry," that enable us to deal more constructively with the negativity we may experience from others.

Yue Sai Kan, businesswoman, television personality, and major producer of cosmetics in China, tried to find a Chinese doll for a friend's child in China. The only ones she could find were very peasant-like characters, so she went off and started a company that is now producing Chinese dolls that are on a par with America's Barbie dolls.

Reeve Lindbergh said of her mother, Anne Morrow Lindbergh, author of *Gift From The Sea, wife of Charles Lindbergh,* "I remember mother saying that it was important to stay open, remain vulnerable throughout one's life, no matter what might happen along the way. I think she has done that herself, and it is one of the reasons why she had an effect upon others. On the journey toward insight, she chose to travel alone, openly, and unarmed. It is a very rare and very brave choice to make."

More shocking were some strong opinions I got from John Walsh. He believes that we should legalize some drugs. John felt that too many women are in prison who were just trying to help a boyfriend sell a few les harmful drugs. He said, "A lot of times these women don't even have a decent education, or marketable skills that would enable them to get a good job."

John felt that somebody selling a kilo of drugs should be penalized for that, but that anybody who had a little bit of marijuana should not face the same punishment.

**Wright**

What would you summarize as the key points? Were those you interviewed negative or positive?

**McCoy**

They were very positive, but what I liked was that they gave me the challenges that all Americans must face. Many of those points most people are aware of, but it's useful to see them written down. These challenges are listed in order of the number of times that they were mentioned. With the 100 people, it is a large enough sampling to show indications of what other leaders might say.

First of all, we all know we're in a period of radical change. For example, it is very hard for people who have not been brought up on the computer to suddenly have to learn this new tool. Second, there is a need to restore the family and community. Third, there is a strong emphasis on the need to revamp K-12 education. However, the leaders felt our higher education is outstanding. They suggested doing more experimentation, opening more charter schools, bringing in new ideas in our K-12. But to try to teach all students by the same approach, and to have the same goal seems not to be realistic. Sandra

Day O'Connor said we also need to learn how to teach values, and also that students should be encouraged to contribute to society. That is not being done at this time.

The fourth point is combating drugs, alcohol, and violence. I am pleased to say that I saw an outstanding program in action. Dr. Mimi Silbert, President of the Delancy Street Foundation in San Francisco, is a little five-foot lady who is doing a remarkable job in that respect. She has learned how to help four-time incarcerated people, who would go to prison forever if they did not make it through this program. Her project enables them to turn their lives around and become productive members of society. It's one of the most successful programs in the country. She has five centers now, and her time is greatly in demand by others for sharing her ideas and solutions to this major problem.

The fifth concern is the need for communicating better verbally and technologically. Sixth is cooperating and competing in business while valuing our customers and employees. Seventh is reawakening our national spirit. The recent election with the huge number of people who voted certainly indicated people's concern for our democratic system. Eighth, raising our ethical standards and ninth, encouraging the media to elevate its message. Tenth, embracing our spirituality. Eleventh, safeguarding the environment and knowing that it does indeed have limits. Twelfth, resolving some pressing health issues. The last section deals with the quality of life. Writing the book and meeting these people was a great journey. It took a long time and at times was difficult. I spent a lot of mornings getting up at 3:30 A.M. and 4:00 just trying to complete the book, but certainly the interviews were never boring. I would come home and be elated for days after hearing the stories of these interesting people."

**Wright**

I know how you feel. Some people have called your *America's New Future: 100 New Answers* a modern-day history book. Would you agree?

**McCoy**

I think that's true. Delores Jordan agreed. She is head of her own foundation and is the mother of Michael Jordan. This book, under one cover, documents what's going on during this crucial time in our nation's history. By putting these interviews with 100 American leaders all in one book, I tried to make it possible for the average busy person to be able to pick it up and get a feeling that they know something about these people, personally as well as professionally. All of these interview can be found in a book called, *AMERICA'S NEW FUTURE: 100 New Answers.*

**Wright**

I'd like to talk about your other book, *MEGATRAITS: 12 Traits of Successful People.* What were the main ideas that these men and women came up with, and were there any that really surprised you?

**McCoy**

*MEGATRAITS* was spurred on by what I heard as a psychologist. Over and over again, my clients complained, "Oh, if my mother only had done this, or if my father had done that." They often were actually using this as an excuse for not getting on with their lives. It enabled them to stay "stuck." They actually could have learned from these situations if they realized that many of our leaders had similar barriers to their success. Since they would not necessarily believe me if I tried to tell them, I decided that I would go around the country and ask some well-known people for their wise advice. I chose people like Malcolm Forbes, Sandra Day O'Connor, and Ronald Reagan. Through the interviews, I formulated a list of 12 traits that were important to their success. The number one trait that I heard repeatedly, which amazed me, was that they were doing what they had a passion for.

**Wright**

That makes sense.

**McCoy**

Today it seems like we have moved, as a country, from doing things that have value and worth to focusing more on how much money can be made. We all know that money is important and it's essential for living and paying bills. However, if you can find a job that really excites you to get up each morning and go off to work, that's what makes it more fulfilling. That trait was found at the top of the list.

Another point was that all of them had negative experiences. Some of us may see a bad situation and label it "terrible." The successful would say the same, but follow it quickly with, "How can I do something about this? How can I turn this into a positive situation?"

**Wright**

Are you saying they were change-motivated?

**McCoy**

Absolutely! Our leaders are so used to change that it's just a part of their lives. But what it also reminded me of was the fact that colleges never have a course called Failure 101. I have never seen it, I don't think it exists. Yet 50% of these people, without my prodding them, would say that their mistakes taught them more than their successes. I think that's extremely important to emphasize, because as parents, we should teach children how to deal with their difficulties. We should tell them there may be difficulties, but these problems should be looked at and dealt with instead of avoided. I think that would be very helpful to our children.

**Wright**

As you go around the country speaking and consulting, do you often use the results of your research for your books in your speeches?

**McCoy**

Yes, I always give a handout like the "12 Traits of Success" to people in the audience. It enables them when they go home to display the list in a prominent place and evaluate their progress. In the research that I do, there is a large enough sampling of individuals that enables me to find trends, so this research is valid. In my talk, I give them the principle, then I support it with a story. This is the same method that professional speaker par excellence Dottie Walters uses. She is a storehouse of knowledge, and in her speeches she will give a statement and then support and illustrate it through a personal example. Some of the examples I use are those of Ray Kroc and Michael Jordan.

Ray Kroc, Chairman and Founder of McDonald's, would say, "Persistence is a very important trait." Most people don't know that Ray was turned down time after time for a loan. Finally on his eighth attempt, the bank gave him the loan that enabled him to start McDonald's. This also points out that we often see the successful part of a person's life, rather than the hard work it took them to attain such acclaim.

If you can believe it, Michael Jordan was rejected when he tried out for his first high school basketball team. He went home discouraged. It was only through his persistence and the support of his parents that he kept working at it. Finally, he was invited to join the team. He is now looked upon as the most outstanding basketball player of all time.

**Wright**

As we consider your speaking and consulting business, what topics do your audiences most often request?

**McCoy**

There are three main topics requested by audiences. A lot of people are interested in the *Traits of Successful People*. At the end of the speech, I always go into the audience and interview two or three people that I have chosen ahead of time, who are willing to talk about their successes. They mention the challenges that they've had, and how they dealt with them, which in the end enabled them to succeed.

The second topic people want to know about is *Where Will America be in the Next 20 Years?* These projections enable companies and individuals to look and plan ahead, giving them an edge on their competitors. It really puts them in a good position to know what they can count on. It provides them with insight on what problems and issues need to be addressed. It helps people project what they want for their American Dream.

The third topic that is a popular title is *The Four Faces of Eve*. This Jungian psychology method looks at the four different personality types, which are the Mother, the Heitara, the Amazon, and the Medial Woman. It will help them to know what kind of woman they are, as well as others, and how to approach other individuals.

**Wright**

You've really fascinated me here on your bio, the fact that you've done three television series and 20 TV specials. Why is this medium so important to you?

**McCoy**

Actually I started doing my first television show when I needed a house payment. I had no background in television. I knew that the payment was coming due, and that something needed to be done for my family, or else I would have to move my children to another location. So I went to the manager of a San Diego television station and somehow this wonderful person at NBC realized my enthusiasm about a program for women and asked me to come and do it. "Of course," he said. "You know how to moderate and produce this, right?" I looked up at the window and could see the money I had been promised sprout wings and fly away, so of course I said yes. I went home that night, called a friend who knew about television, and tried to learn quickly what it meant to produce a TV show. It was a great experience as it turned out, and I was hooked on the magic of TV.

Most people are getting their news information from television these days. I always like to do a TV series in which the viewing audience can learn something that they can take away and use in their lives or with their families. It has been documented that women who do take time to watch educational programs derive benefits for themselves and their families. We see people on TV who are in far away countries, giving us information. It's very exciting because it brings us right into what is going on.

I've covered three of the Women's International Year Conferences, and was able to bring that information and personal interviews back to America. I was asked to do the first of a new series on PBS radio called "These Days," with Gloria Penner, who interviewed me. It happened while I was sitting in my bedroom in Beijing, China. It was the end of the first day of the conference, and it was 12 midnight in Beijing, while it was 9 o'clock a.m. in San Diego. As people were driving down the freeway on their way to work, they were calling in and asking questions about the event. I know it happens all the time. We watch *CNN* and some of the other programs, but it was so exciting for me to experience the speed with which we are able to connect with other parts of the world.

One of my hopes is to be able to get on the Oprah Winfrey's show. Not because I could say, "I've been on Oprah Winfrey's show!" although that would be nice, but because I think that the information from those I interviewed in my new book, *America's New Future: 100 New Answers*, would be extremely important for her audience to hear. She has such a large following.

I'm impressed by what Oprah is trying to do in South Africa and what she did for 50,000 children when she went there, giving them backpacks, tennis shoes, and balls. For some of them, that probably was the first and only gift they may ever receive.

**Wright**

Well, the next time I see her, I'll just ask her. Moving on with our theme of being a remarkable woman, which obviously you are, what are some of the things you enjoyed best about teaching? What was a main lesson that you learned?

**McCoy**

One lesson that I took away from my 17-year experience of teaching communications revolved around the Pygmalion theory. The theory is that if you tell people they are going to respond in a certain way, they often will. I decided to try it out on my students. On the first day of class, I would say to them, "I am so lucky because the dean has given me the best of all the communications classes. I look forward to the interesting speeches that I know you will be making."

Speaking is a very frightening thing for many people. I would always say, "Who has a one minute story to tell us?" or "What about the most exciting thing or the most frightening thing that ever happened to you?" About fifteen students usually would get up and speak. Then at the end of that first class, I would say, "Look, 15 or 17 of you have already made a speech." They would look at one another in disbelief and say, "What does she mean?" Good speaking, I would tell them, is often related to being a good storyteller.

**Wright**

There's one thing that really fascinates me about your career...is it a career or a checkered past?

**McCoy**

I don't know, but I keep doing it. I keep trying to create something new, as I'm doing right now by being a participant in this book.

**Wright**

The Explorer's Club—tell me why you joined this group. It seems a lot different from your other areas of work.

**McCoy**

My first experience in connection with the Explorer's Club was when I was doing a live television show in New Orleans. I was at NATPE, the National Association of Television Program Executives' annual meeting, where I had a chance to interview Jim Fowler, host of *Wild Kingdom*. Jim is a six-foot nine individual and very kind—up to a point. I say that because I was asking him a serious question about endangered species when I felt the pressure of something separating my feet. I started thinking about all the animals that I had seen in his exhibit there in the room. Then I made the mistake of looking down and lo and behold, there was a 12-foot, 150-pound python slithering, pushing my feet apart as it went.

**Wright**

Oh, wow!

**McCoy**

I'm usually pretty cool about that sort of thing, but this time I was totally shocked, and my response was immediate. I threw the microphone in the air, to the great pleasure of my cameraman who said, "I've never had such a good thing happen while I was videotaping." I picked the microphone up and went on because it was a live show. So the whole audience had a chance to laugh along with Jim, who thought it was quite funny. After that experience, Jim invited me to join the Explorer's Club.

The Explorer's Club is a wonderful group of people who are out on the cutting edge of scientific research and exploration long before the tourists get there. I've done a couple of expeditions, and gone to 15 rain forests. One of my last expeditions was in a former headhunting village, which was quite a scary experience for me. What is possible on such expeditions is you can bring back stories of what you've learned in that environment. Ecuador provided an experience that translates into a story.

Paa, the best hunter of the Warioni Indian tribe, spoke to me once for 5 minutes knowing that I couldn't understand him and he couldn't understand me, but we both had respect for one another so we both listented. I watched him all week. He was so enthusiastic about whatever he did. He encouraged others, including children, to win in contests. I suddenly became aware that he had many of the same leadership traits as Malcolm Forbes. I thought, 'Isn't this exciting?' This man had never been out of his remote village. It was way back in the bush, and one could only get there by taking a small bush plane. He couldn't read, and yet his story was something that could be equated with leadership skills that I can use later in the American business world.

**Wright**

Goodness! The last question I have for you is about the American Spirit Foundation. I guess you are the founder. Why did you start it, and whom does it benefit?

**McCoy**

It primarily benefits young people and helps them to identify their potential or what they have a passion to do. I think that we need a system whereby young people can formulate realistic expectations about what a specific career entails. For example, many want to be rock stars or basketball players, but there aren't too many people that are going to be able to really do that. I think they are attracted to the huge salaries and the celebrity status that goes along with those jobs. What I'm trying to do is help young people find their potential.

I'm in the process now of looking for funding to do a television series that would have some of the 100 American leaders talk about the realistic side of job possibilities. So that's what the foundation is about.

I have focused on writing books that could be of help to young people, such as *MegaTraits, America's New Future: 100 New Answers*, and *Movers and Shakers*, to give young people a realistic look into the lives of some of these people before they decide to jump into a career. Now I'm also hearing that there is a mid-life point with both men and women at which they are interested in alternatives to their originally chosen careers. If women have stayed at home, they often want to broaden their lives and go outside. If they can realize what some of these successful people are saying even about those middle years, that would be of help.

**Wright**

Well, what an interesting conversation. You have enlightened me here today. I want to tell you how much I really appreciate you taking time to be with us.

**McCoy**

Well, I'm grateful because, you know, if you work hard on something and you have a passion for it, it's never long or hard. I consider it a privilege to be able to talk to you and other people and share what insights I've received in interviewing these well-known individuals. My advice to readers who are trying to find new alternatives would be: Take a look at the things you do well. Put them down on paper. Some are interests and others are avenues that you could follow seriously as a profession. I always encourage my audiences to choose a field that they see as their passion. Dick Parson, Chairman of the Board of Time Warner, said, "Choose a career that will have an ongoing positive effect and that will be helpful to society. And that will give you great fulfillment." Eugene Lang, founder of I Have a Dream Foundation stated it another way, "Get a good idea and multiply it." Today there are 69 *I Have a Dream Foundations* around the country.

One thing I have tried to do during my lifetime is to show that an average citizen, without necessarily having a lot of money, prestige, or background, is able to make a significant contribution.

I'm sure there are a lot of great ideas out there that women have. They are especially adept at negotiating. Women are gifted in ways that come from the heart and soul. I think their contributions will be appreciated if they just get the inspiration and take some initiative to move on it. Sometimes it's an internal struggle to find the courage and the inspiration just to take the first step, but do it.

**Wright**

Well, today we have been talking to Dr. Doris Lee McCoy. She is a psychologist, moderator/producer of television series, professor, and author of a new book, *AMERICA'S NEW FUTURE: 100 New Answers*. What a remarkable lady you are! Thank you so much for being with us today on *Remarkable Women.*

## About The Author

Doris Lee McCoy was born in Pittsburgh, a high school leader, attended Muskingum College, and received one of fifteen Danforth Foundation scholarships. Following that she received her Masters at Stanford University in Guidance & Counseling. She married, raised three children, helped start Johnson College, went back to college and received a Ph.D. from Claremont University. She is a Psychologist, international speaker, author of three books, moderator/producer of TV, professor. She does research and expeditions into fifteen rainforests, and founded the American Spirit Foundation. She lives in La Jolla, California.

**Doris Lee McCoy, Ph.D.**

President McCoy Productions

President, Founder American Spirit Foundation

Author, AMERICA'S NEW FUTURE:

100 New Answers

www.on.to/americasnewfuture.com

To order call: 1.888.280.7715

Or

www.barnesandnoble.com

www.amazon.com

AMERICAN SPIRIT FOUNDATION

Is a 501 3(c) non-profit organization

www.americanspiritfd.com

To book a speaking engagement contact:

Phone/Fax: 858.459.4971

Email: dorismccoy@aol.com

# Chapter Four

## JOAN BURGE

### THE INTERVIEW

**David E. Wright (Wright)**

Joan Burge is the founder and CEO of Office Dynamics, Ltd, an international leader in the development and presentation of sophisticated training programs and information for administrative staff and business professionals. She also works with high level executives to ensure that they are fully utilizing the talents of their staff and provides insight as to how they can improve their overall working relationships. Joan is the author of four books and 12 workbooks. She is the editor of *Monday Motivators*, and has been published in more than 54 trade journals. She is a member of the American Society for Training and Development, the National Speakers Association, the Southern Nevada Human Resource Association, National Association of Female Executives, and the Las Vegas Chamber of Commerce. Joan, welcome to *Remarkable Women*!

**Joan Burge (Burge)**

Thank you very much.

**Wright**

Well, to start off, when you were growing up, who were the women in your life who most influenced you?

**Burge**

There were two women who had a strong influence in my life. My mother was a huge influence and my grandmother, my mother's mother. Even though she was a quiet influence, I admired many things about her.

**Wright**

So how did their lives influence you and help you succeed in life?

**Burge**

Both women were very strong mentally. They were strong in their beliefs and values. Both were courageous women. My grandmother was born and raised in Italy. When she was pregnant and carrying my mother, my grandfather brought her to America. When I think back to those times, that really took courage for my grandmother to come to a strange country, learn a new language, and leave her entire family behind. She lived in the United States until the day she passed away at the age of 97. My grandmother was a wonderful role model. As I said, she was mentally sharp; very in tune with what was going on in the world and with her family. She always had a zest for life. She had a lot of energy. She loved music, dancing, singing, and cooking for family. I learned a lot in terms of family values growing up in an Italian family. I was raised with the paradigm that family is very, very important.

My grandmother, Mary Adorney, did things that were incredible for her era such as getting her driver's license at 65. Prior to that, my grandfather drove her everywhere. Then he had a stroke and she decided to learn to drive. I'll never forget the day because I was 16 and had just gotten my driver's license. Our picture appeared in the local newspaper. I still have it in my memories! She was a very independent woman for her time. She lived in her apartment with my grandfather for years and then my grandfather passed away. She refused to live with any family members. I believe she was about 94 or 95 before her children placed her in a elderly care center.

**Wright**

Right. And your mother? I understand she had an incredible life.

**Burge**

My mother was an incredible woman! Her life could be a chapter in itself in this book—she truly was a Remarkable Woman! I'll do my best to do her life justice and explain the impact it had on me.

In the early years of my growing up and even through my early teen years, my mother had an almost fairy-tale like life, in my eyes. My father and her were madly in love! We had a lovely home with a built-in swimming pool. Went on a great vacation every year. My parents loved to entertain as well as go out with friends. They lived and loved life to its fullest.

My mother was a very loving and insightful woman. I loved being with her as she was bright, happy, nurturing, and very pretty! She was also tough on me. She wanted to raise me to be a proper young lady. She was strict and was good at disciplining me and enforcing rules.

As I got into my teen years, I noticed my mother liked helping people. She especially liked helping women who were going through difficult situations in their lives, whether it was their husband was cheating on them or they were in financial need. It didn't matter what their problem was; she just wanted to help them cope. She also loved to read and write. During my high school years at Notre Dame Academy (an all girl, Catholic school) in Chardon, OH, she came once a week to talk to us young women about "girl" things like dating. Life seemed to be going along very nicely.

I graduated from high school in 1970. It was about a year later, when I was engaged to my first husband and getting ready for a fairy-tale wedding my parents had planned, when our entire life changed.

It seemed like out of nowhere came bizarre behaviors from my mother. She was saying what appeared to be "crazy" things. It was a very scary time for me, my sisters, and my father. We didn't know what was happening to her. What happened to the mother I knew? Where had she gone, mentally? Why was she behaving the way she did?

One night my father invited several family members to come to our house to see my mother and possibly provide advice for us. He also invited a very good friend, who was a doctor. While everyone was at our home, my mother started saying things that made absolutely no sense. She was on her own "high." As the doctor left our house that evening he told my Dad that my mother was a sick woman and he needed to get her to a hospital. I can't remember his exact words, but he referred to her being mentally ill.

And so the next day, I helped my Dad convince my mother to go to the hospital. We drove her to a highly-recommended hospital in Cleveland. So many years have passed since then that it seems vague to me now exactly what happened. I only remember things like her being locked up; leaving her all alone; her not being able to keep any personal belongings; and my Dad and I going home stunned.

My mother was diagnosed with severe manic-depression. In those days, manic-depression was not something you talked about to your friends. It was seen as something horrible and even embarrassing. The way doctors dealt with it was to put a person in a hospital behind locked doors and drug them till they hit rock bottom. Or use shock treatments. All of which happened to my mother. Then they would have to try to bring the person back to a normal level so they could be more balanced.

This see-saw of highs and lows went on in my mother for more than 20 years! She tried to commit suicide three times. Thank goodness she was unsuccessful each time. But I still remember rushing to the emergency room and seeing her laying in the bed, wishing she would die. That is how horrible of an illness she had. One time, because she thought she could smoke, she started a big fire in our gorgeous big home. There are many stories I could tell you that would be unbelievable to you or our readers. Of course, there were several times when she was on a real high and she would go on shopping sprees and have a ball! My Dad would come home and find all kinds of boxes had arrived with things she bought for the house. We can laugh about it now.

There were many times when my mother was stabilized and her and I would have marvelous conversations about life, kids, family, my work—all kinds of things. I cherished those moments with her because she had so much insight. Sometimes she realized she had an illness and her life had changed as a result. I won't go into all the details. Eventually her and my Dad separated. My mother met a widower who spent several years with her in their little apartment. It seemed like the fairy tale was over. My Dad remarried. They both ended up with great mates for the latter part of their lives. And yet it was still so poignant for me because our family wasn't the same any more. I'm happy to say Dad is still alive, running his business, enjoying his wife, Liz , and will be celebrating his $80^{th}$ birthday in March 2005!

**Wright**

So what was the greatest lesson your mother taught you?

**Burge**

The greatest lesson my mother taught me was, in her own words, "Embrace life with all its hurts, sorrows, and good times. Don't shy away from pain or difficult times. When you are sad, be sad. And when you are happy, be really happy. It's all just part of this wonderful thing we call life." I have never forgotten those words.

A few other lessons I learned from her illness are: Enjoy the good times because the rainy days are sure to come. Make the most of every day. Laugh during the hard times. Try to keep a sense of humor. It helps get through the situation. Love yourself! Love life. Love others! With God, you can overcome anything. After you're married, make sure you and your husband have a night out by yourselves once a week. Don't stop "dating" like when you first fell in love.

**Wright**

It's amazing how you remained strong through her illness. How did you do it when you were working 40, 50 hours a week, married with two children under the age of three?

**Burge**

It was hard. At that time, I needed to work. I was married and we had two little children. While I lived in a separate household from my mother, she was still very much a part of my life. It was not unusual for the phone to ring at night. It would be my Dad calling us to let me know something was going on with my mother related to her mental illness. He would say, "I have to take your Mom back to the hospital." I believe the strength I demonstrated later in life during my own difficult years stemmed from the early teachings of my mother. As a young girl, she taught me to be strong. She taught me to not sit around and feel sorry for myself.

I vividly remember when I was a teenager and I was dating this boy, Jerry, who I was crazy about, and somehow found out that he had been out with another girl. I was crying in my bedroom. I was so hurt. I had the shades pulled down; the room was gloomy to match my mood, and I was very down about what I had heard. My mother walked in the bedroom and pulled up the shades. She said, "Quit sitting around and feeling sorry for yourself! Get dressed and get out of here!" While some young women might have been shattered by that comment, it was just what I needed to hear.

The lesson I gained from that, and I still apply today, is don't sit around feeling sorry for yourself. You take hold of life. You work through tough times. And get the support you need from family and friends.

I think work also kept me sane during those challenging times because I would get to work and be around other people. And because I had people who needed me and needed me to take care of things, I didn't want to disappoint them. As an employee, I always wanted to do a good job so I would be focused at work. Before I knew it, I wasn't focused on the problem or how hard things were. When I came home from work, I had the two little kids, a husband, and dog who needed my full attention.

Going back to your question as to how did I remain strong, I had the solid early teachings of my mother. As we crept through those years of her illness, I learned many lessons by watching her and my father. My mother never blamed anyone for her illness—at least not that I can remember. She accepted her illness. She accepted how her illness had changed her life. That in itself was an important lesson for me.

My father was amazing! He had to be so strong. He had a business to run; a household to maintain; a family to nurture. He had to be mentally strong for all of us plus himself! As a child, my father grew up with a lot of tragedy in his family. And then he had this shock later in his life with my mother's illness. His attitude was, "This is a new day! Who knows what great thing might happen today." "Yesterday is over. Today is all I have. Be thankful."

My father and mother were amazing role models. I was and am very blessed to be their daughter!

**Wright**

Talk about the refiner's fire!

**Burge**

Yes.

**Wright**

Tell me about your first career, the one that lasted for 20 years.

**Burge**

My first career was in the secretarial/administrative field. I started working as a Receptionist when I graduated from high school. I worked my way up to being a Secretary. Eventually I worked my way up to high-level executive assistant positions partnering with Presidents and CEOs of large corporations. I stayed in that profession for 20 years. During those 20 years, I worked for 12 different companies in 5 cities. I worked in various industries from small businesses to Fortune 500 companies. In those days, job hopping was usually frowned upon. But that was just my path. If there were better opportunities for me, I went after those positions. For a good portion of my career, we lived in Cleveland, Ohio, where there were some big companies so I was able to move up internally. Some of the other job changes took place due to company downsizing and we moved several times with my husband's career. But it was great because I worked in small businesses and in Fortune 500 companies. I learned so much from being in all those different environments and in different parts of our country that now when I look back, I realize I was in "training" for the career that I started after those 20 years.

**Wright**

What made you to decide to go out on your own and start your own business?

**Burge**

When I was about 37, for some reason, I just wasn't feeling the same satisfaction in that career. I started thinking that I had had a wonderful career and I worked for top executives. I had worked in wonderful companies, and I worked in some not so wonderful companies, too. It wasn't all perfect. But in terms of that career, I felt I had reached the pinnacle and all of a sudden I started to think, "By the time I'm 40, I don't want to be doing this. I don't want to be an administrative assistant. I don't want to be working for someone else." Then I started to think about what could I do because I didn't know anything else and I didn't have a college degree. All I knew was that by 40 I was not going to be doing that. I guess I then started to open my mind to new possibilities and careers.

**Wright**

As I understand it, you didn't have any money to start your business, and you never borrowed any from your family, friend, or a bank. Is that right?

**Burge**

That's correct.

**Wright**

Plus, you started a business in a market that was untapped. You didn't have a degree. No startup money. You moved to a new city.

**Burge**

Yes. I did all the things you're not supposed to do. All the entrepreneurial or start-up business books I read said you should have six months' salary saved before you start a business. They also said you shouldn't start a new business in a new city where you don't know anyone and so forth. I had broken all the rules.

Before I broke all the rules and started Office Dynamics, Ltd. full time, I kept my full-time job while I started learning about professional speaking, training, and starting a business. I definitely was not in a financial position to quit my full time job. And because I was creating a niche market, I wasn't sure whether there would be interested clients. I started crossing over to this new profession by giving mini seminars to the assistants where I worked, speaking in the evenings at community colleges, and taking a vacation day here and there to conduct seminars where I already knew the business owners. I joined different associations related to training and professional speaking.

This went on for two years. Then my husband got a great job offer that would move us from Memphis, TN to Virginia Beach, VA. He knew I wasn't really happy working as an assistant any more. But I was also scared to let go! My husband was a very smart man. When we were getting ready to move to Virginia, he said, "You have to make a decision. You either have to give up this idea of going into speaking or you need to just do it, and you need to do it full time." He said, "You'll never know if this new career—this new business—is going to work and if it's really what you want unless you go at it full time." In my heart I could not give up the idea of helping others through training and speaking.

When we moved to Virginia is when I broke all the rules! I moved into a new community where I didn't know a soul. I had no money put aside. If anything, we were in debt. And I had too much pride to borrow from family or friends. I really couldn't get a loan from the bank because I didn't have a business plan in place, had not test-marketed my product or service, had no company history, and was creating a niche market in developing professional programs for administrative and support staff.

In the early '90s companies did not invest in professional development for assistants and support staff. All the money was spent on leadership and management training. If anything, they would send an assistant to a one-day seminar and thought that was in-depth training. So, yes, I had everything going against me other than I had a ton of energy, enthusiasm, hope, faith and motivation. Which I think is what got me through those early years. But we also made a lot of personal sacrifices. When we moved from Memphis to Virginia, we did not buy a home. We had owned homes all our married life. Instead of buying a home in Virginia, we rented a home and used some of that money for me to start the business. I set up my office in our rented home. I needed a telephone, computer, printer, desk, and some really nice marketing pieces. Investing in a quality marketing materials was important because that would be my first image going out to the public. It was rough the first year because we had been used to two incomes and the children were still little. I actually started my official business in June 1990. I didn't see my first little paycheck until February of '91, which was only $250.00.

Then it started to pick up in my second year. I started to get speaking engagements and worked with some good clients. Some of that early work was providing training and development for non-administrative staff. As I went into companies and met people, they liked my topics and would ask me, "Can you speak to our sales people on professional image?" And I would say, "Yes," because I could speak on that topic, but I would have to customize the material to make it work for that group.

Just as I started getting known in the community, my husband got a fabulous promotion that we could not pass up. It meant we would have to move to Michigan! And so we did! With that move, though, I suffered a huge step back in my business because all the clients I worked with in Virginia, were not going to pay the expenses to fly me back to that area. Those costs were not in their original agreements with me. Whereas now, all my out-of-state clients pay my expenses.

I thought, "Here I go again! A new community with no contacts!" A little leftover business was all I had along with a huge portion of determination! I struggled for awhile and then I got my first big break with Marriott Corporation. I was hired to conduct 10 seminars within Marriott Corporation, which was wonderful. In my fourth year of business everything started to grow and people started to hear about me. I was hired to teach several of my programs at Michigan State University. This work lasted for a few years. I was getting referrals. Then I actually started advertising in some national trade journals which paid off. That's where I got some of my big corporate clients like Caterpillar and US Airways. That was wonderful. Once I got corporate clients, it was easier to get other corporate clients because if they hear you're working with other corporations they feel your work is quite credible.

During that time I was writing. I had written two books. I was doing everything I could to get published in trade journals. I was aggressively getting out there and trying to get myself known. I was trying to lay a strong foundation for my business. I didn't invest in terms of full time help. I used to get interns from business colleges or high school students to come to the office and help me.

**Wright**

Tell me a little bit more about your journey in running Office Dynamics, Ltd. I know there was a time about three years ago that you thought you might have to close the doors. How did you hold on?

**Burge**

Yes, that is true. What happened was my business had continually grown and sales climbed year after year at a very aggressive rate until the spring of 2001. I was doing extremely well. I had four trainers working with me. We had clients all over country. I was speaking regularly. It was fabulous. In October 2000, we moved from Michigan to Las Vegas to venture into a new kind of life, you might say. Things seemed to be going terrific. Life was good! In the spring of 2001, the economy started to slide. When that happens, companies cut back training. So these huge corporate clients that were giving me tons of business were starting to cut back their training dates and then, of course, September 11th happened. That's when the axe came down. Every day for several weeks I was getting calls from clients who wanted to cancel programs we had booked. Clients weren't canceling just one speech or one day of training. They were canceling 8 to 12 days of training that we had booked several months prior. This equated to thousands of dollars in lost business.

In the training business, much like speaking, you usually book engagements three, four, five or more months out. For example, people normally wouldn't call me today to speak in three weeks. So any business that I had booked for three, four or more months out got cancelled. Do you see the impact of this? There was no way I was going to immediately replenish that business. All I could see was everything I had worked hard for 10 years was going out the door. I was devastated. I wasn't getting new business coming in, either, because companies were not spending money on training, especially for administrative or support staff.

I thought, "How could I go on? I'm going to have to close my business." I remember walking in to my husband's office crying one day because I couldn't handle it any more. Besides the huge financial loss, I had a terrible fear of getting on an airplane after September 11. Yet as a speaker, 90% of my work was out of state. I was dealing with not only am I losing business, but I really don't want to get on an airplane even if I get business!" "Now what?" This was all I had known—helping others through speaking and training. This is what I absolutely loved to do with my whole heart. What was I going to do? Where was I going to go?

Then one day, I woke up and thought, "You know what? I worked too darn hard to close my doors. I don't know how I'm going to do it, but I will hang on with every little bit I possibly can. I'm not giving up and I am going to rebuild this business. I don't care what it takes. And I'm not going to live my life in fear. Those terrorists are not going to prevent me from living my life." Then what helped me was I read an incredible book by Dr. Robert Reverend Schuller called, *Tough Times Never Last, But Tough People Do.*

That was my "bible." I remember I was going on my first business trip a few weeks after the attacks of September 11. I took that book on the plane with me. I was traveling from Las Vegas to Louisville, which is about a 3 ½ hour flight. The plane was only about 25% full. I was a little scared, but I took hold of that book and read the entire trip. I highlighted important phrases and insights I wanted to affirm. I read the book in my hotel that night and finished reading it all the way home. It turned my life around. You know, even motivational speakers need to be inspired once in awhile. I also have to tell you I thought that hard-copy book would come in handy if I had to hit anyone on the head who got out of control on the airplane!

**Wright**

Right.

**Burge**

After I read that book and mentally regrouped, I realized I am tougher than I think. I thought back to a great lesson my mother taught me. That lesson was I am stronger than any obstacle that comes my way. And with the help of the Lord, I can overcome any obstacle. I got to a point (and I still do this) where I say, "Okay, God, get me through this one. Help me. Show me what I need to do."

**Wright**

You've told me about the grandmother, and your mother, and all that you've learned from them. You have a daughter. What do you see in her as a young woman growing up in a different generation?

**Burge**

I see in my daughter, Lauren, openness to express herself. That's something I've really noticed in her and even her girlfriends.

**Wright**

I have a 15 year old. She is ... you're being very kind and it's more than expressing.

**Burge**

When I think back to her teenage years (she's now 25), Lauren wasn't afraid to say "No" to me. I never said "No!" to my parents.

**Wright**

I know.

**Burge**

As a parent, when a teenager says, "no," you think to yourself, "Now what? Where do I go from here?"

**Wright**

Mine doesn't just say no, she says, "Dad, you haven't given this much thought, have you?"

**Burge**

I think the X and Y Generation females are bolder. They are much more comfortable in expressing and saying what's on their mind without a lot of fear or intimidation. This could be good or bad. I definitely see a change in my daughter from my generation in her relationship with her husband, Jeff. In my mother's and most of my generation, we were raised with the belief that females handled all household and childcare responsibilities. I don't see that with Lauren and Jeff. It's great, though. Sometimes when I call their house, Jeff will answer the phone. I'll say, "Hi Jeff! What are you doing?" He'll say, "I'm ironing, mom!" He likes to iron! He likes to cook! After all, Jeff went to college and learned how to take care of himself.

Anyway, I think it's easier for women today because many males of today's generation were raised by working mothers like me. These young men learned early on in life to do things for themselves and pitch in around the house.

**Wright**

Right.

**Wright**

I know you're in your early 50s and are proud of it.

**Burge**

Yes! I don't understand women who are in their mid-50s or early 60s and still want to tell everybody they're 40. I think this phase of my life is fabulous. It has a few downs like little aches I've never had before, but overall I love where I am in my life! I'm confident in who I am, what I can do, and I'm a survivor of life! I'm basically done raising my kids. I can enjoy time with my husband. We're going to be grandparents early in 2005. There's a certain sense of freedom at this stage of life!

**Wright**

You've said that you have so much you want to accomplish. A lot of women feel that their lives should slow down around that age and they're too old to set goals and start a new career. What do you think about that?

**Burge**

Number one, I don't think you're ever too old to set goals. If you're 80, if you're 70, I think as long as you wake up, you're breathing, and you're alive, you can set goals. You may chronologically age, but you're never too old to have dreams even if it's something as simple as learning calligraphy or taking Tai Chi. I think that's actually what keeps us young. People grow old when they stop dreaming, when they stop having a vision or they stop seeing things that they want to do in their life. I'm not about to sit in a rocking chair on the porch yet. I have just too many things I want to accomplish.

It's been fun this year for me because I feel like I'm rebirthing my business. All that hardship the last three years forced me to think differently, look at my business differently, and realize the approaches that worked 10 years ago don't work today. What those events did was force me to challenge myself, to be more creative, which is very energizing. And as a result, my business is picking up, I'm writing and presenting new seminars, developing new programs, and writing new e-newsletters. It's great.

**Wright**

Right.

**Burge**

I feel like I'm getting a second chance to do things even better this time and reaching more people. I just hope I have the physical stamina to keep up with it all!

**Wright**

Right.

**Burge**

It goes back to what we talked about earlier with women role models. I've had wonderful women in my life besides my mother and my grandmother. My mother-in-law is 87. For her 85th birthday she traveled to Ireland. It was a dream she had all her life. She's of Irish descent. I looked at her going on that big trip and thought, "My gosh, look at her. 85!" As I said, she's 87 as of the writing of this chapter. She still has things she wants to do. Yes, she has slowed down a little. She has a lot of swelling and pain in her legs every day. She has macular degeneration and losing her sight in one eye. Do you know what she recently did? She crocheted and sewed more then 12 blankets for her new great grandbabies who will be born in early 2005—my first grandchildren!

I had a wonderful aunt, my Aunt Ida, who lived to be 85. She was busy up until her last days having dinners for friends, enjoying her family, taking Tai Chi, and traveling. To me, this is so wonderful. This is great news because we don't have to become old and just sit on the side lines as if we have no purpose. I like that idea. It's exciting to me.

**Wright**

I suspect that 30 years from now, your daughter is going to be talking about you the same way that you talk about them.

**Burge**

I hope so!

**Wright**

What a great conversation. I really appreciate this time that you spend with me. You know it's exciting. You've motivated me.

**Burge**

Thank you. This was great for me, too. Life goes by so fast that we forget where we've come from and the things and especially people in our lives who helped us get to where we are today. Thank you for the opportunity to share some of that with you and our future readers.

**Wright**

Today we have been talking to Joan Burge. She is the founder and Chief Executive Officer of Office Dynamics, Ltd., an international leader in the development of presentation of sophisticated training programs and information for administrative and business professionals. Joan, thank you so much for taking so much of your time on *Conversations with Remarkable Women.*

**Burge**

Thank you. I appreciate it. Thank you so much.

## About The Author

Joan Burge is the founder and CEO of Office Dynamics, Ltd., an international leader in the development and presentation of sophisticated training programs and information for business professionals. As a professional speaker, corporate trainer, consultant, and author, Joan equips individuals with the proper skills, attitudes, and strategies to be successful in the workplace and at home. Joan is the author of 4 books, 12 workbooks, is the editor of Monday Motivators, and has been published in more than 54 trade journals. She is a member of the American Society for Training & Development, the National Speakers Association, the Southern Nevada Human Resource Association, National Association of Female Executives, and the Las Vegas Chamber of Commerce.

**Joan Burge**

Office Dynamics, Ltd.

2766 Evening Rock Street

Las Vegas, Nevada 89135

Phone: 800.STAR.139

www.officedynamicsltd.com

# *Chapter Five*

## Kathy Slamp

### THE INTERVIEW

**David E. Wright (Wright)**

Today we are talking to Kathy Slamp. Kathy has a rich and varied background. Born in Oklahoma, Kathy has lived all over the United States and traveled to all fifty states and many areas of the world. She has been a full time educator for over 30 years, teaching all levels from kindergarten to college, serving as a public high school assistant principal and as a college adjunct. She has an under graduate degree from Northwest Nazarene University, a Master of Education from Washington State University, and an Administrator's Certificate from West Texas A&M University.

In March 2001, Kathy resigned her position with the Wichita School System, took a step of faith and began *Vessel Ministries*. This ministry is based on II Corinthians 4:7, and Kathy encourages her audiences to be His vessel. Kathy's speaking takes her from coast to coast where she speaks for retreats, seminars, church services, and special engagements. Her sense of human, captivating story telling, and down to earth sincerity endear her to her audiences everywhere. She has spoken to groups from 50 to 10,000, and at five national rallies.

Kathy's first book, *Walking through Life without Stumbling*, was released in 2000. This is an inspirational book based on life experiences and supported with scripture. Her second book, *Our Little House in the Arctic*, was released in 2001. This fascinating book is the retelling of her childhood adventures in Alaska during the Korean War. As a result of *Little House*, Kathy lectures on Alaskan cruise ships during the summer as the ship's naturalist. *Little House* is reviewed in the October 2002, issue of *The Book Reader,* a national bookstore trade magazine, which has a circulation of 125,000.

*You Might Be a Pastor's Wife If,* Kathy's third book, was released in November 2002. It is a cartoon book about life in the parsonage. She's also authored *Mastering Women's Ministries*, a manual for the local church and *Reflection Profiles,* an Old Testament Bible study series. In November, 2004, Kathy released her latest book, *The Word in Real Time.* This is a daily devotional, with a devotion for each day of the year. It includes 25 interactive pages for prayers and reflection. Already, it is being very well received.

Kathy and her husband, Dr. David Slamp, reside in Seattle, Washington. Most recently, he pastored at Central Community Church, in Wichita, Kansas, one of the fastest growing churches of America. The Slamps have two grown children, a married son in Vancouver, Washington, and a daughter in New York City. They have one grandson, Preston. Kathy, welcome to *Remarkable Women!*

**Kathy Slamp (Slamp)**

Thank you.

**Wright**

Boy, you've done a lot in your life, haven't you?

**Slamp**

Well, I've had a lot of years.

**Wright**

Oh my! I've got a birthday coming up tomorrow, so we won't discuss age today. Tell us a little bit about your early family background.

**Slamp**

I was born in Oklahoma where my dad was a pastor. Shortly after I was born my parents moved to Texas, and we lived there during my very early years. I have some recollection of those years, but when I was very small, we moved to Alaska. My dad accepted an assignment in Fairbanks, Alaska, which is pretty far from San Antonio, and we drove across the United States in a brand new '46 Hudson with a brand new baby who was two weeks old. I look back on that experience and marvel at what remarkable people my parents were—and still are. I spent a good part of my childhood in Alaska; then when I was an early teenager, my parents came back to the lower 48.

**Wright**

So, how did you come to know the Lord, and how has that relationship grown over the years?

**Slamp**

Since my dad was a pastor, I was always in church. It's really interesting now, as an adult, to look back on my maturing relationship with the Lord. I can remember the day that the Lord first moved in my heart. I was a small child of five or six. I can remember where I was sitting in church; I can remember what I was wearing; I can remember who I was with. I don't remember much more than that, but I remember the feeling that God was knocking on my heart. To this day, I remember those feelings.

It was at five or six, then, that I gave my heart the Lord. This was, of course, in Alaska. That relationship was very childish, as you can imagine. It was in my college years that I really nailed down my Christian experience. I was always a good kid and never did anything bad. I lived the right life, but I had some bad attitudes on the inside that I kept pretty much hidden—as most teenagers do. During my college years, there was one very quiet moment between God and me. It wasn't a big public thing; rather, it was just between Him and me. I wish I could find the Bible I had then, but I've lost it somewhere along the line. That day, I went to the back of my Bible, and I dated it and I wrote it down. I said, "from this day onward...," and although I can't today remember the exact words, I wrote my confession of faith in the back of that Bible. That was the beginning, I think, of a real mature relationship with the Lord. Of course, that was also many years ago and there's been a lot of things since then that God has continually taken me back to His word and continued to help me to grow in Him.

**Wright**

I've had many friends down through the years that were PKs, preacher's kids, and they always tell me they were kind of treated a little bit differently ...

**Slamp**

That's right.

**Wright**

I think the funniest thing I ever heard, I've got a great friend who is a fourth generation Presbyterian minister. And he used to kid me about getting "DPC" all down through his lifetime. His father was a minister in a large Presbyterian church in North Carolina, and he said when people in the congregation would die, he would get dead peoples' clothes.

**Slamp**

Right. That's happened. Not so much with me, but to my husband. Recently, he was wearing a tennis outfit, and I said, "Is that that thing you got from that dead guy?" He said, "Well, that puts a whole new color on it." I've never heard the term "DPC," though. That's funny.

**Wright**

What and/or who influenced you during your impressionable years?

**Slamp**

My mother and father. Both of them have influenced me in different ways, and I think I could safely say that spiritually my father has had a profound impact on my life. My parents are still living and are in their late 80s. My father still is a very strong presence in my life in that he's such a good man. There were also specific church members in my father's churches that influenced me positively. I can think of one man who died when I was 19. They were members of a church that my dad pastored in Spokane, Washington, and there was just something about him and his wife that really impressed me. They were just dynamic people, and had a "marriage made in heaven." They radiated the love of Christ and made the Christian walk appear winsome, joyous, and fun. And I think, wonderful people like that couple were extremely positive forces in my early years.

In the ministry and in the parsonage, you see the worst and the best of people. Perhaps my nature helped me to see the worst, but concentrate on the best. In other words, I was perceptive and saw it all. Summer camps for some reason were a big deal for me. I would see older kids—those who were three or four years older than me—and think, "Man, if I could just be like them some day." So, I think I could safely say that my parents, some of the terrific people in my father's churches, and those summer camp experiences really impacted me for the Lord.

I guess I have to go back to my father. He came from no place. His dad was an alcoholic and a philanderer, and his mother was a cripple. He didn't have a thing going for him, and as it turns out, I married a man with a similar background. Maybe there's something about that to see God take a life in which the world would say these people don't have a chance, and see what God can do. My dad always believed in me and he still does. I get lots of phone calls from him, and we visit whenever possible. Several times a year, I get a handwritten letter just telling me how proud he and Mother are of me as an individual and how much they believe in me. Those are the things that really impress me and keep me going.

**Wright**

With two children, it must have been difficult for you to get as much education as you obviously have. How has that education progressed, and what were some of the challenges of getting it?

**Slamp**

I had my Undergraduate Degree when my husband and I married, and then everything went on hold while I taught school and put him through seminary. At the end of seminary, we had our first child, and he began his pastoring. It has always been my goal to get a Masters Degree, but that got put on hold for a long, long time. Finally, it just seemed like it was my turn, and so I began to take classes from Washington State University toward my masters. My timing was poor because at the same time my husband was working on his doctorate, and we had two kids in college.

**Wright**

Wow!

**Slamp**

We probably could have done that a little better, but we were able to get it done. The other degree that I have—the third degree—came as a result of job opportunity. When we moved to Texas I was hired as the assistant principal of the high school. It was a pretty good sized school of about 1,500 kids, and I didn't have the credentials that the state required, but the principal really wanted to hire me. He said, "If you go over to West Texas State right now and enroll in two classes, I can hire you." So I did that. For about two years I drove back and forth about a 60 mile drive one night a week to take classes and then I took classes all through the summer to complete that degree. But, I completed it. I thought I would have my masters by the time I was 30. I was pushing 50 before I got it. But I got it!

**Wright**

That's great!

**Slamp**

I never really felt like I sacrificed too much. My husband and I look back on that time, and we think, "We could have done that a little differently money wise."

**Wright**

It seems like most of your focus now is in the secular world. So how have you served the Lord with the commitment that you made a long time ago in this secular world?

**Slamp**

Well, actually, my focus right now is in the church world, but I've come directly from the secular world. Because of my school teaching and what I was doing, I was almost always in the secular world.

**Wright**

I see.

**Slamp**

In the secular world, diversity is a big issue. I think God really helped me to earn a large degree of respect that allowed my Christian testimony to go forward in that secular world. I think the difference comes when He is not only your savior but you allow Him to be your Lord as well. When He's your savior, the emphasis is on the individual; that's very important and that comes first. When He's your Lord, though, then the attitude changes from "What can you do for me to what can I do for you?" I'll just give you an example. It's been now about seven years ago, but that's relatively recent. I just casually met a teacher in a coffee line at a teachers' orientation. To make an extremely long story short, a year and six days after I met her, she died of cancer and left three daughters.

**Wright**

Oh, my!

**Slamp**

Spiritually, she was almost a heathen, but God really helped me to be her friend and through that friendship, my friends and I got involved in her life. My "church friends" and I became her care givers and her lifeline for the last six months of her life. I believe without a doubt that she's in heaven today, but that connection came through the secular world.

I go to a little diner nearly every morning here in town; it seats only 20 to 25 people maximum. I was there this morning. It's on the corner of a little strip mall, and it's very insignificant. The name of it is *The Café* and it's run by a little Portuguese man who is my age. Despite *The Café's* seeming insignificance, the whole world seems to pass through its doors. The people at the diner know who I am, and they are my friends. Last November, the man who owns it dropped dead. We were all there laughing and talking with him in the morning and then, he went home that day and died.

**Wright**

Oh my!

**Slamp**

Before the funeral, the family called me and they said, "We know who you are and what you do. Would you say something at the funeral about our dad?" I've tried to be who I am and live in a secular world, and I believe I've a pretty good savvy about what is going on there. This little incident confirmed that somewhat. You can't be in public education without knowing that.

**Wright**

So what have you contributed, do you think, to your husband's ministry?

**Slamp**

I think he would say I've contributed a lot. He would be a better one to talk to you. Until we came to this particular church where we are today, I've always been very involved in whatever they needed me to do that was in my line of giftedness. I have some gifts in organization and, of course, public speaking and teaching. I've done a lot of that over the years—a ton of it. In fact, the *Women's Ministries Manual* that I published and sell all over the country came right out of some hands on stuff that I dug out with a bunch of local ladies. We figured out how to get uninvolved people involved, and that's really where the manual came from. In this particular church, because it's so large, I've pretty much taken, not a back seat because I sit on the front row, but the main thing I do here is teach an adult Sunday school class. I'm comfortable in saying I am respected, and I believe I've earned that respect.

This church in Kansas seems to be proud of the fact of what I do. I started out with two ladies and now there are ten who call themselves the Vessel Ministry/Kathy Slamp Prayer Support Team. We meet twice a month; they pray for where I'm going and who I'm speaking to and for my traveling safety. I bring prayer requests back to them and they pray for them. It's safe to say that the ministry I have today is impacted highly by this church here in Kansas and the prayers of these women. So this relationship of my involvement in ministry continues to evolve and take on its own shape as years pass.

When I began *Vessel Ministry,* my husband was quite open about his personal support for it. He actually said something of this nature, "You've stood by me and supported my ministry for many years; now I want to do the same for you." I've been side by side in participation with him: I've entertained hundreds of people in our home, attended thousands of services, participated in Bible schools and summer camps, prayed with people at the hospital, sat with people at funeral homes, and those type things. I've never resented it. I've enjoyed what I've done.

**Wright**

Could you tell our readers a little bit about the sacrifices or the values of being the wife of a full time Christian minister?

**Slamp**

To be really honest, I think anybody who's a pastor's wife knows that there are some sacrifices. If I had been out there on my own, I probably would have gone much further in public education than I ultimately have. I suppose that's a sacrifice. Career wise, the other factor I considered was my own two children, and that was high priority. The value far outweighs the sacrifices, if that is a sacrifice. Getting to know such wonderful people and being involved in peoples' lives is a blessing that cannot be measured.

There have been some wonderful experiences of travel and meeting outstanding people, such as missionaries and church leaders. When our kids were home, we made an effort to bring these people into our home and set them at our table. We entertained people around the table from Africa and the Philippines, and other places, and let our children experience that. One particular time we had a missionary from Japan come to town, and I asked him, "What would you really like to do?" His response: "I'm really hungry for Japanese food." We lived in west Texas so I said, "We don't have many Japanese restaurants here." He said, "If I tell you what to buy, could I cook a meal at your house?" And I responded affirmatively. Our adult kids are still talking about that meal, and they are in their 30s. He prepared a genuine Japanese meal.

The biggest value of being a minister's wife is being involved in peoples' lives. Just recently, we sat with dear friends while their son died from a gun shot wound. It was so immensely difficult for them, but it was a blessing to able to be there and do just a tiny bit. I've seen God's church go ahead despite the set backs, and the remarkable people we've had a chance to meet and know far outweighs anything that I sacrificed, if I could call that a sacrifice.

**Wright**

Well, you've authored three books, a study series, and daily devotions on the horizon. I'm always interested in why people do the things that they do. So why do you write?

**Slamp**

For many years as I was speaking part time, people would say, "Where's your book? Where's your book?" So, the thought of a book was always in the back of my head, and I began to formulate some ideas. 1989 was a crisis year in our lives for a lot of reasons, and it pushed us all, especially my husband and me. I can't speak for my children, but it pushed us back into discovering what we're really all about. That's when the concept of the broken vessel began to crystallize because that's really what we were. Life just broke us through some major disappointments, and then there was a period of time where it was like a bottomless pit. But the book was always in the back of my mind. We never gave up, and God was never unfaithful to us. Out of our entire trauma, it dawned on me that what we were experiencing was nothing different than what all of us experience at one time in our lives for a variety of different reasons.

Many people tell me that I have a pretty good gift for storytelling and for turning those same stories to a truth—a tangible moral that people can get a handle on. The story is just the way of relating. My first book, *Walking through Life*, was simply an effort to put down some experiences, and that's what those 12 chapters are. They are all experiences from my life. Some are funny, but in actuality, none of them are funny. You can see there's something funny in everything, and it's based on scripture. From that first book, one thing evolved after another, and now I have so many thoughts in my head for new books that I don't know if I can get them all done.

*Walking through Life* continues to be my best seller, although the last two books have sold thousands also. I believe people relate to and resonate with an ordinary person who has experienced life's traumas just like everybody else. Unfortunately, many Christians give the impression that their lives are perfect and void of conflict and difficulty. Somehow, my husband and I have dealt with life's challenges, disappointments, and traumas through His grace. It is only His grace that has brought us on top of it. With that grace, we face each new challenge.

**Wright**

So tell us a little bit about the stress and the passion of *Vessel Ministries.*

**Slamp**

*Vessel Ministries* is based on II Corinthians 4:7. *We have this treasure in jars of clay to prove that this all surpassing power is from God and not from us.* In 1989, when our lives just got totally sideswiped, I began to really study this vessel thing. The prophet Isaiah put it like this: *You have turned things upside down. And if the potter were to be thought to be like the clay! Shall what is formed say to him who formed it, 'He did not make me?' Can the pot say of the potter, 'He knows nothing?'* (Isaiah 29:16) I realized that God was allowing these things in our lives for a reason.

I didn't realize it at the time, but it began to come to my mind, as time and healing progressed, that God was doing something special—not only in my life, but in my husband's life and in our lives together. Our stress has been similar to another prophet, Jeremiah: *But the pot he was shaping from the clay was marred in his hands* (Jeremiah 18:4). My husband felt as though everything in our lives was just all messed up. But Isaiah continued, *Can I not do with you as the potter does?* It was at this point of realization that we became like clay in the hands of the potter. That has been the stress of *Vessel Ministries* since 1989. We realized that what we had been teaching and preaching was true: Whatever you're going through, God can take it and work good from it—even the most difficult situations. I speak about a lot of different things, but the vessel concept is at the bottom of it all.

**Wright**

So what are some of the disappointments of life that have driven you back to the Lord and into His word?

**Slamp**

In retrospect, our 1989 experience was a "Joseph thing." Joseph said that his brothers and people in Potiphar's house intended their actions for evil against him, but God used them for good. I really can say that there were some people that did and said things in our lives that they truly probably intended for evil. Because of the events of 1989, my husband ended up having a major career change where he went from being senior pastor to a college professor, and now he's back in the pastorate. As a college professor, he trained pastors. What we thought was meant to destroy us God has used mightily. Young pastors all over the country think Dr. Slamp is kind of "it."

**Wright**

Right.

**Slamp**

Recently, a man called to apologize for his part in the 1989 fiasco—fifteen years after the fact and 1,500 miles away. How surprising and unexpected his words seemed to us. When I accepted his apology, I quoted the scripture that says *all things work together for good for them who are called according to His purpose.* The man stopped in our conversation, "Oh," he said, "you believe that God caused this." "Absolutely not," I responded. "But, I believe now from a distance of fifteen years that God *used* the evil intents of some men and women to thrust us out into the ministries we have today."

God doesn't *cause* all things, but to the willing heart, He can *use* all things!

The disappointment that we experienced when we changed life focus and moved in another direction and literally moved from the west coast to the mid-west deepened our depth of love for Him and our understanding of people's hurts and pains. I always enjoyed being the wife of the senior pastor. In the church we are in now my husband is not the senior pastor, but one of ten pastors. I truly believe that if my husband were the senior pastor, it would take an extremely understanding church to allow me to be gone as much as I am with *Vessel Ministries.*

**Wright**

Right.

**Slamp**

There could be unstated feelings, “Our pastor’s wife is never here,” if David were the senior pastor. In this large church, though, it's entirely different. People's attitude seems to be one of pride: “We have one of our pastor’s wives that travels and has an extended ministry. We’re so proud that she’s part of our church.” I've already commented on the prayer support team. Even people in our church who aren't part of the team seem to feel that what I do is an extension of this local church. From that respect (and many others), this church is a mighty blessing to *Vessel Ministries.*

**Wright**

What’s the membership of your church?

**Slamp**

We have about 2,000.

**Wright**

What do you think it means to be a fully devoted follower of Christ?

**Slamp**

As I mentioned earlier, it's the difference from Him being our savior—which is vital—to Him being our Lord. When He is our Lord, our attention is on spiritual things. This emphasis thrusts us back into the community and into the world. It's not about, "What can you do for me, Lord?" Rather, when He is Lord, it's about, "What can I do for you?" I am confident that we could live to be 110 and never be truly a fully devoted follower. When you examine all areas of your life—finances, family, attitudes, abilities, talents—all of those things are really truthfully about yourself. You finally come to the realization that you are a merely an ordinary person. It never takes many minutes in a day for me to remember how human I am.

**Wright**

Right.

**Slamp**

The minute we think we're something special; life abruptly reminds us of our humanness and our ordinary qualities. My dad illustrated this by telling about a young Quaker preacher. With his Bible under his arm, the young preacher climbed the steps into the high pulpit of the church, looked down on the people and was just horrified. He was so totally full of himself as he went up, and he bombed. As he descended from the pulpit, an old Quaker came to him and said, "If thee wouldst gonest up as thee cameth down, thee wouldst cometh down as thee wenteth up."

I believe that the minute we think we're something special; the world has a way of sizing us down because we're all pretty ordinary. As a fully devoted follower when get too full of ourselves God reminds us through others and life experience. The beauty of this is that as we stay close to Him, we recognize His voice. That's when we drop to our knees, either in our heart or physically. Posture isn't the most important thing, but an attitude of humility is imperative. That's when we say, "God, it's just me; please use me."

**Wright**

I find it very interesting that just in the last two or three weeks the opening of *The Passion of Christ*, the Mel Gibson movie, has made such an impact and has driven tens of thousands of people into the movie theaters.

**Slamp**

Right.

**Wright**

I don't know that that means anything. I don't know the impact that will have on people...

**Slamp**

It's hard to tell, isn't it?

**Wright**

But what do you see in the future of ministry?

**Slamp**

Because people are so searching, there's a ... well, you've heard it, there's a God shaped void in all of us that only God can fill. An old hymn that we sang years ago said it well: *I Have a Longing in My Heart for Jesus.* Jesus is precisely what the world is looking for; consequently, there's an endless future in ministry. Jesus said it this way in Matthew, and I quote this a lot: *you are the light. We're the city on the hill but we're the light of the world and we can't be hidden.* (Matt. 5:14).

Interestingly, ministry sort of segways from that particular scripture. My husband was abandoned at birth by his father because his mother had become a Christian. He never saw his dad at all. In the past 10 years he has become acquainted with a woman from Fort Myers, Florida, who is his half sister. She was raised by his dad. There is an unbelievable bond between them, but they have nothing in common. She's a Catholic. He's a Protestant minister. They can't talk about family vacations. They can't talk about their dad. They can't talk about their mom. And yet, there's something that draws them together. They have the same blood.

The blood of Jesus is the arch that connects us with the world, and we become that "city on a hill" that Jesus continued to identify in Matthew 5. My husband's sister has shared with us that all her life she would say to her dad, "I want a brother and could you make him an older brother?" Apparently, David's father never spoke of him—not even one time. But now in her 50s, she's found her older brother.

I believe that's what the whole world is looking for. They are looking for Jesus—the world's older brother. Consequently, there are endless avenues of ministry. You mentioned in your introduction that three years ago I took a giant step of faith and began *Vessel Ministries* as a full time Christian ministry. There continue to be additional steps of faith as far as this ministry is concerned, but I'm not talking about that. I'm talking about our ministry as individuals in the world. The Christian community is faced with endless opportunities and open doors as we're out and about. Each person that we're standing beside has the same older brother—Jesus. They just may not know Him yet. For years we could have been right beside David's sister and not have known her. It's an amazing parallel and a beautiful metaphor.

**Wright**

Kathy, is there anything else you do that you might consider unique?

**Slamp**

Yes, there is. I was raised in Alaska during the Korean War. One of my books, *Little House in the Arctic*, is my family's adventure story of those years. It is a great little book that seems to delight many people. It is a book of adventure, history, and sweet life experiences of a bygone era. This book has opened the door to working with summer Alaska cruises. I am invited each summer to come aboard with one of the major cruise lines in Alaska as their shipboard naturalist and destination lecturer. This new adventure has grown from year to year, until now it is a standard part of at least six weeks or more of my summer. On the ship, I weekly give three multi-media presentations for the guests in the ship's main theater. In addition, I am a guest of the captain on the bridge. From the bridge, I comment over the public address system about glaciers, wild life, and ports of call. It's all quite live and personal, and many of the passengers call me "the voice of the bridge." Presently, I am working on a sequel to my first Alaska book, *Little House in the Rain Forest*. The first *Little House* book was about Alaska's interior; this book is about Southeast Alaska, where our family also lived.

In addition to my Vessel Ministries website, I have developed a unique Alaska website: www.alaskathy.com.

**Wright**

Well, what an interesting conversation. Today we have been talking to Kathy Slamp. She's been a full time educator for over 30 years teaching at all levels from kindergarten through college, and as we have found out today, she fits very squarely within the framework of the title of this book. She is indeed a remarkable woman. Thank you so much for being with us today, Kathy. I really appreciate the time you took.

**Slamp**

Thank you, I appreciate it also.

## About The Author

Kathy Slamp is a woman who wears many different hats. She is a pastor's daughter, a pastor's wife, a mother, and a grandmother. She has been a full time educator at all levels, a high school administrator, and a college professor.

In 2001, she took a step of faith, quit a full time position as "Master Teacher," and began *Vessel Ministries,* a Christian inspirational and motivational ministry. Since then, she has traveled to nearly every state in the union where she speaks to all sizes and genres of audiences. Her sense of humor and down-to-earth style, coupled with her understanding of the scriptures, endear her to audiences.

In the summertime, Kathy puts on a completely different hat when she works with major cruise lines as a naturalist and destination lecturer. In this capacity she makes presentations to the passengers AND is "the voice of the bridge." You just might hear her one day speaking over the loudspeaker on your Alaskan cruise explaining about glaciers, wildlife, and ports of call. She has authored six different books. Everything Kathy does, she attempts to base on II Cor. 4:7: *We have this treasure in jars of clay...*

**Kathy Slamp**

20023 11th Place W.

Lynnwood, Washington 98036

Phone: 316-204-1234

Email: vesselmin@comcast.net

www.vesselministries.com

www.alaskathy.com

# *Chapter Six*

## SHARYN LYNN YONKMAN

### THE INTERVIEW

**David E. Wright (Wright)**

Today we are talking to Sharyn Yonkman. After a lifelong successful career in the New York City area working as a Controller, CFO for various retail and hospitality industries employers, in early 1993 Sharyn walked away from it all, including family and friends, and moved to southern California—if you can believe that. Unbeknownst to her at the time, she was embarking on a journey that involved far more than mere miles. This journey revealed her desire to speak, train, write, and need to empower others. It resulted in her training company, Lynn Consulting Group, and her writing a book for women baby boomers about the transition to life's second act. It's all about the closing of one door and opening of another. Sharyn, welcome to *Remarkable Women*!

**Sharyn Yonkman (Yonkman)**

Thank you. It's my pleasure.

**Wright**

From New York City to California, that's a trip!

**Yonkman**

That certainly was.

**Wright**

That's a mental trip, that's not a physical trip.

**Yonkman**

It was indeed. Actually, it was both. The difference between living on the East vs. West coast is enormous. I sometimes felt I had moved to another country.

**Wright**

To leave behind the life that you had always known, all your financial and emotional security and to go to the opposite side of the country without promise of employment or any social support, one might ask, "What in the world were you thinking?"

**Yonkman**

The truth is I really wasn't thinking. I was feeling. All conventional wisdom was screaming at me to stay, but something, a small very persistent inner voice said to go. Although my checkbook was healthy, I felt emotionally and spiritually bankrupt. Unbeknownst to me at the time, I needed this very move, one of such magnitude, from the safe harbor and nurturing of family and dear friends that I had around me, and really the distraction that it provided. All the social going and doing was no longer in my best interest, and I needed to be isolated, alone if you will, to discover what I was to do, which is to share and empower other women. My life in New Jersey, full of social warmth and activity, as well as financial security, did not challenge me to do the necessary inner work. I was comfortable, busy, and distracted, and was very content to stay upon that path. I needed to travel 3,000 miles to find my true path.

**Wright**

I would think that family and friends and all the social life could kind of distract you from a calling.

**Yonkman**

It can. Actually for me, it kept me unaware I had a calling.

**Wright**

Why did you become a certified trainer, a seminar presenter in 1997, and create your own consulting group?

**Yonkman**

When I was living in New Jersey, I never considered working for myself. The thought was unnecessary and alien. It was the move to California that changed my ideas about self-employment. After being in California a few years, I realized I had not been able to duplicate my past professional financial successes at working for wages positions. Additionally, for the first time I realized that the standard 2 week vacation offered here in America would not fit my needs because I wasn't able to take a true vacation for my time was spent visiting my family. The previous contentment I had of working for someone else was no longer my experience. Always being interested in beauty and glamour, I first dabbled in developing a private skin care line, but due to a glut of products on the market and insufficient capital to really launch the business, it was not successful. However, it did plant the seed of entrepreneurial ship, and one day in early '97 I was reading the *NAFE Magazine* and noticed a small ad for PWN, a Professional Women's Network in Louisville, Kentucky, to become a Certified Trainer. I have no idea why the ad spoke to me the way it did, for I never considered being a speaker/ trainer, it was the furthest thing from my mind, but I decided to follow through and that's how I went to Kentucky to be certified. That decision changed the course of my life both personally and professionally. I want to emphasize that this was not an intellectually planned out, thought out decision. I was attracted to it by a much more primal instinct, intuition if you will, and this choice has helped me with my inner work more than I can say.

**Wright**

In what way, if any, does your previous corporate finance experience lend itself to Lynn Consulting Group?

**Yonkman**

My previous working for wages experience has been invaluable for my current corporate clients, especially those in the hospitality and retail industry where I am well versed in all aspects of the business. Additionally, as Controller I had implemented many managerial training programs which gave me the background for client training and executive coaching.

**Wright**

What unique qualities and special gifts do you bring to the platform for your attendees?

**Yonkman**

For my corporate clients, I bring a vast managerial and financial expertise as well as strategic goal attainment and focusing techniques for my executive coaching clients. I pride myself on my ability to customize training specifically for any organization. My workshop attendees and personal life coaching clients benefit from my sense of humor and wit, as well as my broad based life experiences. I'm empathetic and self deprecating, which helps me to relate with my clients, and I'm always willing to share personal experiences. I'm able to ask the right questions and truly listen to my coaching clients.

**Wright**

So, what inspired you to decide to write a book about baby boomer women and the effect aging, particularly in the area of physical appearance, has upon them?

**Yonkman**

I feel that the old adage, that we teach what we need to learn, is true and it really applies to me. I personally needed to come to terms with my own sense of loss attributed to aging and my appearance and wanted to share my experiences and insight with my fellow baby boomer sisters. In the classes that I have been providing on getting over getting older, I have noticed that there is a great need for fellow baby boomer sisters to share their feelings, validate them, and the need to find tools and techniques to make the next act of life even better. They need to experience this passage on a deeper inward level, one that is certainly not provided by the glut of anti-aging products and plastic surgery techniques that are being developed each day. Our youth obsessed culture in America, stronger than ever, has evolved around the same time that more women are reaching the age of 50 than ever before. As I listen to the many participants of my workshop, I clearly heard their longing and the need they had to be nurtured and empowered during this passage. This was something I felt that I could help them with and I was compelled to begin the research on this book.

**Wright**

So our readers might understand the age group that you're talking about, could you define baby boomer women for us?

**Yonkman**

Yes, it's people born between the years of 1946 and 1964.

**Wright**

I was reading the other day the life expectancy age on the day that I was born, the year that I was born. It was 59.

**Yonkman**

Wow!

**Wright**

I'm thinking, "My goodness!" And then I heard a happy statistic. Most of that was infant mortality.

**Yonkman**

Well, you've passed that.

**Wright**

So I'm going to be okay, I think.

**Yonkman**

I think so.

**Wright**

So, the book that you wrote, did it have a lot to do with that first experience in California in the cosmetics company?

**Yonkman**

Well, that had something to do with it. That business was a private skin care line. But actually it had more to do with my workshops, speaking to women on women's issues, and by interacting with them and seriously listening to feedback.

**Wright**

I see.

**Yonkman**

The sharing that went on in the groups that I was holding and the insights that I learned from my participants inspired me to research the topic. You always, always learn something when you're teaching,

**Wright**

Right. So this project of yours required a great deal of research. Could you share with our readers some findings that came as the biggest surprise to you?

**Yonkman**

I don't know if there were any huge surprises, it was more just eye opening and sort of "Oh now that makes sense" kind of moments that I got from my research. In many of the books I used in my research on the power of beauty, it tells of the human response to beauty. For example, research has established the fact that cute babies are cuddled more in nurseries by their caregiver than less attractive babies. Imagine how powerful it is to set the stage so early on. It starts right from the moment that we're born. We are hardwired, if you will, to respond to symmetry of face which equates to physical attractiveness and its relationship to fertility. Earliest man was attracted to the young, healthy woman for she represented fertility and survival of the species. Women had the same instinct, attracted to strong, healthy vital looking males to provide for and protect them and their children. The formula goes: youth equals beauty, equals good, equals fertile/healthy; as opposed to old equals ugly, equals bad, equals unhealthy/barren. So you see there is a certain genetic hardwiring going back to caveman times that predisposes us to be attracted to the physically appealing to keep the human race going.

**Wright**

One of most unfair things that I think I've ever read, well not just a book, several books now on recruiting, hiring people, that tall people get better jobs faster, higher pay than short people. Pretty women get better jobs than people who are not as attractive. Heavy ladies and heavy men do not get hired as much as thin women and thin men. It just invades every part of our society, does it not?

**Yonkman**

Unfortunately, yes, and that's why I felt that doing this research and writing this book would help let women know that this is not just a superficial vanity issue, or a mistaken perception, that there is research to back up their feelings of injustice, it exists, and that there is a great power in beauty. And for them to recognize it so that they can better deal with the loss of this power that we experience as we age, when our physical appearance is affected by the passage of time.

**Wright**

For your upcoming book, you've conducted a wide spread survey of women. Will you share some of the more compelling replies?

**Yonkman.**

I'd be glad to. One of the more consistent findings, though it was not much of a surprise, but it was meaningful nonetheless, was that women who are above average attractiveness in their youth had a more difficult time coping at mid-life than their less attractive sisters. Women who were constantly praised for their appearances may come to believe that their appearance is them and that their only worth is their look. Less attractive women, however, have dealt with that issue long ago, probably in their early teens; and so at mid-life they've already moved on beyond this, and they've developed the truly important parts of themselves, having not been identified by their appearance, but by the content of their mind, their spirit, their personality. Also women who had difficult childhoods—traumatic, ignored—they weren't allowed to learn who they were due to a lack of nurturing not only suffer from self esteem issues, but have no clear identity of themselves, other than how they look as a package. When their "sell-by date," if you will, on that package is reached at mid-life, these poorly parented women have a particularly difficult time with the loss since they never developed a sense of who they were inside that outer package. Mid-life is the time when the loss of physical beauty needs to be replaced with the person we were truly meant to be.

**Wright**

Now, the next time I see my wife, I'm going to tell her that I talked to you, and now I know why all those women were dragging me into their caves.

**Yonkman**

There you go.

**Wright**

It was just because I was just so attractive.

**Yonkman**

Yes, because that attractiveness related to health, which relates to strength, which equals the best possible provider for the child.

**Wright**

And I'll mention fertility, if you don't mind.

**Yonkman**

Yes, absolutely. It's all about keeping the species going.

**Wright**

So how important do you view this taking for women?

**Yonkman.**

Risk taking is key at any time in life for women and men as well, but particularly important for women at mid-life. Women have a tendency not to take risks. They haven't been trained to take risks as men have been. Men have been encouraged as young men to take risks. Women are not. Many young women also lack the self esteem that's necessary to take risks, but by mid-life they have a better sense of themselves, which gives them the courage to take necessary risks. Also at mid-life we realize that time is running out, and if we don't make it happen now, and if we don't fulfill our forgotten dreams now, then when? When will we do it, if not now? Time is no longer on our side, and we must get the courage to rise to the occasion. The alternative is to live a life unfulfilled and filled with "if onlys," and that's a grim alternative, far too grim for me to imagine.

**Wright**

So what value do you place on inner work and self esteem development for women to lessen the impact of the emphasis placed on outward physical appearance?

**Yonkman**

Going inside is essential for successful aging. It's developing a true sense of self, our life's purpose can only be attained through inner work. One must go within or go without. I cannot emphasize enough the value of inner work, and in whatever form you choose to use to facilitate this work, the important thing is to embrace it and really do the work. The loss of the physical can only be replaced with the finding of the true self. It is worth every difficult moment of the exploration.

**Wright**

I could see where it would be...well it's tough for men, but I could see where it would really be tough for women. All I see are commercials that bombard you with be more attractive, have flatter bellies, you know all the exercise videos.

**Yonkman**

Absolutely.

**Wright**

It really is ridiculous after a while.

**Yonkman**

Yes, our culture has become, particularly in the last 20 years, obsessed with youth. It is obscene. Youth and its relationship to beauty is important in other parts of the world, but not nearly as important as it is here in America. We have really gotten out of control, have completely lost focus on what's important and we're totally oriented toward youth and beauty. I think a part of what makes it peculiar to America is the fact that we have no royalty and have adopted movie stars as our royalty. In early Hollywood we had people the likes of Cary Grant, Jean Harlow, Greta Garbo and we made these figureheads, if you will, our royalty, Since our icons were young and beautiful in appearance, it has become an unnaturally important thing in America as opposed to other cultures.

**Wright**

We had a seminar recently and had a movie star come in and do some things for us. She's now working very diligently with the women's right to do almost everything, it's a Christian movement, I think. By the way she's just, as we say in the south, drop dead gorgeous. As a matter of fact, her name is Jennifer O'Neill. She was in the *summer of '42,* almost a cult classic now. She goes all the way back to the time of John Wayne in *Rio Lobo*. Anyway, she got up one morning before our meeting, and she'd forgot her hair dryer. She just went ahead and washed her hair and didn't dry it. It didn't seem to bother her at all. She was still just as beautiful, but she was so beautiful inside and the fact that she didn't care one way or the other impressed me.

**Yonkman**

Yes, that's most impressive. She is an impressive woman on many levels.

**Wright**

So what message would you like the readers to take with them from your upcoming book?

**Yonkman**

I'd like them to realize that like it or not, fair or not, beauty does matter in life, and aging does take a toll on our physical body and our appearance. This creates a type of loss, a necessary loss; but it's a loss nonetheless. We need to not ignore our responses to this loss. We should recognize them, honor our feelings, and mourn it as you would any loss. This is okay. It's okay to recognize it. It's okay to mourn it. But what is not okay, however, is to stay stuck in that mourning phase. By doing this, we really miss out on the benefits that come with aging, the wisdom, experience, and confidence that accompanies aging. My message would be to recognize the outward loss and replace it with something far more valuable than wrinkle free skin. Replace it with the you that you were meant to be. Get on with life's second act with a different set of assets than you had in life's first, and choose an attitude of empowerment. Life's greatest act is only just around the corner, so we'd better get going.

**Wright**

So your antidote to all of this is self-examination and just being honest with yourself?

**Yonkman**

Yes, partially, but not just self-examination. We need an equal dose of a commitment to self-development. Going inside to develop who it was you were meant to be. In the first half of our lives, we're distracted by our outward appearance and the goings and doings of life. Whereas in the second half of life, when things change around, when our physicality changes, it gives us a fabulous opportunity to go inside and discover the true you that you were meant to be without the distractions of youth.

**Wright**

And then develop that?

**Yonkman**

Yes. Work on that and develop it so that you can be the best person that you can and fulfill your life's purpose by adding more meaningfulness to your existence. It's all a matter of attitude,

**Wright**

Sounds like, to me, that's what you did when you moved to California.

**Yonkman**

It is a work in progress, believe me.

**Wright**

So this is autobiography going on here.

**Yonkman**

We should write what we know, at least that is what you hear writers say, so in that sense it is autobiographical, but it is much more. I did a great deal of research on this project as well as conducting an intensive survey of women across the nation.

**Wright**

I've always believed knowledge as being a cure for a lot of things. I interviewed a lady the other day who's main topic is menopause. And she was absolutely fascinating. I mean, I couldn't believe that I didn't know anything about what she was talking about, and I told her, I said, "You know if I had just known all of this you know 25 years ago." She said, "Yeah, you and every other guy your age."

**Yonkman**

Exactly.

**Wright**

But no one tells you. She says menopause is supposed to be a women's thing, but it's not.

**Yonkman**

It's an everybody's thing.

**Wright**

Right. So is that what you're calling the second act, sometime around menopause?

**Yonkman**

Yes, mid-life.

**Wright**

Mid-life. Just when the physical attractiveness and everything begins to wane.

**Yonkman**

Certainly and other challenges emerge, we're faced with health related menopausal issues as well. So it's like a double whammy. It is at this time that we need to not focus on the body as much as focus on the mind and spirit.

**Wright**

Do you think that people who are more spiritual than others have a better opportunity or people with servant attitudes and the ones that don't think about themselves at first option have a better shot at it?

**Yonkman**

Absolutely. Most definitely. If you can focus on the spiritual within you and to giving and helping others, it really takes quite a bit of edge off the discomfort that many people feel during the aging process. A lot of the discomfort that accompanies aging is associated with being self-absorbed—self-absorbed with your appearance. Self-absorbed with the self and the package that is the self. People who are less focused on that and have a grander vision, one outside of themselves, have a much easier time of it.

**Wright**

What I find really scary, in the past...well actually just in the past year or two, the proliferation of television shows having to do with plastic surgery.

**Yonkman**

Oh my, yes. Especially that hideous thing called *The Swan.*

**Wright**

Yeah, isn't that unbelievable!

**Yonkman**

I cannot believe what a damaging message it sends and that there is a large enough audience that would enjoy this low self-esteem Olympics. Obviously there must be an audience for it. The fact that there is a market for this type of show is extremely disturbing.

**Wright**

Right.

**Yonkman**

And it's sad. It's actually sickening to see what these women will do, to the lengths that they will go to, the pain and opening themselves up for possible disfigurement and death to be better looking. I dislike competitions that pit women against one another just on the basis of pure physical beauty. Healthy competition is great, this however is not.

**Wright**

Well, I will have to admit that at the sock hops, I always wanted to dance with the pretty ones. But the truth of the matter is as I got older, I think that maybe the fact that I was not attracted, physically attracted, kept me from meeting people. But I found that the longer you know someone, the less the beauty really matters because the beauty really is all inside.

**Yonkman**

That's quite true. The problem, the hurdle with that is as you mentioned, many times the less attractive don't get a chance to show what beauty they have on the inside and their true worth because they're not afforded that opportunity. No matter how terrific a person might be, if they don't have that free pass of a pleasing exterior, they are often ignored.

**Wright**

Right. Yeah, that's the down side.

**Yonkman**

That's the down side, yes.

**Wright**

Well, what a fascinating conversation. I could talk to you all day about all these things.

**Yonkman**

So could I.

**Wright**

Today we have been talking to Sharyn Yonkman. She has moved several years ago from New York City to California. I can't think of a more different place. And in so doing, discovered that she has this calling to train and speak and help other people, especially women and especially women in the baby boomer age. Sharyn thank you so much for being with us today on *Remarkable Women.*

**Yonkman**

Thank you so much for the opportunity to share this information with you.

## About The Author

Sharyn Yonkman, founder of Lynn Consulting Group, provides personal and professional developmental training and interactive workshops. A former CFO, she is well equipped in providing executive coaching. A member of several professional organizations, Sharyn serves on the International Board of Advisors for the Professional Woman Network and is the author of an upcoming book for baby boomer women. A passionate advocate of women's self empowerment and life balance, she helps others to achieve their own excellence.

**Sharyn Lynn Yonkman**

P.O. Box 1266

Ventura, California 93002

Phone: 805.677.3117

Email: lynnconsult@yahoo.com

www.protrain.net

# *Chapter Seven*

## DOTTIE WALTERS

### THE INTERVIEW

**David E. Wright (Wright)**

Today we're talking to Dottie Walters. Dottie is president of Walters International Speakers Bureau as well as founding member of the National Speakers Association, and she is founder of the International Association of Speakers Bureau. An internationally renowned speaker, author, and speaking career consultant, she has helped pioneer this industry and continues to shape the world of public speaking as we know it today. She has been interviewed on *CNN, ABC, Good Morning America*, and hundreds of other TV and radio programs, newspapers and magazines worldwide. She has sold hundreds of thousands of copies of her more than fifty speaker products including the globally popular book, *Speak And Grow Rich,* published by Prentiss Hall. Dottie Walters, welcome to *Remarkable Women*!

**Dottie Walters (Walters)**

I am delighted to be on the program with you, and congratulations on doing the book about women. We thank you.

**Wright**

Dottie, in the speaking and training industry, you are a legend. Will you tell our readers why you decided to go into the speaking and training business?

**Walters**

I was getting so many requests from speakers asking me to help them. One day after I had done about seven or eight people, and I wasn't charging for it, I thought, "You know, I think I should add this consulting to my repertoire." So I did and I do quite a bit of it now.

**Wright**

You own an internationally known speakers bureau.

**Walters**

Yes. It's called Walters International.

**Wright**

You've sent professional speakers all over the globe to train some of the world's largest and most successful corporations. How does it feel to know you played an important role in corporate education?

**Walters**

Well, I'd listen to what the customers tell me they want and what they need. The most successful titles for talks solve a problem, like the *One Minute Manager*. They took a big survey of thousands of managers and said, "What's your biggest problem?" They all came back with one word—"time." "Time." And you know he's made a tremendous, wonderful success of that. So if you are very good at one thing, it's a good idea to stick with it.

**Wright**

Fortunately, many legends enjoy star status and recognition while they are still alive and in their industry and active. I understand that you are the only two-time president in lifetime, already a chapter member of the Los Angeles Chapter of the National Speakers Association. Since you've spent twenty-five years working in this organization, how does it serve the public?

**Walters**

Well, you know there are many associations. If you could see here on my desk the directory of all those in the United States, we have two that we work with as a bureau, I mean two directories. One is called Association Meeting Planners. They're the buyers. And the other is called Corporate Meeting Planners. You would be overwhelmed. Nearly everybody, just think about doctors, dentists, chiropractors, lawyers, everybody has an association and all of them really have the same goals. They want to improve it.

**Wright**

Dottie, I read an article you wrote about your daughter, Lily, entitled, *Angels Never Say Hello.*

**Walters**

Yes.

**Wright**

Successful leaders tell me that tragedy can result in a learning and growing experience. Will you tell our readers about your daughter's experience?

**Walters**

Oh, I'd be glad too. The title of that came about because my grandmother used to always say that angels come knocking and kicking and yelling at the door of you heart and most people don't open the door. So I said, "Oh, grandma, if one comes to my front porch, could I let them in?" She said, "No, the angel doesn't have time to come in. They just leave you a message and then they go on. They've got a lot of messages to deliver." And I said, "Oh, really? Well, what would the message be?" She said, "Well, it's always the same one. The angel's message is 'Arise and go forth!' Do it. Now! Who can you help? Who needs you?" You see. That's the way I've always operated.

We had horses here on our ranch in California. I had a speech to make in San Diego so my husband took Lily and two of her friends riding. Then he rented a forklift because they were going to move some hay into our corral. While taking that forklift back, she said, "Let's all get on it and let's sing. It will be just like doing a hay ride. So let's all do that." So he let them do it. They got down to a big curve and he couldn't hold it on the road and it turned over. The other girl was thrown to one side and broke her arm in three places. My husband was hit on the head with a great big rock and he was knocked unconscious. My daughter was pinned underneath the forklift, it landed on her left hand, and gasoline poured all over her body. The boy was thrown clear. He was a Boy Scout. My husband was active in the Boy Scouts and he was one of them. So he got out and he had the presence of mind to stop the traffic because, you see, if there had been a spark she would have caught on fire and had a terrible death. So he told the people to turn around and go back and call for the fire department and ambulances and so forth, and they did. He said, "Don't let them park close." He said, "The rest of you turn around and go back and go another way." And they did.

So when they got a hold of me in San Diego, I immediately drove back and told my client that I couldn't go on. When I got to the Orthopedic Hospital in Los Angeles, here were the doctors standing there. They said, "Well, gangrene has already set in. Sign these papers because we want to amputate the hand." I said, "Amputate it? Can't you save any of it?" They said, "Well, perhaps. But we'll have to amputate more if the gangrene goes on." And they said, "That's not a pretty death." So you know there wasn't any other way to go.

We waited while they were operating. My husband was on his feet by then. I suddenly got an idea. I said to my husband, "I think there's a book about one hand typing. I think I've seen it somewhere. Honey, I'm going to run down to the telephones down here," because she was going to be in surgery for a couple of hours. So I grabbed my purse and ran down. As I ran, I heard a voice speak to me. I think it was God. In fact, I'm sure it was God! And God said to me one word. He said, "Underwood." And I said, "Oh, yes! That's the typewriter I have at home." You see this was back when we didn't have computers yet. I said, "Okay, I'll call Underwood. Maybe they've got that book." And immediately the voice said, "You can't spell 'Underwood'." I thought, "Oh, I wonder why I can't spell it." It was like somebody erased it. And then another name, another company...the same thing. "You can't spell it." And by the time I got up to the telephone and got my dime out to call information, there was just one more word. And it said, "I.B.M." And I said, "Okay." So I asked for I.B.M., and when I dialed the number, I explained to the lady at the other end what had happened. She said, "Yes. We have the book. Thank you. You must have seen the story in the Los Angeles Times this morning." I didn't see any story. And I said, "Oh, what story? Tell me about it." She said, "We are rebuilding used typewriters, portable typewriters, for children who have lost a hand." She said, "We send the book with it."

**Wright**
Goodness gracious!

**Walters**
Oh, can you imagine that? So they did, they sent it to her. And I think that was a miracle. She was able, by studying that book, to type forty-five words a minute within three weeks with one hand. She, of course, has written a lot of books herself too, and many things where she's used computers. I feel that was a miracle. It's interesting how when you need it most, sometimes, its where you least expect it.

**Wright**
Oh yeah!

**Walters**
Yes.

**Wright**
You've written many books, including a featured story in the *Chicken Soup for the Soul* series.

**Walters**
By the way, I wrote eight for them.

**Wright**
Oh, is that right?

**Walters**
Yes.

**Wright**
I talked to one of the authors, Victor Hanson, a few weeks ago. He said they had sold eighty-million of those.

**Walters**
Oh, it's just a phenomenal thing. It's a great honor to be included in that, in any of their books. We are doing a book for them now. It's *Chicken Soup for the Celtic Soul.*

**Wright**
Oh, is that right?

**Walters**

Yeah, for all the Scotch and the Irish. We're working on that now.

**Wright**

Well, your international best seller, *Speak and Grow Rich,* has helped many people build their business in the speaking industry. Why do you think the book became so important?

**Walters**

Well, I think maybe it was because of my own story. I started out speaking because I didn't have any more cardboard for my shoes. My babies, at that time, my two older children, were just tiny little babies. We were going to lose our house. There was a big recession. We had a tract house, like a G.I. house that everybody had then. So my husband put his head down in his hands, and he said, "I can't make the payment." We had bought a franchise for a dry cleaning. That's not such a good business to have in case there's a recession because people just sponge their clothes off. We couldn't get any business. So I asked him if it would be all right with him if I did what I did in high school. I was advertising manager and feature editor of the high school newspaper. He said, "Oh, I don't think you can. You've got the babies and so forth." He was out every day knocking on doors, trying to start routes, but we weren't getting any. So I said, "Let me try, honey." And then I began to make a list of what I needed. I needed a typewriter. I needed paper, and I didn't have either. I began to let that fear come into my mind. "I can't do it because I don't have those little things." Material things are little things. Ideas are big things. So, I thought, "Well, what I'll do, I'm going to think who's got a typewriter. I want to tell all of your people this. I read biographies, and I read four or five a week. I always have since I was in eighth grade, just going into high school. But one of the ones that I enjoyed a lot was Albert Einstein. He said to me, see I hear the voices, when you read a book, if that person's helping you, they're talking to you. And he said, "What you want to do is always realize that you put your whole intelligence on solutions, not on problems." So I thought, "Solutions!" I thought, "Oh, yes, my neighbor's got a typewriter. Maybe she'd loan it to me." I ran over and she did. Then I had to say to her, and I remember looking down at the ground because I was embarrassed, I said, "Would you have any paper?" And she said, "You bet I do, hon." She went back in and she gave me a *ream* of paper. That's one of the most valuable gifts I ever had in my life.

So I fixed up the kitchen table and bang! On the front door they were sampling the newspapers, and the local newspaper...there was their paper waiting for me. I made up a sample column. I got the kids all dressed the next morning. I had everything in the big bag over my shoulder. Now I used to take the two children in the one baby stroller, which was a miserable thing because the wheels don't turn. You have to lift up the weight to turn it. They don't make them anymore like that. So when I tried to put them into the stroller, they wouldn't fit! My children had grown. So my heart sank again. Then I heard Mr. Einstein, and he said, "Solutions!" I thought, "Yes!" ran into the bedroom, grabbed the pillow off the bed, grabbed the clothesline, and rolled that pillow up and made a second seat and off we went. We found the newspaper office and when I found it, I saw the sign on the door that said, "No help wanted." I thought, "Oh, my gosh, I can't go any further." Just then my good friend of the mind, Benjamin Franklin, spoke to me. He said, "Dottie, you're not thinking straight. These people don't have enough money to pay you. So you go in. Don't ask for a job. A lot of people are asking for jobs! You don't need a job. You need a business." Yes! So he said, "Go in and ask if you can buy space at wholesale and sell it as a shopper's column like you did in high school for your high school paper, and I promise you in three weeks you'll have the money to pay for the three week's space." I went in and that dear man, that publisher, he told me thought he'd never see me again. But he said, "Okay." He said, "Dottie, you can pay it in three weeks. It's all right."

So I started out, but I soon ran out of cardboard for my shoes. So I thought, "I've got to think of a better way to do this." So I sat down and I thought and I thought, "Let's think of a better way." And again the newspaper was thrown on my front porch, so I went and got it. It told about all the service clubs in town, Rotary, Kiwanis, Lions Club, etc., and each one of them told where their officers were. They were the very merchants I was trying to reach. They were never in their stores. And I said, "Well, that's where those guys are. They're at all of those luncheons." Then I noticed that it said, "and the speaker was, and the speaker was, and the speaker was." I said, "That's the answer! I'll make up a talk. What could I talk about?" And I thought, "I think customer service. We own a home, and I'm a mother and a wife. So customer service is something that's important to me." I think it is to every woman. "So I'm going to say to them what does your customer really want from you?" So I started called the presidents of those clubs and they all said, "Yes, yes, yes. We want you." So I traded babysitters sitting with my neighbor, and she loaned me her car so I could do it at lunchtime.

**Wright**

Boy, I tell you.

**Walters**

Yes!

**Wright**

You often talk to corporate leaders about their training and education needs. What in your opinion do leaders want from their employees today?

**Walters**

They want them to feel part of the family, to care, and to not say…this is just what my talk was about. If I come into your store and you say, "Well, no we can't wait on you." "I've got to close the cash register." "We're closing now." That kind of stuff, they're not coming back. Right?

**Wright**

You're right.

**Walters**

Yes. So customer service was my topic, and I gave myself a moniker. Now that's free. Anybody can have a moniker. So I called myself "Dottie Walters, Your customer," and that's how I got started speaking. Then the people in difference audiences started to ask me to speak for money and that was the beginning. Then my customers there said, "Next time we're looking for a speaker on a different topic. Do you know anybody?" And I thought, "Oh, I need to start a speakers guild."

**Wright**

You're one of the founding members of the National Speakers Association, which is a four thousand member group with a tremendous service abilities. How does this organization advance their professionalism.

**Walters**

Oh, well they take every piece and they take it apart. They talk about speaking with enthusiasm, and vigor, and to being an expert. Usually a speaker is an expert at something, and that's what they talk about. But you need to have humor, and heart, and you need to be able to not be afraid of the audience. I have heard some speakers who I don't go along with say, "Just imagine everybody's naked and then you can sneer at them mentally." Well, they're going to pick that up. It's a magical thing to be on the stage. Then look at the audience and say, "Here I am. I'm the one you've been waiting for." That's what I say.

**Wright**

Dottie, I've know you for about fifteen years now, and in all of that time you've helped me most by giving me ideas that have worked for me. Fortunately, your ideas have come in conversations and they were free of charge. Your internationally read magazines sharing ideas has helped others as well. Could you tell our readers about your magazine, and how it got started?

**Walters**

Thank you. Well, it got started because I was selected to the first board of the International Speakers Association. A group of us women went out and had dinner to celebrate that night, and then we came back to my room. One of the girls had a guitar and we were singing and having a good time. Then one of them said, "Well, you know your husband has a print shop," which he did by then. I had so much printing to be done and my customers did too, that helped the printing shop, you see. So one thing leads to another, and they said, "Why don't you start a little newsletter for us, Dottie? Tell them what the women speakers are doing." So I did. Another thing I wanted to tell you is that I wrote the first book in the world for women in sales.

**Wright**

That's interesting.

**Walters**

It's called, *Never Underestimate the Selling Power of a Woman.*

**Wright**

Yeah, I've heard of the title. That glass ceiling still exists, doesn't it?

**Walters**

Oh, I don't think so.

**Wright**

You don't think so?

**Walters**

I think we're past it now. Yeah, there's an awful lot of women who are running businesses, and going into every profession. So there's nothing to stop you but yourself.

**Wright**

That's a great thought, especially for women.

**Walters**

Yes. Right, and we have a lot of little things. Like did you know that Jackie Kennedy, there's been a lot on the television about her, when they asked her why all the men she ever met fell in love with her, she said, "Oh, that's easy. I just hang on their eyes." See, these guys don't know about that. But she said whenever they said anything, she would look at them and say, "Tell me about it. Tell me about it."

**Wright**

Oh my. I know when people tell me to get in touch with my feminine side, I have no idea what they are talking about.

**Walters**

Well, that's what they are talking about. Give your complete attention to your customer, you client, whoever it is and illustrate with stories, humor and heart. That's the recipe for a great speech.

**Wright**

I remember years ago, I was talking to you in Atlanta at an NSA meeting, and the first time I ever met you years and years ago. There was a fellow named Terry Paulson from California who was on the platform. He was, if I'm not mistaken, a psychologist, and I though he was one of the funniest men I've ever heard in my life.

**Walters**

He was; he still is.

**Wright**

And I learned more that day than any of the other speeches because he laced it with so much humor.

**Walters**

Yes!

**Wright**

Do you use a lot of humor in your speaking?

**Walters**

Oh yes, I do. I think what you're leading up to is: what does it take to be a great speaker? They asked that of Socrates, and he answered this way. He said, "Well, a great speaker is first a great person who happens to speak well." So your character is really on display there, good or bad. Yes.

**Wright**

I can remember during his presentation that there were about nine hundred people in the room, he had trouble with his sound equipment—the microphone.

**Walters**

I remember that too.

**Wright**

You remember that? He made a joke about it, about how God was getting him back for doing something wrong. Everybody just laughed and they laughed long enough for someone to fix the system, and he came right back. I've never forgotten that day. If you could wave a magic wand and do anything differently with your many business ventures to make them better, what would it be?

**Walters**

I think I would have more confidence from the beginning because I didn't know that I could do it. But I did it because I wasn't going to lose that house. So if you have a goal that's strong enough, it'll lift you up. You go ahead. See, we've all got talents we've never used. People who can sing don't go out and sing. People who can act never went into it. Whatever it is you that want to do, you can do it.

**Wright**

They just never attempted it, huh?

**Walters**

Yes, you really can do so much more than you ever thought you could. Don't listen to the naysayers. I always feel sorry for them. I think they must have nothing better to do than to try to take somebody else down. It's kind of bad. And I never do that.

**Wright**

You know in the past several months, we've had trouble with the economy. The newspapers and everybody was kind of down about them. About two weeks ago, this article came out about how the economy was surging back faster than it has in the last nineteen years...

**Walters**

There you go.

**Wright**

...and all of a sudden business got good again.

**Walters**

Yes.

**Wright**

Strange how that works, isn't it?

**Walters**

Yes, and the people who went ahead and went into that dream they had always wanted to do to start a whatever it was, a pizza place or whatever, instead of standing around waiting for a job and collecting unemployment insurance came out ok.

**Wright**

Right. Hopefully, thousands of people will read this book about women and success and leadership. Is there any last thoughts or advice you would like to give our readers?

**Walters**

I think to read biographies. There's a wonderful book about Laura Scudder, the potato chip lady. She lived right here in southern California. I don't think she is still alive now, but her husband, during the depression right after World War II, just like me, he died and they had a gas station. People were buying twenty-five cents worth of gas. Can you imagine that? So she just wasn't making it, but she was a good cook. So she made a big batch of her potato chips, brought a bowl out in a brown bag, and said to people, "Take you a couple of handfuls and see if you like them and take them home with you." And boy, everybody started coming in do to that, and then they said, "We want to buy the big bags." But brown bags, you see oil goes into the bag, and so she thought she had to have a better way. Then she went out and tried to sell her potato chips to the grocery stores, but at that time they sold them in barrels, open barrels. Can you imagine how they sunk down to the ground.

**Wright**

Oh my!

**Walters**

Oh, terrible. So she got out her ironing board. She didn't say, "I can't do it." She said, "I will do it!" She thought, "What would work?" So she got out a roll of wax paper and her iron and her ironing board, and she invented the sealed waxed bag.

**Wright**

How about that!

**Walters**

There's thousands of stories like that.

**Wright**

I was talking a few weeks ago to Truett Cathy, who is the owner of all of the Chick-fil-A restaurants all over the world, and I think he is seventy-seven now, one of the finest gentlemen I believe I've ever talked to. I said, "You know Mr. Cathy, several years ago I was walking through the mall, and this young lady came up to me with a plate full of little chicken bits on toothpicks and handed me one, and said, 'Taste this,' and I tasted the chicken and I thought this is the best thing I've ever eaten. So I turned immediately and went into his store and ordered the largest one they had for me, my family, and everybody else. Since that day, I have eaten at Chick-fil-A just because of that experience." I said, "Who thought of that?" He said, "I did!"

**Walters**

There you go! You see the ideas are in the air. They are all around us all the time, and you block the door when you say, "Oh, yeah but..." Don't do that! Open the door!

**Wright**

Right.

**Walters**

And that's just the beginning. There are thousands of women that have invented things and done things. We've always done that, but didn't always get the credit for it.

**Wright**

Well, what a wonderful conversation, Dottie, you just don't know how much I appreciate you taking this much time with me today to talk about success and leadership and women. Today we have been talking to Dottie Walters. She's president of Walters International Speakers Bureau as well as a founding member of the National Speakers Association, and a founding member of the International Association of Speakers Bureaus. She, of course, as we have found out today, is a great speaker and her book, *Speak and Grow Rich,* should be on everyone's shelf, not only those people that want to make money in the speaking business, but those people who just want to learn how to speak better and do better presentations. Dottie, thank you so much for being with us today.

**Walters**

Oh, I've enjoyed it so much. Thank you for having me.

## About The Author

Dottie Walters is the co-author of "Speak and Grow Rich" along with her daughter Lilly Walters. She is one of the world's premier sales and motivational speakers! Dottie began a tiny advertising business on foot, pushing 2 babies in a broken down baby stroller, in a rural community with no sidewalks. She built that business into 4 offices, 285 employees, and 4,000 continuous contract advertising accounts. Dottie sold that business so she could concentrate on doing what she loves most, which is speaking, teaching seminars, writing, and publishing her own international speaker's magazine, Sharing Ideas. Dottie's most recent endeavor is co-authoring Chicken Soup for the Celtic Soul, which is an assembly of favorite stories and insights from her Celtic heritage.

**Dottie Walters**

Phone: 626.335.8069

www.speakandgrowrich.com

# *Chapter Eight*

## NANCY HUTSON

### THE INTERVIEW

**David E. Wright (Wright)**

Today we are talking to Nancy Hutson. Nancy, put simply, is a real woman in a real world with real problems just like everyone else, but as a Christian, motivational speaker, author, businesswoman, and certified health and wellness teacher, she takes these experiences and shares them with humor, passion, and realness to motivate and encourage people. Nancy founded and began Shining Star Ministries in 2000 to promote her gift of speaking for the various fields and needs of different groups and organizations. She and her husband, Scott, own Cycle Connection Harley-Davidson/Buell in Joplin, Missouri. Being a Harley owner and enthusiast is one very interesting twist in her life. Through her life, Nancy realized that after many trials and situations that giving God control is the only way to succeed and survive. Nancy, welcome to *Remarkable Women*!

**Nancy Hutson (Hutson)**

Thank you, David.

**Wright**

As we begin our conversation, the first question I would have for you is who were the individuals who influenced your life and encouraged you to be who you are today?

**Hutson**

Well, just like any of us, there are a lot of people who are very influential in our lives. But one of them was my great uncle, Uncle Roy. He was a businessman himself, and at a very young age for me, he started writing me letters. And these letters were filled with all sorts of interesting little tidbits pertaining to having good morals in our life, good backing, making sure that God is the lead of your life and who is guiding you and directing you. Each time we saw each other he would ask me what I had learned, whether I had been to church or to school. It always challenged me because as a child, most generally, you just try to get through those experiences. And as a child, it always encouraged me to make sure I knew something I had learned because I was going to have to tell my uncle Roy. He was very influential in that respect because he was an awesome and very successful businessman. He always strived to be the best at what he could do and to represent himself accordingly. I remember that as a young child and now I have all these wonderful, wonderful letters that I'm able to use when I go out and speak and share with other people the kind of influence that he had on my life as well. Other influences in my life were my parents, who truly gave me direction to guide me and direct me. Also I had some very influential Sunday School teachers along the way that encouraged me. I had some low self esteem issues when I was younger, and I had a lady by the name of Vicky Peters, who was a Sunday School teacher, that was always there to encourage me and to make sure that I believed in myself and that I was a special person that God had made. Very cool.

**Wright**

I've been booking speakers for 15 years, and one of the things, of course, you learn is that public speaking is one of the most feared things in our culture. As a matter of fact, I kid my speaker friends and say, "If you can stand in front of a group and speak to them without passing out or vomiting on yourself, you're in the top 2 or 3% of the nation." Was it easy for you to make that decision going into full time speaking ministry?

**Hutson**

Actually it wasn't easy at all, but not from the perspective of being scared to speak. Having owned a Harley Davidson business for 15 years, it was more difficult for me to leave my comfort zone. I had been involved in doing public speaking as a local host on the Jerry Lewis Labor Day Telethon. I also had done our television commercials, radio commercials for our business, so I was pretty comfortable with the speaking part, and God had blessed me with that gift. My biggest challenge was actually leaving the Harley business because I had been "the queen." I had been the queen of the Harley shop for so long that I was afraid of losing my identity, and I was afraid that I wouldn't have that acknowledgement from people. And that was my biggest struggle when I went into full time ministry. I thought that if I left that Harley world that I would become a nobody, that I wouldn't be important anymore, and it was a real struggle for me to realize that God had a very special endeavor for me in my life in full time ministry. In fact, I felt when I was in junior high and high school that God was calling me into full time ministry. Back then, I thought the only full time ministry position that was available was a pastor's wife, and there was no available pastor looking at me for a wife. So I ended up going a different direction. I went through 18 years of rebellion, and so I skipped the full time ministry calling. So now I've been able to come back to that and God has shown me that He can use me with this gift of gab for His will and purpose in a very powerful way, which is very cool!

**Wright**

How did you hear God's voice for your calling into full time ministry?

**Hutson**

Actually my husband. He kept encouraging me by saying we were both doing the same things at the Harley business, and that it was a waste of my time. Not a waste, but that my time could be used for bettering the kingdom of God by being able to go out and share with people. So as I would read God's word and study, there would be things that would speak to me. Scott's voice kept making it very clear and encouraging me and sort of pushing me a little bit, which as we well know, when our spouse is the one that is encouraging us and pushing us, it's not usually accepted very well.

**Wright**

Um hum, right.

**Hutson**

So that was very...very difficult for me. I kept feeling like he was pushing me away from the business I was so comfortable in, instead of realizing that God was using him as a very powerful voice in my life.

**Wright**

What has been your greatest challenge and perhaps blessing in your life?

**Hutson**

I was married to a gentleman by the name of Ronnie Mills. He died of a massive heart attack on September 10, 1996. Oddly enough, that has been my biggest challenge and blessing. His death was very sudden, of course, with a massive heart attack as they are, and it was the most devastating thing that could have ever happened in my life because he was my life. He was my soul mate. Life was good with Ronnie and I, and when he died at the snap of a finger, there were a lot of things that happened at that point. First, I had been through a period of 18 years of rebellion at that time and was not in God's will. I was overwhelmed with feeling like I was completely alone. Further, I had to decide whether to keep a business that was normally a man's business, the Harley store. I had to decide a lot of things in my life. And what ended up happening, there was a wise gentleman who kept encouraging me to come back to church and to come back towards God's will. Because of Ronnie's death and that devastation in my life, I was searching for peace and a comfort that I wasn't finding without God. One trip back to church and it brought me back to the place where I needed to be with God. Early in 1997, I went back to the place where I needed to be, which was at the foot of the cross and being able to seek God's will in my life. Through a devastation and through something that was just the worst thing I could ever imagine, it actually brought me back to God. It was a tough recovery, but I have learned so many strengths and dependence on God and relying on God making sure that I'm where I need to be.

**Wright**

Were you frightened to be thrown into a man's world when you had to take over the reigns of running the Harley Davidson Motorcycle Shop?

**Hutson**

Oh, yeah, it was scary. There are a lot of women involved in motorcycling now, but that was still back at a time when the motorcycle guys would come in our store and I would be at the parts counter, and they would say, "Isn't there a man I can speak to?" Even though I had been involved in the business daily when he was alive, it was very scary to be put into that position. And it truly was the fact that once I got myself back on track with God, God gave me the strength to stand up and be what I needed to be. And it was only a year and a half later and He presented me with another wonderful blessing in my life, which is my husband now. Scott, who also is a great businessman, joined me in the business and he has enabled me the opportunity to answer God's call and travel to speak to groups and to share stories about some of those big bad Harley dudes. It was a scary time.

**Wright**

What opportunities and doors are opened because you're a motorcycle owner and rider?

**Hutson**

Why actually a lot. I'm amazed over and over again how many groups are so curious and so interested by the fact that I own a Harley Davidson Motorcycle business, and I ride a motorcycle. A lot of the women's groups are very interested in knowing more about that world because to some of them it's completely foreign. Also, I'm able to do motivational speaking for businesses and incorporate the opportunity of being a businesswoman owning a Harley Dealership into a lot of those engagements. Harley is a pretty acknowledged company for having succeeded through a very difficult time of their own. So it's sort of an American success story. So it really does open some doors because of some people's curiosity.

**Wright**

I went to direct a church choral organization seven or eight years ago, and when I walked in I knew these two ladies. One of them was just a beautiful woman. She's in her early 40s, and she was the vice president of a bank and managed one of their branches. And the organist was a retired school teacher, a beautiful lady. She was probably in her late '70s. And one of the biggest surprises of my life, they both came to rehearsal one night, each driving a Harley.

**Hutson**

Oh, how fun.

**Wright**

I almost dropped over. I just hadn't seen … I've seen women hanging on…

**Hutson**

You bet!

**Wright**

But I've never seen them up front.

**Hutson**

That's cool.

**Wright**

And at 77, I think. She was riding out to Colorado and back from Tennessee. Unbelievable!

**Hutson**

Wow! That's great.

**Wright**

Do you ever incorporate your Harley into your speaking events?

**Hutson**

You bet I do. It's always available. Some groups don't want that kind of an atmosphere. But I've always had a lot of interesting comments when I do, especially with business motivational speaking when I go into businesses. They love to incorporate me riding my Harley into a convention hall or a meeting room or whatever. But I did have one really great experience. I had a lady call me about speaking for a group of GA's, Girls in Action, ages six to twelve, and I said, "Yes." Then after I said yes, I hung up the phone and realized that kids frighten me. It is scary for me to speak to kids. Now you were talking about the nerves and all that. When I get up in front of a group of children, it's really tough because they're tough. To keep their attention is difficult. So anyway, I had said yes. Well, I called her back and I asked her if I could bring my Harley to their church, and she said, "Yes." I thought that would be a great way to get their attention and break the ice.

So I took my Harley. My mom and dad went with me because they are so supportive, Daddy opened the doors just at the right moment, and it was meant to be. It was a God thing because there was a ramp that went right up into the two double doors of this church. And so I was dressed full clad Harley. I had leathers. I had the doo-rag, the shades. I had the whole bit on. And so when my dad opened the doors, I started my bike. I revved it up like any good Harley girl does, and rode it up that ramp, and rode it down the aisle down to the front part of the church, and just sort of pulled it in sideways and stopped it. And of course, the kids were just awed. They were just nuts. And the pastor's wife was sitting to my right. The kids were on my left. The pastor's wife did not know that I was going to do this. She was not pleased to begin with, and I proceeded to take my jacket off and throw it over one of the handle bars. And I thought, "Okay, this woman is sort of freaking me out here." And so I looked over at the kids and they were so excited. And I said, "Guys! Do you think that it was really cool that I rode my Harley Davidson into your church?" Of course they're all "Yeah! Yeah!" And I said, "Well, it is pretty cool, but I'm going to tell you about something that's more cool than that, and it's Jesus." And we started talking, and I got to share with them. And at the end of it, the pastor's wife, actually came to me and she said, "I don't know if you knew it or not, but I wasn't very happy when you came in." And I said, "Really? Yeah, um hum." And she said, "That was really cool." Now I don't do any burnouts in churches or any of that kind of stuff. But it is a lot of fun when I do get to incorporate it into it because it's sort of an eye opener.

**Wright**

I've got a lot of minister friends. We talk continuously about their calling. I even kid them and say, "You know most ministers I know get called to higher salaries."

**Hutson**

That's right.

**Wright**

They don't like that at all.

**Hutson**

Oh, I bet they don't.

**Wright**

We do a lot of kidding. It's always fascinating to me this thing of God's calling. Has God's plan always been evident to you?

**Wright**

Oh, I wish it would have been, but a part of my life was spent going through my 18 years of rebellion. I was raised in church. I knew what was right and wrong. I was saved when I was six. My parents taught me well. The church gave me great morals and background. But after I graduated from high school...I went on what I call my little 18 year of rebellious path. God's plan wasn't evident at all because I was completely ignoring it. And it really took a lot of surrender on my part, which took me a long time to get to. I had to quit driving my own bus or driving my own Harley, I guess maybe. I had to give up the keys and give up control, which is really hard for me because I've always been a very controlling person. And being a business woman and riding a motorcycle and all of those things, I've always been very controlling. It was very difficult for me to find God's plan and the surrender part was tough, but the surrender part was the best thing I could have ever done because He makes sure and shows which doors I'm supposed to go through. Once I did surrender to full time ministry, I had no clue how this was going to happen. I had no clue how I was supposed to get my name out there, how He was supposed to work this, and I simply just made a brochure and said, "Okay, here we go God." I prayed over it and asked for God's anointing as each of those brochures went out and people just called and doors opened. So His plan is so cool, but the surrender is so, so important.

**Wright**

So when did you realize God's true joy in your life?

**Hutson**

Well, you know, David, I've told my pastor's wife, "I'm not sure why we have to wait until we're older to find God's true joy." Because it's such a cool thing when you can get into God's will, when you can surrender your desires and allow Him to take care of things. The joy that He gives you just...even the joy He showed me through the loss of a husband, the joy that He's shown me in surrendering to ministry; it has happened only because of my trials and tribulations and my experiences. The Bible tells us we're going to experience them. But part of it is being able to allow God to work through those trials and tribulations to show you the joy, and a lot of times we cut him off. It's taken me a long time to learn that lesson, a lot of hard knocks to realize that.

**Wright**

What is your greatest challenge to share with all your audiences?

**Hutson**

Probably to take the desires of their heart and the knowledge that they have, and to share them with other people. I see so many of us, including myself, that are so busy and we're so crazy with our schedules, and we've always got so many things going on with work, family, activities that we really have gotten to where we're very, very lazy in sharing. I like to say, we need to make the invisible visible. So many of us don't share. So many of us don't show things. Even in business, if I don't share with my employees my vision, then they don't know what it is. They have to guess; then they disappoint me and they don't do the job right and things don't work as well. It's the same thing with sharing God. You know we can be going to church, we can be involved in various different activities that are related to Christian activities and so forth, but we so many times forget the people that we're working with that don't know God. We have gotten very lazy with that. It's really a big challenge for me to be able to encourage and to motivate people that are Christians to be able to share, to go out and to share what's in their heart and try to make a difference.

**Wright**

I looked at all of your civic involvements, and you've got a full plate, don't you?

**Hutson**

I do.

**Wright**

Do you speak to Christian groups, churches only, or do you go into the business venue?

**Hutson**

Actually it's a very wide variety of people, and I'm so thrilled that God has opened that door for me because I've always been involved in a large area of my life with charities, and our Chamber of Commerce, and Soroptomists, and various different things. It's very rewarding to me to be able to give back to the community. It allows me an opportunity to go in to volunteer groups, charitable groups, hospitals and be able to encourage their volunteers to keep on keeping on, as well as with businesses. One of the businesses' number one chief complaints, in any business of any size, are employees, and it's no different with our business. I love to be able to go in and try to help motivate employees, to encourage them, as well as even encourage the employers to make them more aware of how to deal with employees better. And then, of course, the Christian side is wonderful too with women's groups, and marriage conferences, and youth events. I'm just really blessed that God has opened so many doors to allow me to use the gift that He's given me. I'm very grateful.

**Wright**

What an interesting conversation. I really do appreciate you taking all this time with me.

**Hutson**

Oh, David, thank you.

**Wright**

Today we have been talking to Nancy Hutson. Nancy founded and began Shining Star Ministries in 2000 to promote her gift of speaking. She's a motivational speaker, an author, a businesswoman, and a certified health and wellness teacher. And as we have found out today, she loves to help people. Thank you so much, Nancy, for being with us on *Remarkable Women.*

**Hutson**

You bet, David. Thank you for allowing me and giving me that opportunity.

## About The Author

Nancy Hutson, put simply, is a real woman in the real world with real problems just like everyone else. But… as a Christian, motivational speaker, author, businesswoman, and certified health/wellness teacher she takes these experiences and shares them with humor, passion, and realness to motivate and encourage.

Nancy founded and began Shining Star Ministries in 2000 to promote her gift of speaking for the various fields and needs of different groups and organizations. She and her husband, Scott, own Cycle Connection Harley Davidson/Buell in Joplin Missouri. Being a Harley owner and enthusiast is one very interesting twist in her life! Through her life Nancy realized after many trials and situations that giving God control is the only way to succeed and survive!

**Nancy Hutson**

Shining Star Ministries

1420 S. Joplin Ave., Suite B

Joplin, Missouri 64801

Phone: 417.624.5303

Email: nancy@shiningstarministries.com

www.shiningstarministries.com

# *Chapter Nine*

## WENDY PATTON

### THE INTERVIEW

**David E. Wright (Wright)**

Today we are talking to Wendy Patton. Wendy is widely recognized as one of the most inspiring speakers on the subject of little or no money down real estate investing. Her real estate savvy and great depth of experience and knowledge has helped her in orchestrating the most complete and easy to follow lease option program in circulation. After graduating from the University of Colorado, she landed a job with EDS. Unfortunately for EDS, she had an enlightening experience with real estate investing and specifically with the technique called lease options. This experience eventually allowed Wendy to walk away from her corporate job and let her focus her efforts on real estate investing full time. Wendy is now is a licensed real estate broker and a licensed builder with her own real estate company in southeast Michigan called Majestic Realty, LLC. Wendy is the past president and board member of an investment group entitled, D.O.L.L.A.R.S. Wendy has experience in land development, property management, rehabs and foreclosures, but lease options are her favorite. Now investing since 1985, and with hundreds of transactions using lease options, she is extremely excited about the idea of teaching and being given the opportunity to help others achieve the same level of success. In her finely tuned lease option course for beginners as well as for the advanced investor, she demonstrates in the simplest format how to buy and sell lease options. Wendy will give you the knowledge in achieving what you're all striving for FX3—Future Financial Freedom. Wendy, welcome to Remarkable Women!

**Wendy Patton (Patton)**

Thank you, David.

**Wright**

Tell me, Wendy, how did you get involved in real estate investing and why?

**Patton**

Well, actually, I got started by accident. When I graduated from the University of Colorado in 1985, I had received a position with EDS, Electronic Data Systems, in the Detroit area, Ross Perot's old company. I was loading up my moving van to move from Colorado to the Detroit area. My mother was with me getting the moving van ready. Right before I was ready to leave she said, "Hey, Wendy, I've got something for you." I asked her what it was and she said, "I went to a real estate investing seminar last week, and I was really inspired by the speaker and the excitement he shared on buying and investing in real estate. You know I just think it's the most awesome thing and I really want to pursue it. I bought these cassettes and came home with them, and shared them with your dad. But you know what? Wendy, he is too conservative. He will not let me invest in real estate! So would you please take these with you and do something with them? You've got this long car drive ahead of you, so why don't you listen to them on the way?" So I did. I have always been kind of an entrepreneur type and in all honesty that's most likely why she picked me. I grew up with five siblings in my family. I have been by far the biggest entrepreneur in my family. As a child I used to buy things and turn around and sell them for more money. At the time of my leaving Colorado I was buying antiques and selling them for more money to help pay for my college expenses. So here I was listening to these cassettes, on my way to a new state and city and life. I listened to the tapes all the way to Michigan and I was really intrigued with the idea of buying houses and selling them for more money.

I was moved into a hotel due to a housing shortage in the Detroit area. E.D.S. had moved over 14,000 –15,000 people into the Detroit area at one time. There was zero housing available for us. We were all put up into these hotels and put on a six-month waiting list for any apartments in the metro Detroit area. I remember at that point in time I was on this waiting list for an apartment, and one thing on the cassettes that specifically stuck in my mind was, "If you're interested in real estate investing and doing these investing concepts, you really should join a local real estate investor group. They're all over the country. Find one in your area and get involved." So I did. I found a local investment group in my area and attended one of the meetings. At the time I figured I didn't know anyone here, so why not get out and meet some people and learn more about the concept on the cassettes? While at one of the local meetings, the topic came up about where everyone lived. The question turned to me and someone asked, "Wendy, where do you live?" I remember feeling embarrassed and uncomfortable. I was actually homeless.

I replied, "I live in The Red Roof Inn, room 101." You could just see the look on their confused faces.

They all started to say, "Okay, why?"

I said, "Well, it's a long story. You know there are no apartments available and I'm stuck in this hotel."

They all said, "Well, why don't you just buy a house?"

I said, "Well, you don't understand. I am 21 years old. I have negative $20,000.00 to my name. I make $10.00 an hour and I don't have any money. How can I buy a house?"

One person asked, "Do you have good credit?"

I said, "Well, yes, I have good credit."

They replied, "Take a cash advance from a credit card. That can be your down payment on your house, this way you can buy a house."

So I did precisely that. I bought my first home. It was a three-bedroom home, and at that time in 1985 my full payment was $438.00 a month, which was great because apartments were more than that. Being that the home was a three bedroom, I decided to rent two of the bedrooms to two ladies that were in the same situation. They lived with me and paid $250.00 each. So I had "cash flow" in my first deal, and I remember thinking, I have $62.00 a month, which is paying my credit card payment. I thought it was pretty cool! That's how I got involved in investing.

Now I teach people that credit cards are not the way you want to get started in investing. When people hear me speak and I'm teaching people how to invest in real estate with little or no money down, I use a visual display. I have kept all the credit cards I used to get started in real estate whether for down payments or for using credit to fix up the properties. I now have this credit card stack that is in this continual photo album that I unfold in my presentation, it unfolds to be over 50 feet long! It's truly unbelievable. I say to the audience, "Well, I did this over and over and over and over again." I show them this is how I got started investing in real estate, because I didn't know that there were these other techniques.

The techniques that I now teach people are exactly the opposite, which is not using credit to buy property. There are so many other ways to buy property other then using credit as I did.

**Wright**

We've all seen the television infomercials and things about zero down and everything. Could you tell me what is little down or zero down investing? How does it work, briefly?

**Patton**

The infomercials are primarily hype and excitement, and they make investing sound much easier than it really is. I will say if you use those systems and put them into place they can work. They're not as easy as they are portrayed to be and they don't work as easily for everyone as they claim, but there are a couple of ways that do work.

There are actually a couple different types of little or no money down techniques that are legitimate and legal. One of the techniques that I primarily use is what we call a lease with an option to buy and the other is a lease purchase. This is where you find a seller that you know has a home they own and maybe they've already bought their next home. Possibly they've already built a new home or have moved into their next home and they haven't been able to sell their old home. In this specific situation they are carrying two mortgage payments. Well, let's say they are fairly well off financially and they don't need to sell their old home - they would like to, but they don't have to sell it in order to buy the new home. So the biggest concern for this seller is typically just getting rid of that extra mortgage payment on the second home. They're not in trouble. They're not losing their home, but they would like the debt relief of the old payment.

The Lease Option technique works well in this type of situation for the seller that is just moving up in life. They do not need to have the cash from their old home but it's still bothering them that the home is just sitting there taking money out of their pockets each month.

That's the type of seller I really love to work with—a seller that just wants to get rid of that extra payment and the headache of carrying two homes. People in a situation such as that are happy to get someone to take over their payment and be done with it. So that's just one of the little or zero down techniques. There's another one that we call a "subject to." This is a technique I don't use and is usually more effective when a seller is in trouble, financially. They are usually behind in their payments, but not necessarily, they may be almost in foreclosure and are willing to sign over the deed to their home. They actually will deed you the home, being subject to the underlying mortgage. In layman terms this means, "Hey, I'll give you the deed. You're going to be on the title, but there's still a loan on the property and we agree you're going to make my payments." This is done so that their home doesn't go into foreclosure. What you are doing is keeping them from getting foreclosed on and damaging their credit further. You start making their payments, which helps restore their credit. That's a different little or no money down technique that's used pretty prevalently in the real estate investing industry. Lease Options and Subject to's are the two biggest techniques for little or no money down investing.

**Wright**

So how do you find most of your sellers?

**Patton**

Well, there are a lot of different ways. My favorite and most successful way has been working with Realtors, because the typical seller I am looking for is the seller who is not in financial trouble, and I prefer the prettier and nicer homes. I don't chase the sellers that are in financial trouble. It's kind of a different technique. I don't go after the ones that are down and out on their luck per se, although some of them do come to me. I have bought homes in that situation, but I don't chase them. Generally the homes I go after are the ones that are very nice homes, typically a little bit nicer than most investors would normally buy. In my specific neighborhood it might be a $200,000.00 - $300,000.00 home, sometimes even more, and so it ends up being a median price range or above. In Los Angeles, and in today's market, it might turn out to be a $650,000.00 home. In other parts of the country let's say for example, in Ohio, that median priced home might carry a $120,000.00 price tag, either way it usually ends up being higher than the median price of homes in the specific area. The median price range or above is typically what I am looking for, however, it can be slightly lower also. Realtors typically have those type of properties listed. They're working with the sellers who usually are not as down and out on their luck. For example, they have just built their new home and they decide to let the Realtor sell their old one. For whatever reason it hasn't sold yet or it has taken longer than expected, perhaps because the market's a little slower than forecasted. A lot of what I do is work with Realtors to find those specific homes and situations.

I also put ads in the paper to find sellers. I used to use ads and signs more often than I do now and with good results, but now I mostly find my deals through Realtors. I am networked fairly well now. They now call me. There are also some ads I run that will attract specific sellers to call me. There are some signs you can use that you can put out on the streets. I'm sure you've probably driven by and seen some of those "Cash For Your Home" or "Is Your Home Not Selling," "We Lease Homes," you know those kinds of signs. We, in the real estate investor industry, call them "bandit signs" because in many cities they are illegal even to put them out. There are a lot of other ways you can attract sellers that will give you calls too. Realtors are my niche' and that's why I teach my students how to work with them.

**Wright**

So how do you sell the home and how does this make an investor money?

**Patton**

I am the investor, so I would buy the home. Let's say I found a home for $200,000.00 from a seller. Now, I'll be honest with you; that home may be worth $200,000.00, so I might even pay $200,000.00 for that home, but not today. It might be five years from now. Now I'm thinking that in five years from now it's going to be worth more, and that's part of the way that I'm going to make money. There are two things that you make money with when you sell something on an option. The first consideration is appreciation on the property. The second, because my seller doesn't get that appreciation, they're locking in a price today for a future time. The buyer is locking into a future price, and that price is going to include the appreciation. The other thing that the buyer is paying for is the "option premium," which makes that specific property more valuable because they're getting terms. Typically a buyer will pay 5 to 10% more than the retail price in order to get a property with special financing terms like a lease option. This type of buyer typically cannot go get a mortgage today. They need time to improve their credit and start paying their bills on time so that they can get a conforming mortgage at the end of this lease period or sometime during the lease period. Typically this takes 12 to 18 months for most buyers. We call it a conforming mortgage, which means normal rates versus high rates. The buyer can get that even with bruised credit issues.

And that's how you make your money. For example, on a $200,000.00 home, if you've got an appreciation rate of even 5%, it's going to be worth another $10,000.00 for one year of appreciation. It will also be worth $20,000 more for a 10% option premium. So you're talking $30,000.00 total profit, which does not include cash flow potential. Let's say I negotiated $1,000.00 a month with my seller, and maybe my buyer is paying $1,295.00. That could be another $295.00 a month cash flow.

**Wright**

So what is a rehab property and how do you do one?

**Patton**

Well, the rehab property is a completely different type of investing strategy. It is where you buy a property that needs work. You bring in a crew. You fix it up and then you sell it. And I enjoy doing those also. They can be as profitable, but can also be satisfying because you are improving a home in your area or town.

**Wright**

There must be a lot of money in them.

**Patton**

There is a lot of money in both. They are both equally as profitable depending on how you structure each deal. The difference is that lease options take little or no money, leaving less risk, and you don't have to find a mortgage. You don't have to commit to any money out of pocket to make the $30,000-40,000, but you do have to manage it for the 12 to 18 to 24 months. You've got this property and you're working with and a tenant. With the rehab, you've got to get a mortgage or come up with the cash to renovate the property during this time period. You also need to manage a crew to get the property renovated. Then you have to be able to carry the payments until it is sold. They both have their pros and cons, but are both profitable and enjoyable.

**Wright**

So what other real estate investing topics are hot in buying strategies?

**Patton**

Foreclosures are very big right now. Many mortgage companies are seeing a rise in foreclosures. And a lot of investors are wanting to work with the mortgage companies.

**Wright**

You mean prior to foreclosing?

**Patton**

Yes. There are two different kinds of foreclosures. One is what we call pre-foreclosure, where you actually go in and try to buy the home from the owner. Then there's also what is called a short sale, which is where you go in and negotiate with a lender. You go in with a bank or the mortgage company that's going to be foreclosing and try to negotiate buying the note for a discount. There are many mortgage companies right now that are willing to take a discount on those mortgages and notes so they don't have to go through all that headache and hassle of foreclosure. They don't really want to be in the business of owning real estate and don't really want the property back. They just want their money back in the bank, even if it's a little bit less. So those are big: the pre-foreclosures, buying from the owner at a discount, and then also buying from the bank at a discount. They are in the business of loaning, not owning!

**Wright**

So in those, you're going to have to actually have the money to buy it out. You're not assuming a mortgage or anything.

**Patton**

Right. Assumable mortgages are not common anymore and not really available. You may not have to pay it off. The first one you can, which is what we talked about in the beginning, the "subject to" type of investing. Depending on how far along in the process they are in foreclosure, you may be able to do what we call "bring them current." Let's say they're $5,000.00 behind on their mortgage payments. You could wire that $5,000.00 to the mortgage company which would bring them current on their mortgage payments and then have them deed you the home (this is the subject to). They put the deed in your name and you start making the mortgage payments. Now obviously, the lender doesn't like the deed out of the owners name and in your name, so there is a chance of what we call a "due on sale," meaning that the lender may say, "Well, you know we didn't give the loan to you, Wendy, we gave it to Joe. We want the whole loan paid in full – Due now. Give us the $90,000.00 balance of the mortgage." But the chances that this will even happen are very, very rare. Really they just want to be paid on time. It's pretty much paranoia from new investors, but it could happen.

I also enjoy land development. Land development is extremely profitable in areas of the country where land is valuable. For instance, in my area even a very, very small lot (50'X110') starts at $40,000.00. If I can buy just a normal house, even a $150,000.00 house, that might have a bigger lot than normal, and then split off a lot. The home is still worth the original $150,000 and an additional $40,000 for the new lot. It really doesn't change the original home value much, if any, by removing that small piece of land, but having that extra lot split and separate now makes that deal worth $40,000 more for me the investor. This can be even more profitable when the home needs renovation or can be lease optioned out to a new buyer for more than the original $150,000. The numbers get even bigger for my profit margin. You can do something mid-size like an eight-acre parcel and do 5 one-acre home sites. Of course, you can go very big too with it - two or three hundred acre parcels, and put in a subdivision. Subdivisions are extremely profitable but can also take years to develop and can cost millions of dollars in roads, lighting, landscaping, architects, planners fees, engineering fees, politics, surveyors, etc. So there are different things that you can do in real estate investing, some with little or no money, some with lots of money.

**Wright**

So tell me, what is FX3 and why is this your motto?

**Patton**

It's Future Financial Freedom, FX3, and that is my motto because the way that I got started was with those credit cards, and to me that is just such a potential for disaster for our country—living on the edge of credit debt. I just thank my lucky stars and God above that I didn't go over the edge. Financially I was able to pay off all of those credit cards and not go through any financial troubles and get out of debt, but so many people can't or don't know how to. There are no choices for them. They think, "Well, I've got to file bankruptcy. I've just got to get rid of this debt." We keep spending all of this money instead of thinking of ways to get out of debt and ways to build for a future. Right now there's no company that's safe anymore. I grew up in the military, and even that's not safe anymore. My dad always thought for sure he had a great retirement and great medical benefits, but they changed over the years. No one would have thought that back then. With all the companies being laid off we have to create our own financial future. I believe that real estate investing is really one of the only ways for people to create Future Financial Freedom (FX3) for themselves.

**Wright**

Tell me, why do you like being self-employed versus working for corporate America?

**Patton**

That's a whole book in itself. I did work for corporate America for 10 years plus little jobs before that. I liked what I did, but the bottom line is that you'll never ever be truly financially free working for corporate America. First of all you have no time freedom.

I don't like someone telling me I have to be there at 8:00 tomorrow morning or every day from 8:00 to 5:00. Even my employees who work for me, I don't tell them those types of rules. I do have employees that work for me, but I won't tell them they have to be there from 8:00 to 5:00. They know what needs to be done and what it takes to do it. If they weren't responsible enough to take care of the tasks at hand they wouldn't be on my team. I don't want anyone to feel like they have to be pinned down to a time period. So that's one thing for me. I didn't like the dress code thing. I dress up when I should. I'm tired of rules and regulations. I could be a rebel at heart, that could be part of it.

**Wright**

I can't wait to hear what you had to wear.

**Patton**

I had to wear pantyhose every day, so now I think I've had the same pantyhose in my drawer from 1995 from when I left corporate America.

**Wright**

Trust me, I wouldn't know what you're talking about.

**Patton**

I wear pantyhose when I speak but that's about it. The truth of the matter is it's the Future Financial Freedom. I tell people, "Look, if you love what you do for your job, you shouldn't quit," because there are jobs out there, employee job wise, that people love, and that's wonderful. You are blessed. I feel that real estate investing is the only way to invest right now that is the safest way to build a business on the side that will give you Future Financial Freedom. It's not going to be in the stock market, and it's not going to be from your employer. So if you love what you do, that's great, but you need to invest for the future. I've worked as many or more hours than I did before, but if I want to golf tomorrow afternoon, I just want to be able to say, "I'm going golfing." I don't want someone to give me permission. My employees have the same freedom.

**Wright**

I went into business for myself in 1969, and with the exception of one year, I've been in business for myself all this time. And I work harder for myself than I ever worked for the corporate. But you truly get the rewards for it.

**Patton**

Right. When you work for a company, no matter what you do, or no matter how good of an idea it is, they truly cannot pay you what it's worth. They can't or they wouldn't be in business. They have their overhead too. I remember my bonus from EDS is what threw me over the edge. And thank you, Lord, that it was so bad that it made me leave, because if it was really good, I may have not left that soon. I worked very hard for the entire year on this project, and they were having financial problems and starting to cut budgets. At the end of the year, my boss called me in and said, "Here's your bonus." It was $2,000.00. I had been traveling and working extra hours, and I said, "You know, I could have worked at Burger King and made more money." I was so angry! But it made me realize that they couldn't pay me what I was worth. I can only earn what I'm worth by being self-employeed. That bonus was the best and worst bonus I have ever received! It was what I needed to leave corporate America and be a full time real estate investor and speaker.

**Wright**

What do you feel are the most important qualities that make a person successful?

**Patton**

Commitment. I had one lady who bought my course. She called five people to try the lease option system. They all said, "No."

She called me up and said, "I want a refund on your course."

I said, "Please send it back."

She said, "It is that easy to return your course?"

I said, "Yes. You don't have enough commitment to make it work."

She said, "What do you mean?"

I said, "If you're only willing to call five people and you think that after five people you should be successful, you don't have what it's going to take, honestly. You should send it back."

How many times have I been rejected or things haven't gone right? I have a building that got broken into two days in a row just recently and I have not thought twice about it. I forgot about it until my office called today and said, "Do we need to send someone to clean it up?" I said, "Oh yeah, you know what? We do. I forgot about it." You need commitment, endurance, creativity – the ability to look for solutions when you come to a roadblock and not give up easily. Sometimes you come to a roadblock. It's okay and you may want to just die that day. You think the world's falling apart. Cry, fine. Just leave it for the day. It's okay. We all have those days. Come back to it tomorrow morning and figure out how to solve it. But it's that endurance, that commitment and just looking for a solution that is important. It's not getting down when you feel like everything is falling apart, especially when in you're in business yourself or you know that even in a job or anywhere that things do go wrong. Sometimes you feel like everything goes wrong in one day and you have a bad day or a bad week or a bad month. I really truly believe that the successful people are the ones who are able to continue and not give up.

Goal Setting is of course one of my favorite topics and something near and dear to my heart. Those that set goals are by far more successful than those that don't. It is a proven fact. I am very goal oriented and driven by my goals. One of my goals this year was to write a book. I am completing that as we are doing this chapter in this Remarkable Women book.

**Wright**

Well, what an interesting conversation. Wendy Patton is widely recognized as one of the most inspiring speakers on little or no money down real estate investing. Her real estate savvy and great depth of experience and knowledge has helped her in orchestrating the most complete and easy to follow lease options program that we can find today. You can find out more about Wendy and her courses at www.WendyPatton.com. And as we have found in this conversation, she knows a whole lot about all kinds of real estate investing. So, Wendy, thank you so much for being with us today on *Remarkable Women*. You are truly remarkable.

## About The Author

Wendy Patton is widely recognized as one of the most inspiring speakers on "Little or No Money Down" real estate investing. Her real estate savvy and great depth of experience and knowledge has helped her in orchestrating the most complete and easy to follow, Lease/Option Program in circulation. After graduating from University of Colorado, she landed a job with EDS. Unfortunately for EDS, she had an enlightening experience with real estate (lease/option) and walked away from her corporate job and decided to focus her efforts on real estate investing full time. Wendy Patton now is a licensed real estate broker and licensed builder with her own real estate company in southeast Michigan called Majestic Realty, LLC. Wendy Patton is the past president and board member of D.O.L.L.A.R.S. Wendy Patton's finely tuned Lease/Option course for beginners as well as the advanced investor. Wendy demonstrates in the simplest format, how to buy and sell Leases/Options. This program will give you the knowledge to achieve what we are all striving for, "Future Financial Freedom" FX3.

**Wendy Patton**

Limitless Options, Inc.

P.O. Box 144

Lake Orion, Michigan 48361

Phone: 248.394.0767

Fax: 248.394.2126

Email millrealty@aol.com

www.WendyPatton.com

# *Chapter Ten*

## Sasha ZeBryk

### THE INTERVIEW

**David E. Wright (Wright)**

Today we are talking to Sasha ZeBryk. Sasha shows people how to stand out and shine in the marketplace...in *Technicolor*. She inspires people in organizations to speak and network with purpose, power, and passion. She earned a B.A. Degree in English, a Business Woman of the Year Award, and serves on the Board of Directors of the New England National Speakers Association. She is a speaker, keynoter, executive speech coach, voice-over artist and the author of *NetWork the Room like a PRO—99 Tips & Techniques*. Her *Technicolor* seminars guarantee more contacts and more business with less sweat and more fun. Sasha, welcome to *Remarkable Women*!

**Sasha ZeBryk (ZeBryk)**

It's good to talk with you.

**Wright**

Sasha, this book is titled *Remarkable Women*. In your experience dealing with women, what characteristics do you think remarkable women have in common? To put it in another way, what do you think makes a woman remarkable?

**ZeBryk**

A remarkable woman has a clear sense of her life's purpose, and knows her purpose is bigger than she is. I see remarkable women exuding passion, not only about their work, but how they connect to other people. They have this ability to...kind of excite people, and in a way, teach us how to be more alive. Julia Child, for example, showed us her zest for living and expressed it through her unadulterated desire to share her love of food and fun.

The remarkable women I know are also very generous. This past summer I met with a college president in her office to talk about my first Tips Booklet that I had just published. Despite her busy schedule, she gave me her undivided attention. I wasn't in her office six minutes, when she became as animated and enthused about my project as I was. She said to me, *"...and Sasha, here's an idea for you about the alums,...and you could market it this way...and etc."* And as she went on, I thought, "How remarkable!" in just a few minutes she tuned in and lifted my mission and me to a higher plane.

**Wright**

My company just published a book of first and second graders' comments. One of the questions we asked was, "What do you want to be when you grow up?" This little second grader said that she wanted to be a doctor so she could save lives and help people through their sickness and cure them—even if they were a boy. So she's already growing.

**ZeBryk**

Yes, at a young age, she's already expressed the idea that serving others can be noble. Even though she might think differently about boys in 7 or 8 years, she's showing early signs of becoming a remarkable woman.

**Wright**

Will you tell our readers a little bit about your background and the journey that you took to get where you are today?

**ZeBryk**

My father died when I was ten, leaving my mother widowed and alone with 11 children, aged 15 months to 17 years. We didn't have a lot of money. There was no such thing as an allowance in our family of 11, so we had to find our own way to make a little money for the things we wanted. My first ""job" was singing Christmas carols every night for the two weeks before Christmas...me with all of my brothers and sisters old enough to stand up. Our favorite location was the high-columned Oliver Building in downtown Pittsburgh, PA. We collected donations in two of those round, 12 inch high Mother's Oats boxes, wrapped with Christmas paper, with a slot cut into the top for coins and bills. I was six when we began. Mother would pay each of us twenty-five cents for an entire night's work (that's about 36 songs). People are surprised to learn how, to this day, I still know *all* of the verses to most of the carols. We found many other ways to make money—like scouring the neighborhood to find empty soda bottles and selling loads of products door-to-door. We even tried to establish our family as THE neighborhood babysitting service. We'd look for prospects by canvassing the streets, scouting out every house that had a baseball, bike or baby doll in the yard.

In high school I became very competitive by entering (and usually winning) every sales contest, whether it was selling the most Easter candy or raising money for veterans. Out of necessity, at this early age, I'm sure I was developing entrepreneurial leanings. When I was 25, I graduated from Franciscan University with an English degree and for six months taught high school as a substitute teacher. I learned I really am a teacher at heart and love being in front of a group, but pure academia was not for me. During the next 21 years, I worked with 7 different companies, and while prestigious and rewarding, none of them had that combination that'd allow me to use all of my natural teaching and entrepreneurial talents. Though I was successful and got excellent business experience, I was never fully satisfied. I felt I was always "under-employed."

**Wright**

How did you know the work you're doing now was the work for you?

**ZeBryk**

One Sunday morning in 1994, I was reading the Lifestyle section of the Sunday paper. Smack in the middle of the front page was a woman standing next to a seven foot ladder. Her name was Judes, and she had just given a keynote speech at a women's conference about how she motivates women to "climb the ladder of their dreams." Her story as unfolded in the article literally started my body vibrating. I mean, I was stirred with a passion...that I'd never felt before. I thought to myself, "She's showing me how to *live* my dream." I could really SEE it. So I phoned her to ask for a couple hours of her time to help me form the Big picture view of the ladder to my future. That two hour meeting turned into an inspiring six and a half hour conversation. It was a conversation that changed the path of my life. We discovered we had much in common, formed a mentoring friendship, and soon after, made a very bold decision to jointly produce our own regional *Whole Woman Conference.*

One thing I learned from Judes was never be afraid to go "to the top" to seek advice. She told me how she had once called then-Secretary of Education, Bill Bennet, to ask an intriguing question no one locally could answer. He actually called her back, which led to her being invited to Washington. She even got photographed with President Reagan. I'll forever be grateful to Judes. Because of her, I finally recognized how to meaningfully combine my natural, God-given talents with very worthwhile work. And, because of her, I make a special effort to mentor other women to help them identify and fulfill their life's ambition. I might be working with up to three or four women at any given time.

**Wright**

After that women's conference, what made your speaking career grow?

**ZeBryk**

The first conference proved to me I was now on the right career track. We did a lot of things wrong and a lot of things right. People related to my message. I loved it. That conference gave me the courage and confidence to seek out big name company sponsors and produce two additional regional ones. This time, by myself. From these I learned two things: one, I love working with women…women are so open to learning (and we laugh quicker and more easily than men); and two, I knew the road to build a speaking business would be a long, dusty one. Yet, *never* had I felt so clear. I was fully, viscerally energized. For the first time in my life I saw how I could combine all of my gifts, talents, strengths and yearnings in work that had meaning and thrilled me. Daily, I would pray for insight; and I sought guidance and advice from many people I admired including former teachers, a gifted pastor, and, of course, my sisters.

Then one day a flyer arrived in the mail advertising business seminars. I sat at my breakfast table and said, "Why not work for the companies that already give seminars nationally and learn from them from the bottom up?" Two seminar companies hired me as a part-time program manager (PM). The PM handles the logistics, hotel arrangements and help with product sales. In the 18 months working as a PM, I met some of the best speakers in the country. I watched everything they did; listened to how they opened and closed every training session and I took scads of notes. I observed how they dealt with audience questions, with hecklers; how they increased books and tapes sales at the back of the room; and *I visualized myself in their position.* Visibility is vital to growing a business, so I sought out opportunities to develop my own adult education workshops at four local colleges; I volunteered to head committees, gave a lot of free talks, and listened very carefully to the feedback people gave me.

**Wright**

What are some of the things you learned from feedback people gave you?

**ZeBryk**

One thing many people said again and again was, "Nobody connects with people in a room like you do." In my earlier business career, I learned I had a knack for creating spirit and rapport within a group. Whether I was a management recruiter, a sales manager, whether I was training or just holding a meeting, my bosses would say, "Go out there and get things going."

When I started going to networking events, my rule was to get there early and stay late. I always came prepared with a goal and a bag of questions, eager to learn. I'd ask business owners and other professionals about themselves, listen to their successes, their woes and their needs. Then I try to connect people who could benefit one another.

People would comment on how I "worked the room" and frequently asked, "How do you do it? Tell us." I recognized a need and demand for what I did. I saw a specialty niche market and knew I could satisfy it with programs designed with my own personal imprint. So I broke down, step by step, my way of "working a room," did a lot of research and developed my own philosophy and principles, centered on this one belief: that great networking is the art of listening and helping others without expectation. People recognize generosity and the reward it in unimaginable ways. Networking has become the hallmark of my speaking business and many call me an expert. When

I reflect on it, though, I suspect I started developing a lot of these skills while growing up around my family's long, oval dining table.

**Wright**

You come from a large family, eight girls and three boys. How has your family influenced your choices down through the years? And tell us more about the long, oval table.

**ZeBryk**

Our dinner table evokes many wonderful memories of growing up in a big family. All 11 of us had our individual place, and if anyone were missing, we could feel their absence. I loved dinner time in our house. Around this big, long, oval table was the chance to share the highs and lows of your day. It was a boisterous, mostly joyous experience where you had to be on your toes to get not only your fair share of the meal, but also the attention and the conversation. As a teenager, I felt very self-conscious in public. The two things that helped my confidence to grow, were getting braces for my teeth and telling stories and jokes at the dinner table (which later turned into skits performed for the family).

If I knew we were having guests, I'd privately rehearse a song or a skit or a poem, anything, because I knew my mother would often ask one of us to perform. I was always ready with my *impromptu* song. I've brought this pattern into my business life. And I tell my audiences today that, to be successful, the pro is always prepared. *Luck is simply opportunity meeting preparation.*

**Wright**

Who had the most influence on your life to date?

**ZeBryk**

The first is my mother. She had a very hard life in my early years, widowed, no money; and oodles of decisions to make with 11 young children. So I admire her perseverance. She never cried out, "Why me, Lord?" As a woman of strong faith, she knew that God had a plan for her. Even with her daily load of responsibilities, she was optimistic, loved to celebrate everything; she's a great cook and loves to dance. Mother was tireless. She'd think nothing of rising at 3:00 am to mix yeast and knead dough so that her famous home-made *paska* could be enjoyed at breakfast.

My mother was also resourceful. I recall a Saturday night around 1962; just before closing time we rushed into a bakery to buy some rolls for Sunday breakfast. (Pennsylvania Blue Laws at that time prevented stores from opening on Sundays.) As my mother eyed all of the baked goods that hadn't been sold, she asked, "What do you do with all the extras?" The owner answered, "Some we take to the nuns; and the rest we throw away." Seizing the opportunity, my mother said to him, "I'll pay you a dollar for everything you throw away. And my children wouldn't mind coming down here every Saturday to give you a dollar for the leftovers." That was one of Mother's ways...and I seek to emulate her resourcefulness, ever-present faith, and her buoyant optimism.

And my husband, John, had a strong influence. As a musician I would say, John heard the song in me long before I did and he didn't rest until I heard it too. From our marriage in 1984, he saw that the jobs I had up to then didn't fully use my natural talents. He urged me to reach very, very high, and encouraged me to make the most of and market many of the people skills I took for granted. His strengths were my weaknesses: he helped me to conquer procrastination (the *real* thief of success); to think more logically, and to prioritize. John's a man of action, and he'd say things like, "Marsha, (using my baptismal name), let's put this marketing plan down on paper...today."

**Wright**

In your workshops, you skillfully use stories and anecdotes to make your points. I was intrigued by your challenge to your participants to relive their stories and anecdotes, not just tell them. What's that all about?

**ZeBryk**

When we tell a story, we want to re-create the expectation that "once upon a time" produces. We remember stories more through our emotions than by recalling facts. Some people tell stories exactly as they happen, accounting for every minute, chronologically, every fact. "And then we went home, and met so and so, and then we...." That's *telling* it. But the storyteller *relives* the experience, pulls us into the moment as if we are there with him. Stories are successful when they involve us emotionally.

**Wright**

You also teach four parts of storytelling. Could you share with our readers what they are and how to develop these four parts?

**ZeBryk**

Yes. Get right into your story. Avoid starting with "I'm going to tell you a funny story," or "something really interesting." Don't tell listeners how to feel; let them discover their own emotions *in* the story. So, part one is, hook the listener quickly, in the opening. *Last Tuesday, around four am, my car had two flat tires. At that time, the snow was only about seven or eight inches deep.* Part two, develop your story by creating pictures in the person's mind using the five senses. *"She was sobbing so loudly, all I could hear was a teenager on the brink of heartbreak."* Paint pictures in people's minds through their senses with colors, sounds, smells, and comparisons. *"She smelled like a gardenia at midnight."* We don't remember the facts as much as we remember the emotional pictures created. And part three, create a dilemma. A good story has a cliff hanger or a surprise that's pointed and sharp. And part four, solve the dilemma. It's the "aha" moment that makes the whole story meaningful and significant. Clarify and reduce the lesson to be learned to one thing: how have you changed and what insight can you now pass on to the listener?

**Wright**

That's good. You know, most of us find it difficult to meet new people and simply be comfortable in new surroundings where we don't know anyone. Could you give our readers a few tips on how to overcome these fears and so we can widen our friendships and/or client and customer base?

**ZeBryk**

The easiest way to overcome such fear is to focus on the other person. When first meeting someone, make them feel at ease by *your* body language: look them in the eyes and linger just long enough to notice the color of their eyes—and smile! Smiling, you know, boosts your own likeability and reduces the emotional distance between two people. Next, find something positive to say or compliment them about. Admire an accessory, like a necktie or earrings; tell them their energy is catching or that they look great in that certain color. Be upbeat; concentrate mostly on them and less on yourself. Whatever you say, really mean it; insincerity is quickly recognized. By doing these simple, easy things, your confidence will go up while your anxiety will fade away and your circle of friends will grow.

**Wright**

So you're saying that fear and anxiety in social situations come from thinking about ourselves too much?

**ZeBryk**

Absolutely. I can't overemphasize how much more important it is to be *interested* than interesting. So, to overcome fear and anxiety, get the other person to talk as soon as you can. People like to talk about themselves once they sense some trust and interest from you. Use questions to stimulate conversation rather than trying to think of something clever to say. Whether you're shy or not, asking questions is a learnable skill that can be perfected with practice just like any other skill.

One of the best ways of doing this is to think up questions in advance. If going to a small party or group, find out who's going to be there and think up a question for each of them. At a larger business, social or networking event, come with three or four general questions you could ask most anyone—about current events, business trends, sports, community. Your questions should be ready and on the tip of your tongue. Remember, "the pro is always prepared."

**Wright**

You have a reputation for remembering names. Tell us how you do it and how you teach people in your audiences to do it.

**ZeBryk**

Yes, we do love the sound of our name. So, to remember names, I use and recommend this: *Decide, Repeat, Picture, Write.* Anyone can do it. *Decide* that you will remember someone's name; then listen with your eyes, ears and mind. You see, all of us have a photographic memory; some of us just don't put in the film. So, putting in the film is the act of paying attention. Give people your full attention. Don't dart your eyes to the left or the right, or over their shoulder. *Repeat* the person's whole name as soon as possible by including it in a comment or question. You might ask how it's spelled, "Is that Anne with an 'e'?" *Picture* the person in an absurd and vivid way in your mind: does the person remind you of Abraham Lincoln, or your red-haired

Aunt Kate? Lock in that picture. Lastly, *write* down the name ASAP, on a business card or even a cocktail napkin. You're three times more likely to remember a person's name when pay attention with *all* of your senses.

**Wright**

You know many people reading this book are in sales-related occupations. Simply put, the income is in direct proportion to their ability to make an impact on others. Could you talk about the number one secret for being remembered, recalled, or referred, and explain it to us?

**ZeBryk**

Gladly, and let me say that this concept applies equally to all people who interact with others. The number one secret, I believe, to being remembered, recalled, and referred is this: always think of yourself as a *host* not as a guest. Hosts feel responsible for other people by greeting them, starting conversations, mingling and offering to be of service to them. You don't have to be an extrovert or the life-of-the-party to be remembered. Some of the most successful people I know are low-keyed and reserved and create immediate rapport by putting others' needs above their own. Their antenna is always up and operating: they think "outward" not "inward," showing curiosity and interest by asking questions. When it's their time to talk, they don't preach, teach or sell; they just tell. And, they're great listeners.

These people may in fact be guests, but they act like hosts. For example, they'll start a conversation with someone who looks shy or alone; they offer to pass the refreshments; or they may position themselves near the entrance and greet people as they enter and help direct them to the coat room, rest room or toward the real host. The secret of being remembered, recalled and referred is this: people remember *you* when you concentrate on *them*.

**Wright**

So true! One of the things you emphasize is that the art of asking questions is the key to making people feel important. What are some of the *no sweat* questions master networkers use to make people feel important?

**ZeBryk**

The best way to get people talking is to ask open-ended questions... questions that require more than one-word answers like "yes" or "no." I call them *no sweat* because you can prepare them in advance. Begin your questions with "How? Which? In what way..? What was the first...?" *How did you come up with that idea...?* Or, I might ask a seasoned CEO: *What changes have you seen take place in the XYZ industry over the last 15 years?* You get to learn and the CEO gets an opportunity to shine. One of my favorite *no sweat* questions is: *What did you learn the hard way?* Delightful, incredible answers follow. Asking interesting questions, makes people feel important.

**Wright**

You mentioned earlier that you enjoyed working with women and have experienced some success in working with them. Tell us a little more and why.

**ZeBryk**

The glass ceiling still exists. Women haven't yet reached an equality with men in pay scale and recognition. And women remain shy about allowing their light to shine in the marketplace, and I seem to be able to give them the techniques, as well as the strength and courage, and sometimes the pizzazz, to release their talents. I show people how to brand their uniqueness and brag in the marketplace, by transforming ho-hum introductions into *Technicolor* ones where people say, "Tell me more." Early on as a woman business owner, I learned that you need to promote yourself, often shamelessly, because if you don't paddle your own canoe, it doesn't move. So women see in me, I think, a fellow traveler (although not the most glamorous) who is successful in her field and who's dealt with the obstacles they face.

Whether I'm coaching or teaching, I make it a point to offer every person at least three specific things they can do immediately to enhance their life. They draw confidence from the energy I bring to my seminars, from my stories, the strength of my convictions, and from what my husband calls my "joyful, eternally optimistic attitude." We have a lot of fun together.

**Wright**

You emphasize the importance of inner peace to release the power source we all have within us to live a more productive and joy-filled life. What do you mean?

**ZeBryk**

Many of us are weighed down with the excess baggage of regrets, self-doubt and past hurts which hinder us from rising to our full potential. Part of my mission is to help people believe that they can let go of regrets and embrace the present; reject work that's meaningless or ask for forgiveness and receive it. Joyful people get through life's bumps, others' criticism, even self-doubt more easily. Joy comes when we make peace with ourselves; when we count our blessings not our bruises.

**Wright**

I've got friends who don't speak to their mother or siblings. I'm thinking, "Isn't it time to forgive?" When we do forgive, it then becomes God's gift to us.

**ZeBryk**

Yes, and the gift is one of peace. When we do make peace, our heart has much more room for joy. Joy, then, gives us the inner power to live deeply, not on the surface or in boredom. We're more open to life's abundance and much more creative, more grateful...and experience God's love more.

**Wright**

I completely agree with you. I understand that 87% of the population of the U.S. gets up every morning and goes to a place that they don't want to be.

**ZeBryk**

I've been there.

**Wright**

So, let me give you a *no sweat* question I learned from you. If you could do anything else with your life and career, what would you choose to do?

**ZeBryk**

Well, it took me 46 years to find the special work that I now do. Wonderful, interesting people have come into my life. They have showered me with friendship, and they've trusted me with some of the intimacies of their lives. When I work with an audience, and they respond to my message and say something like, *"You helped me reach down and bring out my best self,"* I absolutely know that I'm in the right place. To have such an impact on people's lives is a privilege. I don't know how many people can say at the beginning of every workday, 'I am in the right place and can't wait to get started.' And I can say that. So, David, I don't think I'd change a thing, except that, maybe, I'd like to be about 11 pounds lighter doing it.

**Wright**

Well, Sasha, I have really enjoyed this conversation. I've learned a lot and I think our readers have learned why you are so remarkable. I want you to know how much I appreciate your taking so much of your time. You've just done such a great job and I really appreciate it.

## About The Author

Sasha ZeBryk is a recognized networking expert, speaker, speech coach, and voice-over artist. She shows audiences how to release their inner powers to speak and network with her trademark 3 P's: Purpose, Power, and Passion. She is author of *NetWork the Room like a PRO-99Tips* and *Techniques and Introduce Yourself in Technicolor*. Sasha earned a Business Woman of the Year award and serves on the New England National Speakers Association Board of Directors.

**Sasha ZeBryk**

SashaSpeaks Seminars

210 Beekman Drive

Agawam, Massachusetts 01001

Phone: 413.821.0086

Email: sasha@sashaspeaks.com

www.sashaspeaks.com

# Chapter Eleven

## KAYE BERNARD MCGARRY, M.ED.

### THE INTERVIEW

**David E. Wright (Wright)**

Today we are talking to Kaye Bernard McGarry. Kaye earned a degree in Secretarial Science from Barry University in Miami, a BA degree in Business Administration from the University of South Florida in Tampa, and holds a Master's Degree in Education in Guidance and Counseling from the University of North Carolina at Charlotte. In 1992, Kaye started a company, Survival in College Seminars, and has been presenting programs at various high schools, churches, and colleges throughout the United States helping college-bound students and parents. Since publishing her first book in 1998 titled *A New Beginning: A Survival Guide for Parents of College Freshmen*, she has been invited to speak on college campuses as well as serving as a guest on various talk shows. She has also presented at numerous educational seminars. Her book was featured in *U.S.A. Today* and a newly updated second edition came off the press in 2001. Kaye is a former teacher of high school and college students, is a member of the North Carolina Counselors Association, the National and Carolinas Speakers Association, Toastmasters International, and has long been involved in the Charlotte community as an active volunteer in the arts, her church, and for the past 12 years as a Trustee at Central

Piedmont Community College. In November, 2003, Kaye won a four-year term as an At-Large Member of the Charlotte-Mecklenburg Board of Education. Kaye, welcome to *Remarkable Women*!

**Kaye Bernard McGarry (McGarry)**

Thank you, David.

**Wright**

Boy, you're busy, aren't you?

**McGarry**

Yes!

**Wright**

Oh my! When I think of professional speakers, I think of motivational or inspirational speeches designed to inspire sales or marketing people. With a 15 year old daughter, who is a high school sophomore, I was fascinated by your book titled *A New Beginning: A Survival Guide for Parents of College Freshmen* and surprised to learn that you actually offer workshops and seminars on the subject. So what led you to this line of work?

**McGarry**

David, when I reflect on that question, I realize many seeds were planted along the way for a good many years.

Basically, I think of three distinct turning points in my life that led me into this career path. Let me tell you a story to illustrate the first two turning points. I grew up the 3rd of 8 children. I was VERY SHY. In my high school class, I was voted "Friendliest" in my class. Being shy, I only smiled and said hello, but I smiled and said hello to every single person. When I was a freshman at Barry College, a Catholic women's college, in Miami, Florida, I was taught by the nuns. At that time they wore those habits you see in movies with Whoopi Goldberg. They were my professors. One of my professors, Sr. Christopher, asked me to give a report in front of my class. Being so shy, I replied that I couldn't do that. "I can't get up in front of anyone and speak." In no uncertain terms, Sr. Christopher made it clear that I would not get the "A" I had earned to this point if I did not give that report in front of my class. Lo and behold, I remember to this day what I wore, my pin striped suit with red buttons and red shoes. I remember how I sweated thinking I would literally not live through the day. Sr. Christopher was definitely one woman who influenced my life dramatically. What happened that day when I was a freshman in college was that someone believed in me when I did not believe in myself. That was a turning point in my life. I want the parents and students I interact with to know that they, too, will experience many turning points in their lives. When these opportunities present themselves, we need to be aware, to listen, and to open the door to experience that opportunity. Only in this way will we each grow as a person.

Some years later when I was completing my graduate work in Education in Guidance and Counseling, I was assigned to Queens College as an intern. My job was to interview incoming freshmen students in the residence halls regarding their roommate situation. I found I loved working with college freshmen and understanding the transitions they were dealing with at this point in their lives. I still have all those roommate surveys.

At the same time, I was raising four children. I continually attended all the parent seminars and meetings at schools with experts who come and tell you how to raise your kids. I was at every one of them. So you know that meant I was in many auditoriums over several years sitting there listening to all of this knowledge. At one time it seemed that I just wanted to be on stage instead of sitting in the audience, but yet I didn't have a viable topic. I had lots of ideas for topics, but nothing that would warrant such an audience. And, then it came to me one evening as I sat listening to a speaker tell about the transition from high school to college. It was a light bulb going on and saying to me. "This is your topic." I knew I was fully qualified to address this topic. All the pieces eventually fell into place.

I share these stories with you because in the last 15 years, I have stood before hundreds of audiences, many of them parents of college freshmen, and many of them seniors in high school. I love doing what I do. I feel I am using the talents God gave me through speaking and writing and I sincerely hope I am making a difference in people's lives and will continue to do so.

**Wright**

You mention that Sr. Christopher, one of your professors at Barry College, was an inspiration to you and planted a seed that changed your life. What other women have dramatically influenced your life and career?

**McGarry**

My mother, Anna Bess Dineen Bernard. She gave me the greatest gift of all, the gift of a strong faith in God through the Catholic church. By her quiet example of raising eight children, she exemplified the best of what a woman should strive for and become. She was very patient and a terrific listener. She was a homemaker, yet her job was the most important job of all and all of her children appreciated her dedication to being a homemaker. She encouraged a healthy lifestyle through proper nutrition and regular physical exercise. She also taught me how to volunteer and give back to the community in which I live.

I also think of Barbara Walters. For years, I loved hearing her interview personalities on TV and I respected her sincerity and work ethic. I read her book on speaking and treasured every word. She was a role model to me. She represented the most skilled in bringing out the best in others through her interviews.

Mother Theresa of Calcutta captured the world by lifting up the neediest persons and helping one person at a time. Wow. She is at the top of my list. She lived her life truly loving to pray, because she felt prayer gives a clean heart and a clean heart can see God. I treasure the memory of her visit to Charlotte, North Carolina. In person, she appeared as a very tiny woman, soft spoken, yet she held the world on her shoulders and by her example, she could move mountains. She moved millions and even after her death in 1997 at age 87, she has many who are following in her footsteps.

These are the truly remarkable women who have helped me overcome obstacles in my life and inspired me to succeed in life, by striving to make a positive difference in many people's lives.

**Wright**

When I read the story of your first phone call to your son three days after he had gone off to college, I laughed. That was before I put myself in your concerned position. You stated that after that, your next three children afforded you the opportunity to let go and enjoy the process. Can you tell our readers a little bit about the process?

**McGarry**

Letting go is really very difficult for most parents, even those who say, "Oh, it's no problem. My kids have gone, isn't that wonderful." But there is a process, and I think it happens with any transition in our life. When a child goes off to college, whether it's your first or second or fourth or tenth, there is change in your household. One's gone and there's a different pecking order again. Therefore, it offers parents, as well as students, an opportunity. We always focus on the student saying, "Isn't it wonderful, they're off to college!" "They have all these opportunities. Isn't that great?" Yet just as important are the parents, and the wonderful opportunities they have during this transition as well. When I took my fourth child to college, even though I have learned that I have to let go, I did shed a few tears as I left him. It was dark and I hoped he didn't see my tears. After I got home, he wrote me a letter explaining how he felt about the transition and he actually felt the same way I did. He said it was "Exciting and a little bit scary!" That is how I explain the transition process to parents, it's exciting but it is also a little bit scary because our roles change. Maybe it's time we reconnected with ourselves at another level. No doubt, when a child goes to college it leaves a void. The challenge is deciding what to do with it. Some parents decide to spend more time with other children and some become more involved in their community. For me, starting this company, Survival in College Seminars, before my kids went on to college was an effort to look ahead and have a plan for filling the inevitable void that would occur once they all were gone and in college. I encourage parents in my seminars and in my book to plan for that time when your kids are gone. With a plan in place, parents have a much easier time with the transition and can really make it a fulfilling experience.

**Wright**

So those of us who are used to talking to our children every day, how do we best communicate with our college freshman when they are away? For example, how often should we visit?

**McGarry**

Well, generally you visit a college freshman only when you have announced that you are coming. I would not recommend surprise visits because we are trying to treat them as adults, and just as we generally expect people to let us know when they are coming to visit, we want to extend that same courtesy to our children when we visit their new home. The first visit should be during parent weekend or what some campuses call family weekend. Generally it is in the fall, on occasion it might be in the spring, but most campuses hold it in the fall. I encourage parents to schedule the date on the calendar and plan to attend. Often kids may say, "Oh, it's not important that you be there." But listen carefully to what they don't tell you. They really do want you to come. They are a little timid about making a big deal of it because they have been told they are supposed to handle all the stress of college life on their own. Also, being a freshmen, they don't know yet if it is "cool" to have your parents come or not. Will all of their new friend's parents be there or will their parents be the only ones? The answer is yes, parents do come to parents weekend. And when all of the parents start arriving, anyone whose parents do not come feels left out and lonely. This is the perfect opportunity for parents to see how their kids have decorated their room, meet their new friends, and see how they move in their new environment. When parents go home, they should have some idea of how well their student has progressed and transitioned to college life. Another important visit to consider is the first visit home. This will usually occur about six weeks into the semester, around fall break. I promise you, six weeks at college is just about six years for a college freshman because they have changed a great deal. They are going to look the same, but their lives have changed. During that first visit home it is very important to be a good listener and hear everything your child is telling you about their new life.

**Wright**

You write of seven communication styles that do not work for college freshmen. Could you tell our readers what they are?

**McGarry**

One is the General Patton style. "You know you're going to do what I tell you and you're going to do it right now." General Patton's toughness and blunt speech earned him the nickname "Old Blood and Guts." Parents who communicate in this style create a habit difficult to change. However, now is the time to be better communicators when children are leaving the house and navigating into adult status.

Another one is what I call the Goldie Hawn style. We all like to be around people who make us happy, and she once said that when she was born God said, "Bing, okay you're going to be happy. You've got that little button of joy, now you're going to pass it around." Sometimes as parents we get so preoccupied with our day to day routine, even with small children, that we don't always realize that we are not listening to our children. Trying to listen while we are cooking dinner, watching the news on TV, feeding the dog, doing several things at once does not make us a very good listener. We are spaced out like

Goldie Hawn is in many of her character roles. When children get to be juniors and seniors in high school, they really want your listening ear. We may think we are listening, but they know when we are not. So it behooves us to give them 100% of our attention and to really listen to them before they just stop talking to us. I always say, "Why did God give you two ears and one mouth?" As parents we need to remember to listen more and talk less.

My third one would be the Perry Mason style. These parents are the investigators. I was always good at this—asking a million questions. Where are you going? When will you be home? Who are you going with? How much drinking's been going on? Why are you home late? When are you going to clean up your room? Why are you being rude and disrespectful to your parents? Having parented this way, I now remind parents that after three questions they stop listening and the communication door is closed. So again we have to think of better ways to communicate.

The Pollyanna style—Haley Mills played this part in the movie with her perfectly braided hair, full of wide-eyed curiosity and boundless bubbly enthusiasm, always just in a state of being uncorked. The parents in this category will generally say, "Today's going to be a wonderful day. Everything is going to come out perfect." Unfortunately for these parents the reality that life is not perfect, especially for teenagers, is a difficult blow when everything has been sugar coated for so long. Our days do not always turn out perfectly, there is an awful lot that goes on in our kid's world and they need our listening ear.

Then there's the Bill Cosby style. Now I love Bill Cosby, he's a famous comedian and actor who is known for his humor and jokes. Parents who tell jokes all the time and use humor in raising their children need to use discretion. Maybe it was okay for a period of time, but there are times when teenagers really want to talk seriously. They may want to share something with their parents and perhaps endless humor is inappropriate and will result in shutting down that communication channel.

And then we've got the Sigmund Freud style. He was the father of psycho analysis. He analyzed everything! I think I feel like I was one of those parents. I read all of the self help books. If I didn't find an author that would tell me what was wrong with my kids, then I would keep reading until I found an author who did. Again, this type of parenting has a time and place, but when you are at the point where your child is going off to college, stop analyzing them and start listening and accepting them for who they are. You will discover that they are wonderful human beings.

Finally, the Oral Roberts style. He is the American missionary and revivalist, whose preaching made him known in all parts of the world. Now if you ask students at our student seminars which categories their parents fall into, they are very open and honest. But parents, they're not always as astute at which category or categories they really fall into. I normally tell parents if they are trying to get a point across to their teenager in three minutes and 15 minutes later they are still trying to get the same point across, they fall into this category.

These are the communication styles that can really turn kids and their communication with us off. As parents of college students, we need to make the transition. Learn to communicate on an adult to adult level. The result of doing this early enough to build rapport with our children is that we can enjoy our college students now and long after they've graduated. I always ask parents to consider changing from governing your kids to talking with your young adults because that's real, real important.

**Wright**

You pull no punches when you discuss college campuses being microcosms of society. Could you talk about colleges and personal safety issues?

**McGarry**

When I first started speaking about a dozen years ago, safety was not very high on the list of concerns for parents. But I'd say in the last six or seven years that has become the number one concern of parents—not of students, but of parents. I think the federal privacy law, demanding that colleges be more open with their records of crime on campus has generated more awareness. These need to be available to both students and parents. At parent orientations in the summer time, parents need to ask about the crime statistics. Most colleges have a website on safety, as they do here at UNC Charlotte, which shows very clearly where crime is occurring , what types of crime are being committed, and what you can do to prevent it. I know the University of Georgia publishes a newsletter which actually pinpoints locations and types of all crime in the area. This really promotes crime awareness with the students. On the other hand, University of Georgia students seem to feel very safe. I think, David, as parents we don't realize that these students have had to deal with many issues on their high school campuses, in their communities, with friends they know, and when they visit colleges, they are more aware than we think they might be. Colleges have instituted many practical safety measures. They have lighting, and phone boxes where you can call campus security and request a ride back from the library or other campus location any time day or night. Some of the libraries are open all night long giving students a safe place to study. Their hours are far different than they were when they were living at home in a high school scene. There is cause for concern by the parents as well as the students about where they should and shouldn't be at various times. Parents need to encourage their students to attend the safety seminar during orientation in the summer. Freshmen need to go and find out what's happening on their particular campus.

**Wright**

For students in college, time management seems to be directly connected to grade point averages. Can you tell our readers about the dangers of not managing time?

**McGarry**

Managing time is one of the biggest challenges for all college freshmen. Any study that has come out recently shows that poor use of time is the biggest single reason freshmen do not maintain at least a C average. Surveys of undergraduate students continually show that 70% or more report learning to manage their time more effectively is their greatest personal need. I encourage my students to make a schedule. I promise them they will do better that first semester if they make and maintain a schedule. Granted, they have to learn how to work through it, but you can give them some hints on how to create and live by a schedule. You know when they first get there and someone has asked them to go out for pizza at a time clearly marked for "study" on their schedule, they may go. But if they choose to go, they need to move that study time to another time slot on their schedule. I tell them to look at it like a work week. Just as our parents and their parents work 40, 50, 60 hours a week, they must also. When they finish the work and if they put in those hours on their schedule, they will find they still have time for church activities, extra curricular activities, exercise, and mingling with friends. If they put all of that together and you show them how you put in two to three study hours per class hour, they will have their work week of

60, 50, 40 hours depending on their goal. Do they want A's or B's or are they content with C's? Then they will see how much other time they have and can pick and choose. They know where their strengths are. Do they study better in the morning or at night? They can arrange their classes to suit their time schedule. They can choose professors who teach the way they best learn. There are so many opportunities for them. But as we all know, they have to take advantage of those opportunities or open doors for better opportunities.

**Wright**

When my daughter goes off to college, she'll have no restrictions as to when she gets home, where she goes or with whom. So do her mother and I put restrictions on her when she visits home on breaks?

**McGarry**

This is what I call the first visit home. It will probably come about six weeks into the semester when they have fall break, because that's normally when residence halls close. I encourage parents to rethink the process. There are many students who complain to college administrators about being treated like a senior in high school living at home when they are in college and living away. Parents are thinking, "You just left, you know. You couldn't have changed that much." But we all know they do.

**Wright**

We just don't want them too.

**McGarry**

They've been working a 24 hour schedule, and I promise you it's far different from the home schedule. I also encourage parents to remember that it is still their home. If a parent is getting up at five in the morning in order to get to the office and their kid is coming in at three in the morning, this is not going to work. I think there's a respect issue here and it's better communication to say, "Okay, this is just not going to work." The same as when my teenagers were home from college and I went out. I would let them know this is where I'm going to be and I expect to be home at this time. I expect my visiting college kids to do the same thing for me. If they're going out, let me know where they are going, who they are with, and about what time to expect them. If that changes, they can call. As far as time restrictions, it's something I think parents have to deal with. It is something to think about, discuss and make some adjustments because even a simple thing such as doing the laundry a little bit differently brings criticism and kids will complain when they get back to their administrators. On the other hand, some kids will say, "Hey, I just do it like I did in high school because in a couple of days I will be back at college and can do what I please." Therefore, parents need to consider making some adjustments during their first visit home, i.e., curfew, chores and home responsibilities.

**Wright**

Right.

**McGarry**

I think students really understand, but I think it will help in the communication process for students to know that their parents have considered it and they can talk about it and see what will work best with the people at home. But very definitely, I encourage parents to remember that it is their home and I feel they are the decision makers.

**Wright**

What about finances? How do we figure out what the student's responsibilities are and what the parent's responsibilities are?

**McGarry**

Well, that's a big one because some students have more pressure with money matters than they do with time management matters. Although I would say 99% have time management issues first and money management is second. Part of the problem is they feel so independent and on their own, yet many of them are dependent for at least some if not all of their college expenses. That makes it very difficult. Even my older daughter when she was at UNC Chapel Hill, would say, "But Mom, these people spend so much money and it's just flowing..." I said, "Denise, it doesn't matter how much somebody else has because you will always find someone who has more money than you. You will always find someone who has less money than you. But what's most important is to learn how to budget the money you have." Because, in most cases, we know they have enough money to adequately go through college, considering both needs and wants. I promise you what parents consider needs are not necessarily what students consider needs.

**Wright**

Right!

**McGarry**

Ask any pizza man about the $25.00 pizza in the middle of the night.

**Wright**

Yeah.

**McGarry**

Consider the $20.00 or the $10.00 for the pizza and the $15.00 for the credit card fee or the insufficient funds fee at the bank.

**Wright**

Right.

**McGarry**

It's just the same as years ago when people were deciding whether to give their kid a credit card. It's only for an emergency, you know. Well, tell me about what they consider an emergency.

I have tons of examples of that, and again I used to tell my kids, "Your poor planning is not my emergency." I think the way we can prevent some of that or ease some of those pressures is by sitting down in the summer before they go off and making up a budget. I have a sample budget in my book and it is mainly a tool to discuss budgets and the expenses that come up at college which may not be your expenses at home. For example, at home when doing your laundry, you have a washing machine and there are no slots to put coins into. At college you're going to need soap powder and make a decision about doing dry cleaning. Are you going to wait until they bring all of their laundry home and send it to your dry cleaner? Who's going to make all of those copies at Kinkos?

Certainly they don't have a kitchen and mom's refrigerator 24/7. It is institutional cafeteria food these kids complain about, so they always want to go elsewhere. So what is a realistic budget? Parents need to help them learn how to budget and know that at the end of the month, if they are out of money, that is their problem not their parents'. Too many times, we as parents tend to make up the difference. If you do that too often, what's going to happen is kids will take over the planning and budget. I've got a two-year-old granddaughter and she already knows just who's in charge. She is!

Kids know how to do that and they are not intentionally saying you must give them money but that's what they have learned. We need to transition into having them take responsibility. It is hard, but the budget is really key to this. They need to understand the budget, credit card issues, and responsibilities. People use their credit cards all the time, but do kids ever see the parents paying those bills? In most cases, when my kids were growing up, I was paying my bills in the middle of the night. So, do they understand that if they don't pay that credit card that month, they are going to have finance charges that will exponentially increase week by week by week by week. I've seen credit card debts from $2,000.00 to $40,000.00 with college freshmen. It happens very quickly, and it happens to students you would never think would be a candidate for that behavior. It's just very tempting.

**Wright**

You have said that college freshmen are creating their world and they need some space to blossom. As a parent, how do we help in this process? Or do we help?

**McGarry**

I think we do. I definitely think we still need to parent the college freshmen. They still need our support and encouragement in helpful and meaningful ways. We do that by continuing to ask questions when they call with problems and by understanding. Sometimes they really don't want you to solve their problems. When my kids used to call after they first went off to college, I was so excited. I thought, "Ooh, they want to talk to me!" Well, little did I know it's not that they really wanted to talk to me, it's that during those first few weeks they have not formed their own friendships yet and they don't want to dump their problems on their new friends. I promise you after they call home in tears and tell you what's on their minds, the problem is gone and they are on to the next thing as soon as they hang up the phone.

**Wright**

Right.

**McGarry**

So, after a call like that, whether it's the mom or the dad they happen to reach, they are kind of in a quandary. Parents immediately think, "My poor kid, this isn't working for them." In the meantime, the kid has gone on to the next item of his day. They just needed you to listen to them, I promise you. So I say treat them as adults, encourage them, love them, and eventually they will become your best friends.

**Wright**

Could you give our readers any thoughts or tips on how to be the best parents of our college students?

**McGarry**

In addition to what I have already said I would advise parents to just be aware their child is going through changes. This is an important transition for them. It is important to not judge the success of the entire college experience by just the first semester. Don't make judgments. There really aren't any right or wrong answers when it comes to your student learning or setting his or her own values. Communication is most important because it's how you respond to them that validates their decisions as an adult. Even if you need to set up a time to call each other on a weekly basis or write letters, e-mail, etc. Then you will avoid them saying, "Well, you're always checking up on me." Or a parent saying, "Well, you're never in." We need to remove those communication barriers because if we call, we really want to have a conversation. We really have to understand and acknowledge it is different from high school and it is all new for them. We want to give support, yet we want to create some distance. Parents need to relax and just have faith. As parents, we've done the best we could during that molding period at home and now we need to treat them as adults. They are going to make mistakes, but I say, "Hey, you and I still make mistakes and that is how we learn." I would also say, "Pray!"

**Wright**

What a great conversation! Today we have been talking with Kaye Bernard McGarry. Since publishing her first book, in 1998 titled *A New Beginning: A Survival Guide for Parents of College Freshmen*, she has been invited to speak on college campuses as well as serving as a guest on various talk shows. She's also presented at numerous educational conferences and her book was featured in *USA Today*. Kaye, I really do appreciate this. And I'm going to take all this information to heart since I've got a 15 year old, and buy one of your books. It sounds like good information. I really do appreciate your taking all of this time to talk with us on *Remarkable Women*.

**McGarry**
Thank you, David.

## About The Author

Kaye is a graduate of Barry University in Miami, Florida, and the University of South Florida in Tampa, Florida, with a degree in Business Administration. She also holds a Masters Degree in Education in Guidance and Counseling from UNC-Charlotte. Continuing her life-long learning, she has taken additional courses at UNC-Charlotte in Journalism and English. In 1991, Kaye started a company, **SURVIVAL IN COLLEGE SEMINARS**, and has been presenting Survival in College programs at high schools, churches, and colleges in North and South Carolina, Georgia, and Wisconsin to college-bound students and parents of college-bound students. Since publishing her first book in 1998 titled, ***A New Beginning: A Survival Guide for Parents of College Freshmen,*** she has been invited to speak on college campuses as well as being interviewed on television. She has also presented at numerous educational conferences. Her book was featured in *USA Today*. A newly updated 2nd edition came off the press in 2001. Kaye is a businesswoman, respected author, educator, wife, mother of four, counselor, and community leader.

**Kaye Bernard McGarry, M.Ed.**

5101 Gorham Drive

Charlotte, NC 28226-6405

Phone: 704.366.8971

Email: kbmcg@carolina.rr.com

www.kayemcgarry.com

# *Chapter Twelve*

## ROBBIE HOUCEK , SHAMAN, CHT, APP

### THE INTERVIEW

**David E. Wright (Wright)**

Today we are talking to Robbie Houcek. Robbie is a gifted intuitive, healer, ceremonialist, speaker, and an Apache initiated shaman. She has committed her life to supporting her clients in leading abundantly rich, emotionally authentic lives – which all yearn for, but few achieve.

Robbie's focused mission is to *empower women to become the conscious creators of their own electrifying lives, systematically examine the devastating beliefs that sabotage their freedoms and breed self-betrayal, alter destructive behaviors that undermine relationships, and reshape their personal visions of what's possible.* She uses a unique approach combining hypnotherapy, bodywork, energy healing, and sacred, mystical ceremony. Robbie draws on 20 years of experience leading women in sacred ritual including full moon and dark moon ceremonies, blood rites, solstice ceremonies and more all delving to the core of internal authenticity and self-discovery. Clients describe her as "my template for a woman."

She is a nationally certified Clinical Hypnotherapist, an Emotional Integration Practitioner, an Associate Polarity Practitioner and an ordained minister.

Atlanta is home to Robbie's private practice where she lives with her beloved husband.

**Wright**

Robbie, as a practitioner for many years, no doubt you have helped several troubled clients. What are the top issues that clients bring to you?

**Robbie Houcek (Houcek)**

Actually, most of my clients are women. And a large percentage of them are in life transition. They're seeking to find a deeper connection to their spiritual side. Several of my clients are experiencing an identity crisis which results in failed or miserable romantic relationships. I empathize with them because I've found myself facing the same challenges, the same obstacles. A young client recently told me that I'm not only a healer and mentor; I'm her role model for emotional integration. As a woman, I feel that this is my most important role.

In the patriarchal paradigm, women learn that men are the "Keepers of Power." We've learned to look to men and plead for confirmation of our worth. This is particularly true of women who have had little or no meaningful interaction with their fathers. We relentlessly seek approval as though their love is a salve that soothes the searing pain of inadequacy. We ask them over and over, "Am I beautiful enough? Am I thin enough? Am I smart enough? Am I enough for you to stay? Am I enough for you to love?" Then, based on the responses we receive, we proceed to betray ourselves again and again in an attempt to fit the mold. We spend hours at the gym. We go on ridiculous fad diets. We abandon our intuition to what we know to be true, and then adopt popular opinions in a desperate attempt to be worthy of love. We fracture ourselves into several pieces, each sporting a different mask to be brought out should the need arise. We attempt to be enough by using masculine energy, by "doing" instead of "being." And we've inadvertently reversed the process. We attempt to change the exterior, yet what's calling to us is a yearning. It's a longing, a longing to recognize our inherent splendor. We've neglected the most important questions. "What do I think?" "What do I want?" "What's important to me?"

In working with my clients, I've often posed the question, "When everything has been stripped away, what do you yearn for? When you take yourself out of the roles that you've chosen as wife, mother, boss, friend, employee, when you focus on you, what's your deepest passion?" And the astonishing answer is: "I don't know. I'm not sure." What we've failed to realize is that no one can save us. No one can deliver us from our self imposed worthlessness. It's not the responsibility of our boyfriends, our husbands, our lovers to remember who we are and remind us of our magnificence. The journey of self discovery is ours and ours alone. It's up to us to embark on this path with dedication and deliberation, to begin the work of listening to the whispers of newly emerging wisdom and acknowledge burgeoning intuition. We learn to love ourselves by keeping the company of women who have dedicated their feet to this path. And under their tutelage, we absolve ourselves from our sins by embracing the essence of who we've always been and surrendering to our feminine nature. When we surrender, we become intimate with life and intimate with ourselves. We recognize the magic and embrace the mystery of being a woman. Actually, the journey is to come home to the wonder of our own hearts and in so doing, discover that we are indeed divine. When we have the courage to surrender to vulnerability, to remain true to our nature—which is open, receptive, attractive—we flourish. When we are the source of own our approval, our edges soften and the opportunity exists for kindness and compassion. Then we become truly radiant. When we reclaim the deep sensuality of our nature and then, firmly grounded in this knowing, extend ourselves to love, it will most certainly respond in kind.

**Wright**

You're an energy healer. What is it and how do you use it with clients?

**Houcek**

Basically, energy healing is the manipulation of energy through the human body to bring about the natural state of health. The human body is made of energy. There are various schools of thought or different models that explain the energetic road map of the body. In the Polarity Therapy model, the human body is much like the earth. It contains both longitudinal and latitudinal lines. The electromagnetic currents flow down the long lines of the body, there are five currents running on each side of the body. Each of these currents corresponds to a natural element, earth, air, fire, water, and ether, or space. The polarity of the downward or negative flow changes at the ankles and wrists. As the current exits the ankles and the wrists, the flow changes and turns upward, or positive, towards the crown of the head. Once the currents reach the crown of the head, the process begins again to keep a constant flow of energy. In addition, electromagnetic currents circle the body from top to bottom. These lines correspond to the latitude lines of the earth.

Another example is Oriental Medicine. Oriental Medicine is based on the principle of energy meridians or pathways that correspond to a particular internal organ and carry vital energy, similar to a transportation system. Along the lines of the meridian system are small dots. Actually, they are spots of heat and electromagnetic energy which run along the surface of the skin. These spots can be manipulated with needles, which is referred to as acupuncture, or they can be manipulated manually, which is referred to as acupressure. Both of these therapies release blockages and regulate the flow of energy. Although these spots are on the surface of the skin, the corresponding meridians run deep into the organs and the muscle tissue. There are several meridians or energy pathways that regulate the major organs of the body – liver, spleen, heart, lungs, bladder, and kidney, just to name a few. When a person is mentally, emotionally, and physically healthy, the energy is regulated and flows in the proper direction. The physical body, both energetically and physically, has a good strong look and feel. If I'm working on a healthy client, I can actually, psychically see the long lines of the body and can feel the pulsing energy. But when the energies are out of alignment, the pathways feel stagnant or sluggish. Sometimes the energies will run in the opposite direction of the normal flow, or the pathway becomes blocked. Sometimes, the energy of a compromised path feels weak, dry, and almost brittle. Other times, it can feel damp, sluggish and congested.

My clients ask, "How did my energy system become compromised?" Actually, modern lifestyle contributes greatly to the disruption of our energy system. Pesticides and herbicides are in the food we consume. Air pollution, heavy metal toxins, lack of sleep, lack of exercise, excess caffeine or alcohol, even airline travel, and of course stress, can all overload the body and disrupt the energy system.

The next question my clients ask is: "What can be done?" The good news is the human body was designed to heal itself, and an energy disruption is easily rectified if treated shortly after the initial imbalance. Long term disruptions can be more complex and can take longer to correct.

Recently, a client came to see me complaining of intestinal problems – diarrhea, gas, and severe abdominal pain. She also mentioned a severe sweet tooth. These are symptoms of a compromised earth pathway in the body. This energy meridian affects the knees, the bowels, gastrointestinal system and the neck. So using Polarity Therapy, I opened the energy pathway in her head, or what is referred to as the north pole of the body. Then, I opened a pathway in her feet, or what is referred to as the south pole of the body. And as described earlier, there are five currents running on each side of the body. What's interesting is that the toes and the fingers carry the same charge as these five energy currents. So when I worked on the toes, when I actually just held her toes, I noticed that the energy in her little toe was slow and stagnant. The energy in the little toe corresponds to the element of earth; it felt like the earth element had been impacted. So, I worked on the earth points by applying pressure with my index and middle finger until the energy began to move, and then I enhanced the earth flow by working the water points. By the end of the session, her pain had disappeared and she said she was feeling much better. Later in the week, I called to check on her. She reported that she was feeling great and had been free of her symptoms since our last session.

**Wright**

Do your clients come to you primarily with emotional or physical complaints?

**Houcek**

Clients come with a variety of issues. Yet, in my experience, even the strictly physical complaints have an emotional component. I have a client who came to see me after having been diagnosed with Type 1 Diabetes. With Type 1 Diabetics, the pancreas is unable to produce sufficient insulin and as a result, daily insulin injections are often required. Before she came to see me, my client eliminated sugar, alcohol and caffeine from her diet, began to exercise regularly and take yoga classes. Due to her healthy lifestyle, she does not require insulin. Although, medically, she has learned quite a bit about the disease, she felt she could improve her insulin production through alternative methods.

During the first session, she was primarily concerned with eventually needing insulin. She felt that somehow, being insulin dependent was a personal failure. We began the session with hypnosis, exploring the pancreas and its ability to manufacture insulin. What emerged was something very different, what emerged were old, unresolved childhood issues.

She had come from a large family. She was the second of seven children, her father a successful businessman, her mother a housewife. Her father focused the majority of his time and energy on his business while her mother devoted her attention to caring for the younger children. Because she was an older child, she was expected to fend for herself. From these early experiences, she learned that asking for love or attention rarely met with a satisfactory response. Her parents had limited resources and she was not at the top of the priority list. As a result, she made the decision that asking for love and attention was futile so she learned to stop asking. Yet, she still carried a deep fear that her needs would continue to be ignored.

In the next session, we explored the diabetes in light of this new information. The pancreas is responsible for metabolizing food, but it also effects our ability to metabolize ideas, concepts, emotions such as worry, fear, love and joy. I asked her "What does the diabetes allow in you, how does it serve you?" After a long pause, she said "It gives me permission to give myself what I need. I feel I have permission to take care of myself. Because of the disease, I am justified in eating right, exercising daily and going to bed when I am tired." I asked "Would you be doing these things if you were disease free?" "No, probably not" she replied.

During subsequent sessions we explored her willingness to risk asking for what she wanted regardless of the disease. As she became more comfortable with her own authentic expression, she became less anxious, her relationships improved and she experienced more joy. During our sessions, the focus shifted from her pancreas and insulin production to enhancing her emotional metabolism. The parts of ourselves that have remained hidden most of our lives are often the source of our deepest healing.

**Wright**

I'm sure you've been involved with some very unusual life crisis. What's the most touching case you've ever worked with?

**Houcek**

That's a good question. I have more examples than I can count, but this is the most heart wrenching. A client brought in a young 11 year old girl. I usually don't work with children, but this girl had been through a series of deep emotionally traumatic events, and as a result, had stopped speaking. She would either respond with a single word or refuse to speak altogether. The background I received was that the child's father had been in prison. While he was in prison, the mother had died; the result of a car accident. The young girl and her siblings had been shuttled out to foster homes. Angry and frustrated about the children being placed in foster care, the father had escaped from prison. He kidnapped the children, and had taken them deep into the mountains. Eventually, law enforcement officials caught up with them. Unwilling to face losing his family again, the father opened fire on the law enforcement officials. A gun battle ensued while the terrified children watched in horror. After several hours, out of ammunition, outnumbered, and totally defeated, the father surrendered. The children were taken into state custody and returned to foster care. Since this incident, the child was listless, detached, and usually refused to speak.

Before she climbed on the massage table, I explained the type of work that I would be doing with her. Then, I asked the child if she would allow me to work on her. She nodded her head, "Yes." As I gently placed my hand on her small back, the psychic impressions started to emerge. In my mind's eye, I saw her as an infant in the arms of an adult male. He was walking slowly, but unsteady. He was wavering, stumbling. As I watched the vision, his arms began to relax his grip on the child. She slipped from his hands, tumbling to the floor where her wails of fear and anguish went unattended, a child abandoned and utterly alone. From the psychic impressions, it was evident that like an infant, she felt helpless to change the situation and had lost all hope that anyone would even notice, much less change it for her.

In order for the session to be effective, I needed to keep myself open and vulnerable. I needed to hold a strong vibration of love. During a healing session, the practitioner can support the client's process by holding an energetic vibration. The most effective vibrations are peace, love, comfort and compassion. If the vibration is constant, the client will instinctively begin to attune to the same vibrations. It's the same principle of resonance used when working with tuning forks. If two tuning forks are in resonance, meaning that they vibrate in the same pitch, you can strike one fork to set it vibrating and then touch it to the second fork. Both forks begin to vibrate.

I began quietly to talk about the feeling of safety and trust. I asked her to remember a time when she felt safe and happy. I talked about body memory and how our bodies have inherent intelligence that can remember feelings and recreate them. Using color and sound, we anchored the feeling of safety in her body. I watched as her small frame began to release. Her breathing slowed and became more regular. Gradually, her body began to shed its protective emotional armor. As infants, we are unable to support the weight of our heads. We trust that those who care for us will support us in our vulnerability. So when issues of trust or safety develop, they often emerge in the neck. I asked her to turn over so I could support her neck and sat quietly. From the expression on her face, I could see that something was moving deep inside of her. Energetically, it felt as if some dark, massive wall of protection was tentatively melting. I moved my hands to cradle her head, as tears slid down her cheeks. "What are you feeling?" I asked. She looked at me with tear filled eyes and in a pleading voice said, "Don't drop me." It was confirmation that she was feeling safe and emotionally supported, and desperately needed to trust both me and the experience.

During my body work training, instructors would often caution us, "When you step to the table, remember that at any moment your heart can and will be broken wide open." And that was certainly the case with this child.

**Wright**

We discussed energy work. How did you get into body work?

**Houcek**

I was working in the technology industry in Silicon Valley, and I was experiencing chronic lower back pain. And I had been to a few traditional doctors, but none of them could determine the reason for the chronic pain. A friend of mine suggested I look into alternative methods of healing. She suggested Rosen Method Body Work. The foundation of Rosen Method is that the physical pain is often caused by repressed or unconscious emotional issues. It really sounded interesting, so I booked my first session. It was such a profound experience! I found the work to be slow, deep, and quiet. As I lay on the massage table, the practitioner gently put her hands on the small of my back. She sat quietly, occasionally asking a question. I could feel myself becoming more and more relaxed. Then, like browsing through an old photo album, memories flashed in my mind. Vignettes of my life danced across my field of vision. And eventually, deeply buried feelings, long forgotten angers, and resentments began to snake their way to the surface. As the session progressed, I noticed that the pain in my back was slowly releasing.

After the session was over, I walked a short distance to a park overlooking the Bay to ponder the experience. I sat by the water watching the sun reflect on the waves. What I realized was that I was experiencing intense pressure at work, and I was not feeling supported by upper level management. I remembered the practitioner telling me the lower back and pelvic girdle support the spine and the weight of the torso, so it made sense that an issue regarding support would develop in my lower back. That experience opened up a whole new world for me, and I began to explore the connections between my emotional state and how it was reflected in my body. I booked a session every week for an entire year. It was an incredible journey. It created an opportunity for me to discover aspects of myself that at first I denied, exiled and finally abandoned. At times it was difficult, full of fear, pain, depression, and sometimes grief. But it led ultimately to liberation, the gifts I received are beyond measure. For me, it was a process of reclaiming the scattered fragments of myself and weaving them back into the core of my being. It was actually my path to emotional integration.

**Wright**

Your first career was in the technology industry. How did the transition to alternative healing occur?

**Houcek**

Several years ago my mother was diagnosed with ovarian cancer. When she started the chemo treatment, the effects were devastating. She was sick for days after a treatment. Finally, the family decided that it wasn't enough to depend on conventional medicine alone. We wanted to utilize every method available. So we began a search for anything that would eradicate the cancer, or at least restrain its progress. There were days when she would be at the hospital for chemo treatments. Then there were other days that she would have an appointment with an energy healer, an oriental doctor, an acupuncturist, or even a medicine woman.

I realized, unfortunately, my time with her was limited; and for me, it was important to be an integral part of her process. I wanted to do more than just drive her to appointments and help with the household chores. I wanted to actively participate in her emotional journey. So, I started searching for the modality that would lead me to a deeper understanding of her experience through the disease. I spoke to my Rosen Practitioner, Rosie. We discussed using the body work as a way to help facilitate my mother's emotional process. Rosie was not only a practitioner, she was also an instructor. And fortunately, she had a training scheduled later that month. I attended the workshop and it changed not only my career, it changed the entire course of my life.

**Wright**

So what happened during the workshop?

**Houcek**

My experience of the work, both as a practitioner and a client, was deeply moving and profound. During the workshop, lectures were given in the mornings while the afternoons were reserved for the actual body work. And since we were new students, volunteers had been recruited to function as clients. As the students walked into the room, several massage tables had been erected, and volunteers were lying on the tables draped in sheets. We were instructed to use our intuition and stand by the table that called to us. I walked to a table with a pleasant looking, middle aged woman. As I began to work, I quietly placed my hands on her back, and we both settled into the session. Then, something strange happened. Within a few minutes, her breathing changed. She was panting rapidly and her face contorted into an expression of fear and pain. She began to cry and whimper. A deeply buried, emotionally charged memory was emerging.

During the introductory lecture, we were told that once a client began to process, our hands were never to leave the body. I didn't know what to do! The client was clearly in distress and I couldn't move my hands from her body. Eventually, Rosie came to my table. Before she checked the client, she gently placed her hand between my shoulder blades and very quietly said, "Breathe…relax….stay present." Through her supportive touch, I immediately felt my body relax; I took a deep breath, and was able to center myself. Then she moved her attention to the woman on the table. She placed her hand on the woman's shoulder and with great tenderness asked, "How old are you?" " Fa fa fa four," the woman stuttered. "Where are you?" Rosie asked. "In, in, in, in the cl..closet," she stammered. In a very small, childlike voice the woman proceeded to explain that she was hiding in a closet, terrified that her abusive father would find her and beat her yet again. And so my training began.

As I watched, Rosie adroitly followed the energy of the client's emotions, never leading, always following. Her quiet strength and intense focus created a safe container for the client to explore the dark, shameful secrets long forgotten; secrets abandoned but still trapped in her body. Using only gentle touch and a few quietly spoken words, Rosie helped the client move through the wretched tempest to begin to heal a very old wound. In that one very clear, heartbreakingly, tragic moment, I knew what I wanted to do with the rest of my life.

The value of that experience was absolutely priceless. I realized what an honor it is to touch another human being. When we open our hearts with deep reverence and respect, we reach out to touch another person; we create the opportunity to change a life. We create the space or the opportunity for the body to begin an authentic expression. In the spirit of allowing, there are no expectations about what should happen during a session. The practitioner doesn't say, "This is what you should experience," or "This is how you should feel." The opportunity is kept open, empty, expectant, waiting to be filled by the client. The client has the freedom to experience what is there to be experienced, express what needs to be expressed, and everything that emerges is welcome. Everything is honored from grief, joy, pain, fear, even anger! And through this work, the client is supported in navigating their own unconscious terrain. They begin a dialog with the body, exploring the mystery of their inner realities. And because the process is allowed to unfold in its own time, in its own way, the movement is deep and emotionally significant. The client has the opportunity to resolve the barriers that inhibit an emotionally rich, authentic experience of life. The opportunity exists to break the pattern of emotional bondage. And the interesting point is, the client actually learns to experience their own feelings, and in so doing, opens a new arena of choice. The energy that was used to suppress the emotion is released and can now be utilized in a more productive way. Through this work, I realized I had the opportunity to profoundly impact the life of another person. I realized I had found my calling. I wanted to create opportunity, create the empty space that would invite miracles. I immediately enrolled in the next residential training and my journey was underway.

**Wright**

You utilize ceremony as a growth experience with your clients. Could you tell our readers more about that?

**Houcek**

Sure. As participants, ceremony gives us the opportunity to validate ourselves through personal experience of the divine. In our culture, validation is external. Training, education, and experience is verified by a diploma or a certificate or some other form of material verification we can hang on the wall. We can frame them, display them as proof that we've accomplished something important, proof that our efforts are worthy of recognition. We look for the *Good Housekeeping Seal of Approval* as evidence of authenticity. It's what we've been taught to value, this is our cultural experience.

So making the transition from external, material validation to internal, ethereal validation can really be daunting. There are no templates to teach us how to do this, and little support to sustain the effort. During my Shamanic training, I had to complete a vision quest. Basically, a vision quest is an exercise in communing with the spirits. The person seeking a vision goes out alone into the wild and calls to the spirits, asking for a vision. I had been instructed to call on a specific group of elders. I hadn't worked with these particular spirits before, and wasn't sure they would come if I called. I discussed the issue with my teacher, an Apache Shaman. To allay my fears, he had given me two feathers and said, "Call the spirits. They'll know I've sent you by the feathers that you bear." So I went out into the night and called to the spirits. When I returned, he asked if I had received a vision. I told him that the spirits had indeed come and I had been given the gift of a vision. We discussed it at length. But before he left, I asked him, "What if I just imagined it? How can I tell if it's real?" He looked at me in shocked disbelief and said, "Did you see the elders? Did they come to you?" "W...w...well, yes." "Did they give you a message?" "Yes." "Then how can you dare to doubt them? It's exceptionally rude to question the existence of the spirits, particularly if you've been given the gift of a vision." He turned on his heel and stormed out.

Even though I had been given a vision, it was difficult to accept it's authenticity without external validation. My experience was very real, yet I didn't have external proof to validate it. The lesson was to learn to shift my focus and trust what I knew to be true. My communication with the spirits didn't need external validation. What was important was the value of my own experience and where it led me. I didn't need to ask for authenticity from this vision; I needed to use the vision to find my own authenticity. This is what ceremony provides, intimate communion with our spiritual side; an understanding of what is inherently true for us by using the path of personal experience. The value of personal experience is that it can not be denied.

The ceremonies I lead are based on the Native American wheel of life and are specifically designed for women. Within the safety of the circle, like minded women can gather to explore the movement of energy in our bodies and in our lives. We can learn to trust an experience of the invisible and heed the ethereal guidance of spirit. When we bring all of who we are to the sacred circle of ceremony, we bear witness to our own unborn potential. It is both overwhelming and undeniable.

**Wright**

But doesn't prayer have the same effect? Why is ceremony different than prayer or meditation?

**Houcek**

Actually, you're right. Prayer and meditation do create an experience of the divine. Yet in my experience, ceremony is more expansive. It's more interactive. Prayer, meditation, and even chanting are utilized during the ceremony. Through the use of symbols, ceremony brings into form that which is formless. It breathes life into the concepts that reside in our imagination. It's an effective way of balancing the internal world of the imagination with the external world of our daily lives. There are groups of women who have formed ceremonial circles and kept them active for several years. Through regular communion they have supported each other through life transitions like marriages, birth, child rearing, divorces, and even diseases. They have created a community and a spiritual support network based on the foundation of ceremony. We learn to be women of substance by keeping company of leaders, philanthropists, and matriarchs. The ceremonial circles provide a forum for this education. In my experience, I learned valuable life lessons sitting at the feet of elders and matriarchs. I learned that ultimate strength is vulnerability, that compassion and forgiveness heal what modern medicine can't. I listened to stories about the cycles of the moon and its mystical effect on the female body. I learned to watch the cycles of the earth, to honor the changing seasons as I honor the cycles in my own life. I spent countless hours listening to stories; stories about women as wives, mothers, daughters, women in the work place and women at home. I listened to stories of grief, courage, compassion and deep joy. Each story was as rich and uniquely woven as the woman who told it. Stories are the way life teaches us, the way wisdom is passed from generation to generation.

Ceremony creates time, time for stories, time for listening, time for pondering wisdom. It also reconnects us to the mystery and magic of life. It engages our souls, it ignites our imagination, and it reminds us of infinite formless possibilities. Through ceremony, we are granted access to deeper parts of ourselves, access to a reality beyond the confines of ordinary life. And through ceremony, we are reminded that it's both a privilege and an honor to be a woman.

**Wright**

You mentioned using ritual for life transitions. Can you give me an example?

**Houcek**

Yes, my mother passed as a result of cancer. Death is such an intense transition that the only way for me to approach it was through symbols and rituals. Having lived in New Mexico, I was fortunate enough to have spent time learning from an Apache Shaman. I attended sweat lodges, fire ceremonies, dances, and prayer ceremonies. I learned the importance of stories, myths, and legends. And through these experiences, I learned that the language of the soul is symbolic. Symbols speak to us in the deepest parts of our being; they're metaphors for the internal experience of the psyche. Symbols arouse powerful emotions and bring them to the surface for conscious recognition. Death, a transition of such immense magnitude, called for symbolic representation that was far beyond words and well beyond the scope of my current comprehension.

In ancient cultures, families created altars and shrines for the safe passage of their departing loved ones. I decided to create an altar for my mother as a ritual marker for her journey. One night as she sat in bed, the family gathered around her and proceeded to construct the altar. The foundation of the altar was a large tray lined with rabbit fur. Rabbit is an animal whose face is close to the earth. He takes one step at a time and sees only what is directly before him. Since the Dance of Death is uncertain and demanding, it seemed wise to walk with deliberation, taking only one step at a time. We placed a small purple satin heart on the altar, representing the love of her family. We included a white pillar candle so that her path would always be lit. There was a small obsidian arrowhead to point her in the right direction. There were small bowls of herbs – Mint to ease difficult life transitions, Cinnamon for protection, Echinacea for strength, Thyme for purification and courage, and a braid of Sage and Sweetgrass. We consecrated the altar and chanted prayers until she fell asleep. It was a symbolic acknowledgment of her process without an attachment to a specific outcome. The prayers were for her healing in whatever form she chose. If she chose to die, she would be supported in the death process. If she chose to continue treatment, she would be supported in that choice as well.

As the months passed, the cancer spread throughout her body and she lapsed into a coma. On a cold December night, my father called and asked me to come home. He sensed that the end was near. He had brought her home from the hospital as there was nothing else that traditional medicine could do. When she got home, he had placed her hospital bed in the sunroom. It was a beautiful glassed in porch, and the family had decorated a Christmas tree and placed it by her bed. Brightly colored holiday banners hung in the windows.

When I arrived, I walked into the room, and noticed how beautiful it was. There was a reverence and a deep stillness, reminiscent of a church. It was such a poignant moment; in her darkest hour she was surrounded with the symbols of Christmas – love, light, joy, hope, and peace on earth. Christmas music was playing softly in the background. I noticed that her altar was on a table near the bed. It was dusk, so I lit the candles. I sat with her, stroked her cheek, and spoke quietly. Within a few minutes came the harbinger of her passing. She began the labored breathing known as the death rattle. My young niece summoned the rest of the family. As we stood around her bed, my sister opened the chakras in her head. I opened the chakras in her body, while my niece rubbed the soles of her feet. The chakras are energetic power centers attached to the spine. During the final phase of the death process, they can be opened to assist the spirit in exiting the body. The herb, Rosemary, stimulates the memory of home. We anointed her feet with Rosemary oil to ensure they would always remember the path home. Breath is symbolic of the spirit. I blew my breath across her feet indicating that her earth walk was complete and her spirit walk was about to begin. As we sat around the bed, we chanted and prayed. There's an old Native American legend that says our loved ones are carried to their final resting place by the sound of our prayers. During the death process, hearing is the last sense to go. So, each of us bent close and said our tearful goodbyes. We told her we were proud of her courage, her strength and her fierce loyalty. We told her we were grateful for her love, her laughter, and her passion for life. We told her how empty our lives would be without her, yet we gave her permission to go. Her struggle was finally over. We urged her to fly home on the sound of our prayers. We chanted for hours, singing her home. While we sang, she gracefully passed—a silent exodus, a final emancipation under the star filled, winter sky. In retrospect, it was the most valuable gift I could have given her. She gave me the gift of life and I gave her the gift of a sacred death.

**Wright**

Well, what an interesting conversation. It seems that all of the study and practical experience has really paid off for you.

**Houcek**

Yes, it really has.

**Wright**

And now you can help others?

**Houcek**

Yes, I do. It's my passion and my life's work!

**Wright**

Fascinating! Today we have been talking to Robbie Houcek. She is, as we have found out this afternoon, a gifted intuitive. She's a healer, a ceremonialist, and an Apache initiated Shaman. She has committed her life to supporting her clients in leading abundantly rich, emotionally authentic lives. Robbie, thank you so much for taking this large amount of time to discuss this important subject with me, and you've given me the impetus to read more to learn more about something that I know very little about.

**Houcek**

Thank you, David.

## About The Author

Robbie Houcek is a gifted intuitive, healer, ceremonialist, speaker, and an Apache initiated shaman. She has committed her life to supporting her clients in leading abundantly rich, emotionally authentic lives—which all yearn for, but few achieve. Robbie's focused mission is to empower women to become the conscious creators of their own electrifying lives, systematically examine the devastating beliefs that sabotage their freedoms and breed self-betrayal, alter destructive behaviors that undermine relationships, and reshape their personal visions of what's possible. She uses a unique approach combining hypnotherapy, bodywork, energy healing, and sacred, mystical ceremony. Robbie draws on 20 years of experience leading women in sacred ritual including full moon and dark moon ceremonies, blood rites, solstice ceremonies and more all delving to the core of internal authenticity and self-discovery. Clients describe her as "my template for a woman." She is a nationally certified Clinical Hypnotherapist, an Emotional Integration Practitioner, an Associate Polarity Practitioner and an ordained minister. Atlanta is home to Robbie's private practice where she lives with her beloved husband.

**Robbie Houcek , Shaman, Cht, APP**

P.O. Box 88190

Atlanta, Georgia 30356

Phone: 678.579.9250

Fax: 770.393.0076

Email: rvhoucek@mindspring.com

www.spiritceremonies.com

# Chapter Thirteen

## JANET HATCHER RICE, D.D.S

### THE INTERVIEW

**David E. Wright (Wright)**

Today we are talking to Dr. Janet Hatcher Rice. Dr. Rice is a dentist, lecturer, writer, and laser enthusiast with over 30 years experience in the dental field. She is now focusing her efforts on teaching other women how to succeed. The focus of leadership training in the professions has always been on men. Now with over 50% of enrollees in professional schools in the United States being women, a growing need exists to help women acquire skills that will prepare them for achieving success in their business, professional, and personal lives. But Dr. Rice takes it one step further. As a wife, mother, professional, small business owner and spiritual being, she has personal insight in how to balance the multiple roles of women so that success is redefined and attainable. Women can have it all, but on our own terms. Dr. Janet Hatcher Rice, welcome to *Remarkable Women*!

**Dr. Janet Hatcher Rice (Rice)**

Thank you.

**Wright**

What led you to the male dominated field of dentistry?

**Rice**

Well, I grew up with a father who was a dentist. I never thought about dental school because I *was* from a small town with no women dentists. Instead, mine was a journey that headed down the traditional paths of women in the dental profession. Because of this, I ended up working my way up the ladder, so to speak. I started working in my father's practice at age 16. I was an assistant and a receptionist during high school; went to college and became a dental hygienist; worked a couple of years and then one day, about age 22, I realized that I could be a dentist. I wanted to be a dentist. And it was so totally right for me, but wrong in the sense that I had no female mentors. It never, ever entered my mind or my parents' mind for me to be a dentist. So I really don't fault them or society, that's just the way it was.

**Wright**

I've been trying to think of a female dentist, and I can't think of one. I know a lot of dental hygienists, but I cannot think of one female dentist.

**Rice**

Well, that's going to be changing.

**Wright**

Is it already changing?

**Rice**

Oh, yes!

**Wright**

How long does it take? I guess you go to dental school after you get your college degree, right?

**Rice**

Yes. It's typically four years undergrad and four years of dental school.

**Wright**

Wow!

**Rice**

I changed my major three times so it took me even longer. My first year I was an English major, I wanted to be a writer. And then I went to dental hygiene school, a two year degree. I thought that way I could at least get a job and be able to support myself while I wrote. And then I went back to the University of Tennessee to do my pre-dental, which took me about two more years after that. And then I went on to dental school, in Richmond, Virginia, for four years. I had nine years of college.

**Wright**

Goodness. That takes quite a commitment.

**Rice**

I didn't see it as a commitment. It was desire and sheer determination. But I think that my journey was saner in that I had a chance to experience the working world. Even in dental school I worked as a dental hygienist. I don't regret my choices. I had time to make the right choice for me and to truly want it. It was difficult, but the difficult part for me was finding my place. Dental school was enjoyable because I knew that more than anything I wanted to be a dentist. I finally found where I was suppose to be.

**Wright**

How were you able to gain leadership roles in this profession?

**Rice**

Once again, you know, just starting at the bottom and working my way up through the ranks, paying my dues so to speak, to acquire skills and to gain authority. Of course, a little gray hair and bifocals doesn't hurt either. I was young, attractive and female; it was very hard to be in any kind of leadership role. But I learned that I had to join professional organizations and be willing to put in the hours on any project that I was asked to do. I just had to talk their talk and fit in as best I could. But as the years went by and as I gained more and more leadership positions, then I was able to develop my own style. My style is to involve others in the leadership process. I enjoy bringing new leaders up behind me, setting an example for others to want to follow. And I'm not afraid to give up control or to give up any of my power in a leadership position. As long as I chose who to give it to. But it is a difficult balancing act.

**Wright**

Can I ask you what might appear to be a sexist question, but I assure you it's not? Are most of your patients female?

**Rice**

No, actually I have a fair amount of male patients. Women typically do seek medical and dental care on a greater average than men. So...a typical dental practice will always have more females than males. But mine is closer to being 50/50, and that's unusual for a dental practice.

**Wright**

Can you explain to our readers what you mean by balance in life when mentoring women?

**Rice**

Yes. It all began when I was asked to write an article for a national dental magazine, *Women Dentists Journal*. They asked me to write about how I was able to balance my life—how I was able to balance family, work, play, and spirituality. And so that really led me to think on this topic. I realized I had no role models early on and it has taken me many years to achieve balance in my own life. I wanted to be able to share these insights with other women dentists. So I started thinking about my journey. How it has been a road worth traveling towards balance in my life. That's what I've been working on for these last 20 years in dentistry. I love dentistry, but I needed to be able to balance other aspects of my life. When I first started my career, I was all mixed up. I was trying to become someone that I thought I should be, a stereotype. Of course, we all probably do this. I was using my left brain too much, thinking too much instead of just intuitively knowing who I was. And I just didn't take the time to really process that when I first started into business. I just thought, "Well, a dentist does this, and a dentist does that." And I really didn't look inside and see who I was or how my gender influences my happiness. I guess I looked at my male colleagues, and it's funny, but it's true. I emulated them. For example, I learned to play golf. My father was a dentist and golfer and we lived on a golf course. I remember going to him my senior year in dental school and saying, "Dad, you've got to teach me how to play golf. I'm going to be a dentist and I have to do that." And then I joined male civic organizations. I was doing all of the things I thought dentists did. I joined the male professions and all the things that I saw male dentists do. But then as I went through my thirties, I realized that I was really in conflict between who I really was and this persona that I was trying to put on. So since that time, I guess since my late thirties, I have really worked towards achieving a balance so that my life feels complete. I found my authentic self. So I'm not just a dentist or business owner. I'm a wife, mother, stepmother, daughter and sister. I'm all of these things and I have my own unique hobbies and interests.

**Wright**

Tell me about your family, your family life and hobbies.

**Rice**

Okay. I'm married and have a teenage daughter and together we live on 100 acre horse farm adjoining the Cherokee National Forest just south of Bristol, Tennessee. Bristol is where I have always practiced dentistry and where I grew up. It is a small city but beautiful and surrounded by mountains. About six years ago, my husband and I made a choice to change our lifestyle to give more emphasis on family and faith. We wanted to find land to build a home on and to raise horses. We thought developing a retreat away from the pressures of the workplace sounded refreshing. It was just the best decision we ever made. My husband has four children and they love to come visit and see the horses. They have learned to ride and have grown to appreciate our farm lifestyle. The thrill of raising horses, which is not just a hobby but has become a way of life, was exactly what all of us needed. We raise the American Appendix Horse, which is a cross between a thoroughbred and a quarter horse. They are very versatile and many are trained to show in hunter jumper classes and are very popular for fox hunting. They're just magnificent animals. It's indescribable to watch the foals being born and they get up almost immediately and stumble around wide eyed. It's just thrilling. And then to see them as they grow and to be able to watch that incredible transformation, it's just the best thing we ever did. Everyone in the family is caught up in it. My husband manages the farm business and also has a full time job. He educates and trains dentists on laser technology. That's how we met and having these common interests (lasers and horses) has given us much to share. My daughter loves horses, too, but she is also developing her own unique likes and dislikes. I encourage her to explore her own hobbies. Right now that is art. She also likes to hike and run cross country.

**Wright**

So you gave up your dentistry practice?

**Rice**

Oh, no!

**Wright**

Oh, you still do that too?

**Rice**

Yes. I do that too. I work Monday through Thursday, 8 to 5, but then the rest of the time I'm down on the farm. In fact, I rode two of the horses this morning up on the trails. This is separate from my business persona, which helps me tremendously. I have to be neat and clean as a dentist. I work in a sterile environment and sit for hours in a chair in very uncomfortable positions and during highly emotional situations. At the farm I get to put on my blue jeans, get my hands dirty and do physical labor. I need to do both.

**Wright**

Has this lifestyle helped you in dentistry?

**Rice**

Oh yes! If I'm grounded and happy, I can give more of myself to others. I am able to have healthy relationships because I am my authentic self. For me, life is about relationships. In my personal life and in my business, I enjoy the relationships I have built with my family and friends, my staff, patients and other professionals. Dentistry has given me an opportunity to grow and to learn and develop these relationships. So it has been very satisfying. I also get to learn new things, and I try to do the job a little better each day, knowing that it can always be better but not driving myself crazy if I don't ever get it perfect. Because that's not the point, getting it perfect isn't the point. The point is the journey. It's the people. It's the relationships. I've also developed my down time, a time with my family and with my friends and with my horses so that I am able to go back every Monday morning and do dentistry again because I've really allowed myself some time to get away and to be who I am.

**Wright**

When I was reading your bio, I said that you take things a step further as a wife, mother, professional, and spiritual being. What's that about, the spiritual being?

**Rice**

Well, we live in a hollow, as they say in Tennessee. That is a series of foot hills. We are adjacent to the Cherokee National Forest. I am many, many generations removed, but my great-great-great grandmother was a full blooded Cherokee Indian. And we, my husband and I, have studied Native American teachings and I really like that philosophy. I take time to step away from the my busy workaday world and explore my surroundings. Native Americans viewed the earth and animals as co-habitants and as wise teachers, and that they're part of us, that we're all in this together so to speak. I've also found that spirituality, that looking to nature, and to mother earth helps heal me. All I need is a walk in the woods or a ride on a horse or watch a sunset to give me inner peace. It's being quiet and living in the moment. I spent too many years waiting to accomplish this or that and then I would be happy. When happiness never came I realized I needed to change. I have to be happy first. It sounds so easy, but it has taken me years to fully understand. It is the simple pleasures that bring so much peace to me, to my soul. And I think that a lot of people are missing that. I want to share this with young professionals. They may seek a different path but the human desire to find peace is the same. This is what I mean.

**Wright**

Yeah, one of the theories that I ascribe to is that, terrible illnesses not withstanding, we're all dying day by day of too much stress. Just hearing you talk about watching a sunset or walking in the woods, I relaxed a little bit more.

**Rice**

Studies have shown that the power to heal ourselves is actually within us and that's why illness is called dis-ease. It's not being at ease with yourself. Today's women are getting more disease because they are following the career paths of men and it does not always suit them. They have to find their authentic self to be at ease in their bodies.

**Wright**

So what do you see for the future of dentistry and for the future of women in dentistry?

**Rice**

Well, I see great things for dentistry. I see a noble profession, which has worked harder to please the public than any other health profession. We've always given back more to the communities than we take. And I think we are appreciated for the efforts made a half a century ago to decrease pain and suffering with a preventive program of fluoridation. I see dentistry staying ahead of other health care professions because of this emphasis on prevention. We are managing our practices and our care without the intrusion of government and are able to keep down costs better than medicine. I also see dentistry emerging as a woman's profession. It's a field well suited for women because of the relationships and the trust building that occurs, the nurturing that has to occur in order to touch and heal patients. And for women that comes second nature, that nurturing. Really women have been healers for centuries. It's only modern medicine that took away that role. But now it's coming back around. Women are emerging in all areas of health care and dentistry. Dentistry has long been a stronghold for males because of its mechanical nature but dental schools are now close to 50% female, and that's a huge leap in just 30 years when it was less than 2%.

**Wright**

Goodness.

**Rice**

Yeah. It's amazing isn't it?

**Wright**

So what are your goals for the coming years?

**Rice**

Well, I plan to continue practicing dentistry. But I realize that the workload and the physical nature of the business will not be sustainable for me as I age. So I do have plans to combine my love of horses into future plans. My husband and I, along with our trainer, are breeding the Appendix bloodline, and once again, that is a cross between a thoroughbred and the quarter horse.

**Wright**

I'm trying to think how that would look.

**Wright**

Quarter horses are stout and...

**Rice**

Stout and stocky...

**Wright**

...and stocky, and the thoroughbreds are taller and...

**Rice**

Skinny. You've got the perfect horse when you blend the two. They're just right. They combine the best strengths of both breeds...the quarter horse is known for its gentle disposition and calm manner. And the thoroughbred, of course, is known for its speed and pure bloodlines.

**Wright**

Thoroughbreds are hyper, I think.

**Rice**

Yes, they are, but when you breed them to the quarter horse you've got a horse with spunk, but one that has a good mind and a calmer disposition so that you can put them to work such as teaching them how to jump courses and fox hunt, and things like that. This is a wonderful breed, and in fact, I'm so excited because the American Appendix Horse Association (AAHA) was founded this year and we were able to register our mares and our stallion as founding stock. And I can just image that this will be the next organization I'm going to be involved in. But for now, I will continue to write and lecture on dentistry. My husband lectures on laser dentistry all over the world and I hope to be able to work and travel with him soon. He helped me become a pioneer in the laser dentistry field. His background was laser medicine. So we will continue sharing our knowledge with other dentists. Another goal is to take the skills that I've learned through my work with professional organizations and put them into a format for the main stream market where I think they'll be valuable to women in other professions. Women need to develop leadership skills specific to their gender. I believe I have much to offer.

**Wright**

How would you define your leadership style and how did you develop it?

**Rice**

Well, after being president of my local Rotary Club, President of the American Association of Women Dentists, and currently President of the Academy of Laser Dentistry, which is an international organization; I can say once again that my style has evolved. I developed skills for attention to detail and delegation of duties early in my dental practice and just expanded on these. As I became involved in organizations, I remembered an old Cherokee saying that goes, "One finger cannot lift a pebble." This is true in leadership. You have to have a shared vision. A vision that isn't seen by others is only a mirage. So the first thing I do is clarify my vision; then I keep putting it out in front of others to see; and then I involve them in developing it from a vision to results. I help them take ownership of the process with me by asking for input and delegating what their ideas are. This works much better because I may have the vision, but those following must have the desire to take that and put it in their own structure. Working together will make the vision a reality. I also try to give credit to as many people as I can because this isn't giving away my power, as I have been told before, but it actually strengthens it. It makes you humble. And all these things make a great leader, but you won't really be remembered for your works or your vision but for relationships built. In fact, if you take joy from helping others, then it's much more satisfying.

**Wright**

How do you set goals?

**Rice**

I write my goals down. I write long and short term goals. I look at them often and revise them. I visualize what I want in my life and what I don't want. Sometimes things happen beyond my control and I go with it rather than fight it. Many times this points me onto a new path I needed to be on but hadn't thought of.

**Wright**

Tell me again about your ideas of balancing life.

**Rice**

Well, life's hard. And we spend most of our energies on all of the wrong things. And family and spirituality seem to take a back seat. I love business. I love work and professional organizations, but I set aside time for family, friends, fun, and what I call "me" time. And that's where I recharge my batteries with family trips, with touching, smelling, and galloping horses or go on solitary walks in the woods or one of my favorite things, spa days.

**Wright**

Spa days, oh, yes.

**Rice**

I have a daughter and two step daughters, and we all love spa days.

**Wright**

Oh, yeah.

**Rice**

But it took me years to realize how important these things are to my well being. And they're my touchstones, but business is my pulse. So I really need both. And I really believe women can have it all if they balance work with these things.

**Wright**

Do you think men are learning how to balance?

**Rice**

Oh, I most certainly do.

**Wright**

Do you?

**Rice**

I do. I see men learning not just to relax and to go for a massage, but I see men able to let go of some of the stereotypes that they've been brought up with. A lot of the stereotypes are out there about being a manly man. I don't know how else to express it, but I think men are learning to be themselves and not to have to live within society's stereotypes. I think they have it much harder in a way than women because from day one, men are brought up to follow a certain role model, and whereas I didn't have any role models, it gave me the freedom to kind of explore on the ground. Having set role models, in my opinion, has contributed to making men too rigid. Many times they are so set in how they're supposed to act, they miss opportunities for growth. But I see them changing too.

**Wright**

It's strange. I haven't always done interviews, only for the last few years in the publishing business, but the thing that surprises me more than anything when taking into consideration all you've said this afternoon, when I ask men who the influencing factor was in their life, as they reflect on it, almost every time it's their mother.

**Rice**

Isn't that interesting?

**Wright**

But they have all these manly qualities, but the influence has always been female. What legacy do you hope to leave for your children and your grandchildren?

**Rice**

Well, I don't have any grandchildren, yet, but I do think about my impact on future generations, whether they're relatives or not. As a descendent of a Cherokee Indian, I know from Native American teachings that what we do today will affect seven generations. That's profound for any of us to contemplate. Many times we think, "What could I do?" But the reality is that each of us will make a difference. My husband and I care for the land we live on, the horses we raise, and our children. And in just a small way we're making a difference by loving these things and taking care of them. So I guess if I don't leave anything else behind, I mean monetarily or even if I do, I hope what my kids really remember about me is the love that I've shown for all things.

**Wright**

Well, if we don't consider the ecology, we're all going to be in trouble a few generations from now. I think that's kind of a given. Everyone's saying it now. There are a few that deny it, but most people are at least thinking about taking better care of the land. Well, what an interesting conversation. I've learned a lot here and I wish you all of the success in the world. I'll bet you are going to be a mentor for all kinds of females.

**Rice**

Well, I hope so. I hope I'll be able to give back just a little bit of what I've learned and what others have given me.

**Wright**

Most of the teachers that influenced me tremendously down through the years have always been female. I think women are just so good at nurturing, and their intuition skills are just unbelievable. Sometimes I feel I don't have any at all.

**Rice**

Well, men can develop intuition. It's not just something that women can. And in fact, I've had long conversations with my father and my husband about this very subject because I'm quite interested in intuition. And I do use intuition in my dentistry. I don't try to block out that part of me that might just intuitively know what somebody's feeling or going to say. I don't think I'm the one that has all the answers, so I approach people with a kind of a questioning or quiet manner. And I see many times beyond the spoken word. People don't always tell you how they feel. We all have that ability to really intuitively tell what others are feeling, we just have to let go of our desire for control.

**Wright**

That's right, something us men have a hard time doing. Well, I really appreciate you spending all this time with me and for our readers in this book. And I really learned a lot today.

**Rice**

Thank you.

**Wright**

Dr. Janet Hatcher Rice is a dentist, lecturer, writer, and laser enthusiast. She's got years of experience in the dental field and as we have found today, knows a lot about balancing in life and skills necessary to become a leader. Dr. Rice, thank you so much for being with us today on *Remarkable Women.*

## About The Author

Dr. Janet Hatcher Rice is a dentist, lecturer, writer and laser enthusiast with over 30 years experience in the dental field who is now focusing her efforts on teaching other women how to succeed. The focus of leadership, business and professional training has always been on men. Now with over 50% of enrollees in professional schools in the United States being women, a growing need exists to help women acquire skills that will prepare them for achieving success in their business, professional and personal lives. But Dr. Rice takes it one step further, as a wife, mother, professional and spiritual being, she has personal insights in how to balance the multiple roles of women so that success is redefined and attainable. Women can have it all… but it will be on our own terms.

**Janet Hatcher Rice, D.D.S.**

136 Edgemont Ave.

Bristol, Tennessee 37620

Phone: 423.989.7733

Fax: 423.989.7632

Email: JHR902@aol.com

www.quantumdentistry.com

# *Chapter Fourteen*

## REV. DIANA MCCRACKEN

### THE INTERVIEW

**David E. Wright (Wright)**

Today we are talking to Diana McCracken. Diana has a hunger for learning. In April 2002, while attending a workshop at Trinity Seminary in Newburgh, Indiana, she met Linda Fitzgerald. From the moment they spoke to one another, they knew that God had planned this meeting. In July of 2003, Diana was transferred to a small town in east central Indiana. She found herself just a few miles from Linda. God has given them the opportunity to work together in various projects. One of those projects includes the implementation of speaking and teaching ministry for women. Diana is a strong faith filled woman. She has faced many challenges. One challenge was the tragic murder of her oldest daughter. This experience has taught her wisdom and has strengthened her relationship with Jesus Christ. Her story is one of courage and how Jesus Christ has shown her how to improve. Diana, welcome to *Remarkable Women*.

**Diana McCracken (McCracken)**

Thank you.

**Wright**

Tell me about your life as a child and a little bit about your family.

**McCracken**

Well, I was born into a family of farmers. In fact, I was born on the kitchen table in our farmhouse.

**Wright**

Oh, my!

**McCracken**

My mother was so upset because I was going to be the first child in our family to be born in the hospital, but I was in too much of a hurry. I have an older sister and an older brother. I'm the baby of the family. My father was a farmer as well as a Ford mechanic. My mother was a cook at our local school. I lived in one house for 18 years until I married. I can honestly say I know about hard work. The chores had to be done. No matter what happened, you had your job to do and you did it.

**Wright**

So you got married at 18? That's about the time all the kids are ready to go to college now.

**McCracken**

That's true. I can remember people saying, "Oh, you need to go to college. Don't get married so young." I thought I knew it all. I knew how my life was going to be and it was going to be perfect.

**Wright**

Yeah, right.

**McCracken**

That's the way it is when you're 18.

**Wright**

I remember in a school assembly once, we had a speaker, she said, "Look around you." And everyone all looked around. She said, "The person that you're going to marry you've never even met in 98% of the cases." And we snickered because we had our little sweethearts.

**McCracken**

You're all thinking, "Ah, what does she know?"

**Wright**

That's right. But she was right. Tell me, what was your faith turning point? How did you respond to it?

**McCracken**

My first faith turning point was when I was young and I had a grandfather that was such a gem. He was also a farmer. I didn't realize until I was older what an influence he had on my life. He and my grandmother both lived a Christian life. I grew up appreciating what God had done for me. The life changing turning point came when I was diagnosed with cancer at the age of 23. I was told that I was pregnant at the same time.

**Wright**

Wow!

**McCracken**

The doctor told me that I was going to have to abort my child. I wouldn't live to see her born if she lived. At this point in my life, I had already lost three children, and I said, "No, this one's in God's hands. It's going to be okay." I carried the baby full term. The Doctors took x-rays every month to see how the tumor was growing. They didn't have ultra sound back then. During the delivery they kept saying, "Don't look because she probably will be deformed." But she was perfect! How could she not be? She was in God's hands the whole time. After that they took me to be prepped for surgery. As I was waiting to go into surgery I had a visitor. I can only describe him as an elderly man. He had on a priestly collar, had white hair, and had beautiful blue eyes. He came into the room and asked if I wanted prayer. Well, of course, I wanted prayer. I always want prayer. I had been told I wasn't going to live to see my baby be born and I got to see her and she was perfect. Perfect! I wanted to hear prayers of Praise and Thanksgiving. When he prayed for me, he prayed this strange prayer. He said, "Because of your faith you will be made whole." I thought at the time, this guy has no clue what is going on in my life, but it was so nice and kind that he came in and he prayed for me. They took me into the operating room. Before they operated, they wanted to take one more X-ray to see how the tumor was laying now that the baby was out of the way. They estimated the tumor to be about a 10-pound tumor.

**Wright**

Goodness.

**McCracken**

But when they got the X-ray back, the tumor was gone. It was then that I knew that I had been in the presence of God.

**Wright**

Goodness.

**McCracken**

I knew that God had something special for me to do. I had no idea what I would be called to do, but I knew that God would have me do something special with my life. I was sure that whatever He asked me to do, I was going to say, "Yes."

**Wright**

Going into surgery after childbirth, if you aren't well, the surgery could kill you. Goodness gracious. What were they thinking?

**McCracken**

Well, they thought they were going to try to save my life, but it took Jesus Christ to do that.

**Wright**

Tell me about the unique challenges that you faced as a woman pastor in a traditionally male vocation.

**McCracken**

It's been interesting. I have been the first woman pastor in every church I have served. A lot of people are very open to having a woman pastor, and a lot of people are very closed to having a woman pastor. It's has been God working through me and teaching me—I hate the word "patience"—but teaching me patience to let the Spirit work. For me to understand that as a person I need to step back and let God do what God needs to do. There have been times when I've been directly challenged as I meet with a committee. I have had them say, "We don't want you here." Then I have said, "But God wants me here. I wouldn't be here unless God had wanted me here. So are you going to do what you think is right for this church or are you going to do what God feels is right for this church?" The majority of the time I've stayed. I was at my first full time church for eight years. They've never had a pastor there that long, and I wouldn't have moved when I did if it hadn't been for our Bishop. I knew that when I needed to go somewhere else, I would have a new challenge. But it has been an eye opener. You're either loved or hated. There were many times that I could preach saying I understood what Jesus felt like moving from one place to another, being accepted or rejected, but also knowing that God is the one in control.

**Wright**
You sound like a Methodist.

**McCracken**
I am.

**Wright**
Oh my! When you said Bishop and move around a lot, you can mean only one thing.

**McCracken**
That's right.

**Wright**
I was in the conference that had the first black Bishop, and also the first woman pastor.

**McCracken**
Wow!

**Wright**
And I tell you, there are challenges, aren't there.

**McCracken**
Yes, there are. And I tell you, as long as you depend on Christ, you make it through. There are times when you look back and say, "Oh, I don't understand how I did that." But you did what needed to be done because the Lord has led you through it.

**Wright**

Tell me about the challenges you faced when your oldest daughter was murdered.

**McCracken**

I was a mother who lost her daughter through a violent death, but I was also a pastor who lost a daughter through a violent death. You see, as a mother, I wanted to find this young man, and I knew who he was, and wanted to make sure he paid for what he had done to my little girl. As a pastor, I wanted to find this young man, minister to him, and help him find Christ. And so there was always that struggle going on within me. This person stalked me after the death of my daughter. He knew I knew who he was. This went on for several years. Did I tell you that I prayed constantly for him? I was at a Pastors' Spouse Retreat when I was told about Lisa's death. I had 128 pastors' wives around me, wanting to take care of me, but my first thought was, "We need to pray for this young man because he had to be living in a world of torment in order to be this angry to do something like this." And so my first request was for all of us to get together and pray for him. I haven't stopped praying for him to this day.

**Wright**

So he was convicted?

**McCracken**

Yes, just this past year in 2003. He killed her in 1987.

**Wright**

My goodness!

**McCracken**

I was able to talk to him at the courthouse. I was able to go up and talk to him with the police present. I shared that I forgave him for what he's done to Lisa, and for what he's done to my family. God showed me that if I didn't forgive him; guess who's not going to be forgiven? It's like God saying, "I mean these words, you know."

**Wright**

I think He said them four times, didn't He in different places?

**McCracken**

Yeah! You read that book too!

**Wright**

I read the book, yeah. I know how it all comes out in the end of it. Now because of Mel Gibson, I got to see the movie.

**McCracken**

There you go.

**Wright**

So during all of these years of being stalked, how in the world did you live with that? Was he incarcerated during those early years?

**McCracken**

No, he was walking free during that time.

**Wright**

Oh, my!

**McCracken**

And it was 16 years before we got him convicted.

**Wright**

16 years?

**McCracken**

Yes. I've known who it was all this time. For many years I couldn't preach on forgiveness because I couldn't forgive him. If I couldn't forgive, I couldn't preach about it. It was such a freeing experience to finally let go and put it in God's hands. The day that I was able to speak with him, I think he expected me to hit him because when I walked up to him, he stiffened up. And I said, "I just wanted to give something to you." I told him I wanted to give him a gift of forgiveness, and I did forgive him. He looked at me with such a funny look on his face, and he said, "I don't want it. Take it back." I just chuckled; his words just struck me as funny. I said, "Well, it's a gift. It's free." He said, "I don't want it. Take it back." I said, "Nope. It's a gift. It's yours." And as I left the courthouse he was still yelling at me, "But I don't want it!" I just waved at him and went on out the door.

**Wright**

Oh my. So then...so he never admitted to his crime?

**McCracken**

He admitted it through plea-bargaining. He sat there and admitted he intentionally killed her. And you know I knew he had done this. He had told me before that he did, but it wasn't until I heard those words "I intentionally killed her" that it just really got to me. I can't imagine that kind of anger and that kind of rage.

**Wright**

How old were you at that time?

**McCracken**

At the time of the murder?

**Wright**

Yes.

**McCracken**

That was 16 years ago, how old am I now? Oh, I was 40 years old.

**Wright**

Oh my!

**McCracken**

Yeah, I'm 56 now.

**Wright**

That's a lot of years to live with that kind anguish. How do you get to a place where you can forgive those who hurt you so deeply?

**McCracken**

Mostly through prayer and trying to understand that other person, trying to see them through God's eyes instead of my eyes. That was one of the gifts that God gave to me. When I looked at Jeff, I saw him through God's eyes, and saw a tormented soul. I literally hurt for him. I still hurt for him. I really do. And my hope and desire is that while he is in jail, for the rest of his life, he will find Christ. What a joy that would be! I have truly been blessed to be able to say, "Okay, you've hurt me. You've hurt my family. You've changed our lives forever, but God loves you and I forgive you. This only happened through the grace of God. It's only through the grace of God."

**Wright**

I bet your whole family just went through a private hell for years, didn't they?

**McCracken**

They did. My son, Rob, and daughter, Michelle, were devastated. Both were still in high school at the time Lisa was murdered. In fact, it's only been recently that my husband and I separated and divorced. This is largely due to him not being able to go on with life. He doesn't want to talk about her. He's still waiting for Lisa to come home. I couldn't do anything to help him. Nobody else could do anything to help him. He had to do that himself. Sixteen years ago we were a happy family. My husband was a minister. I had two children that were in high school, a daughter in college, and life was pretty doggone good. Then all of a sudden our world changed. The world is like that anyway, you never know what the next moment is going to bring. You don't know what's going to happen and that's why it's so important to be able to let God have the control in our lives. Because if we stay in control, we mess it up really bad, really bad.

**Wright**

What specific ministry and work do you feel called to now that will empower women and help them become remarkable as well?

**McCracken**

I don't consider myself remarkable.

**Wright**

Well, I do. It only takes me to think it, so you don't have to believe it.

**McCracken**

God is opening the doors to a speaking ministry. I have been asked to speak at retreats and conferences', sharing what Jesus Christ has done in my life. Also sharing what Christ has done for my family, and sharing what Christ can do for all of us. I try to help women understand that no matter what they've been through, or what they are facing, they're not alone. That's one of the hardest things for us women to understand. We're not alone. To have somebody sit there and say, "You know, this is what I've gone through and I've been able to get this far in my faith journey, and through all the trial I know that life is good. Life can be filled with joy and happiness no matter what you go through, what you face, because you're not alone. Not only do you have Jesus Christ, but also you have others who have been through similar situations and circumstances. Goodness can come into your life because forgiveness is the freeing moment in your life."

**Wright**

What a testimony! Well, this has been an interesting conversation.

**McCracken**

Unusual anyway, huh?

**Wright**

I've learned a lot. I just kept thinking of my daughter. She's 15 now. I just kept thinking how in the world would I get through that. I profess to be a Christian, but I'll tell you what. I haven't been that tested.

**McCracken**

We never know until we are faced with different situations on what we would do and how we will handle things. I was 18, I was getting married, and I thought I knew everything, that I could face anything. I loved my husband, he loved me, and we'd be together forever. But life changes, not necessarily with anyone at fault, but life does change. I don't know what people do if they don't have Jesus Christ in their life.

**Wright**

Well, in your case, since you're so young, you still have a lifetime ahead of you anyway, and with all that behind you, I don't know what could move you from the right path. If that doesn't do it, I don't know what would.

**McCracken**

Well, there's a new challenge every day.

**Wright**

Well, it certainly has been an enlightening experience talking to you, and I wish you the very best as you serve and in your speaking career to try to reach more folks. Being a pastor, I've been on a church staff myself for about 47 years now, and pastors are kind of limited. The same people hear them every Sunday.

**McCracken**

That's true.

**Wright**

And those same people never change. That's the comment I give my entire minister friends, and I have many. How can you stand there and talk to all those people for 52 weeks and they never change.

**McCracken**

Or you give the same sermon that you did last year and nobody recognized it.

**Wright**

Yeah, that is a bad sign, isn't it? If you change the color of your hair, or cut it, or wear cowboy boots, they will notice that. Well, what a pleasure it's been talking to you.

**McCracken**

I've enjoyed talking to you.

**Wright**

Today we've been talking to Diana McCracken and we're laughing now, but she's been telling us some things that for most of us would not be a laughing matter. And to have gotten to this place is miraculous to me. No wonder they call you a Remarkable Woman. Thank you so much, Diana, for talking to me today.

**McCracken**

Thank you.

## About The Author

Diana McCracken is an ordained minister, in the United Methodist Church, with over 18 years in the ministry. She has a Bachelor of Arts degree in Psychology from St. Mary of the Woods College, a Master of Divinity degree from Louisville Presbyterian Theological Seminary, and is a Doctoral candidate in Ministry at Trinity Theological Seminary. Diana lives in East Central Indiana. She is a Mother of two and a Grandmother of 5.

As a Pastor, Diana's message has focused on "being the best at what God wants you to be." She emphasized that God's teachings are not monumental or overwhelming expectations but accomplishable tenants of faith and salvation. Moreover, Diana understands that following God's word is not always easy. She was a pioneer in becoming an ordained minister when there were few women clergy in the United Methodist church, moreover, she has a profound testimony to the power of forgiveness as she and her family endured the murder of her oldest daughter, Lisa, in 1987 and the capture of Lisa's assailant in 2003. Diana's life work has been to serve God and the church. She has also done extensive work with women suffering from many forms of abuse and has helped them experience empowerment in their lives while enjoying a deeper relationship with God.

**Rev. Diana McCracken**

423 W. 27th Street

Connersville, Indiana 47331

Email: McCrackenDi@wmconnect.com

# Chapter Fifteen

## JEANNIE DESANTO

### THE INTERVIEW

**David E. Wright (Wright)**

Today we are talking with Jeannie DeSanto who had been a successful massage therapist for over 12 years until breast cancer surgery and the subsequent chemotherapy and radiation forced her to retire. She holds a BA in Psychology and Theology/Philosophy, certifications in Religious Education and Youth Ministry, and spent many years working with natural healing. She is the mother of three, a daughter and twin boys. She had been considering writing a book about and teaching holistic health for a long time, and is now pursuing her passion for writing and teaching, to inspire, encourage, and guide others toward healthier, more fulfilling lives. With practical logic and plenty of humor, she helps others make the connections they need to create more balance and abundance in their lives. Welcome!

**Jeannie DeSanto**

Thank you, David! I'm delighted to be talking with you today.

**Wright**

Now Jeannie, you say you're a person of passion. First tell me, what does that mean?

**DeSanto**

Well, people are driven by different desires, right? I believe that we're all intrinsically creative and hard-wired as social beings to contribute to the larger community. It's fascinating and wonderful the way our diverse interests and abilities intersect. I'm so grateful, for example, that there are people who love accounting, people who want to grow food or plant trees, and people who love the details of lab research. And what if no one wanted to start a garbage collection company? Isn't it great that somebody did?! There are people who are building safe houses for victims of abuse, people who can manage investments, and people who love geriatrics, or the rush of an emergency room. There are people willing and able to be soldiers, people who make beautiful artwork or music, and people who love endangered animals so much they dedicate their whole lives to conservation. The world needs all of our gifts.

Part of our challenge in life is to find our personal passion and then pursue it. No one person can deal with all the issues, so when we each tune into our inner driver and really follow our hearts, the right things will get done and they'll get done well. We need to bother to ask ourselves, "What meaning do I want my life to have? What energizes me? What do I (or could I) contribute that is my unique gift?"

Myself? I find that I'm very passionate about making connections—helping people make connections with each other, connecting with ideas, and connecting ancient wisdom with modern knowledge, technology, and methods. I see this as a path to a better world for all of us—personally, in our individual lives of course, but also socially and globally.

**Wright**

Why do you believe the ancient Greek phrases "know thyself" and "nothing to excess" are keys to solving modern problems?

**DeSanto**

Well, it turns out that Mom was right. When she would urge restraint by saying, "moderation in everything" I would secretly dismiss the idea as "square." Ooh, I'm dating myself here, aren't I. Well, incredibly enough, this little phrase turned out to be an ancient philosophical proverb. How was I to know she was a fountain of Socratic wisdom?! In Latin it's, "*Ne quid nimis.*" Nothing to excess. While our passions are really the basis for fulfilling our purpose, we still have to develop balance.

"Know Thyself" therefore becomes a key to success on virtually every level. When we become conscious of our inner driver, we are better able to safely stay on the road to heath, wealth, and wisdom. If we unconsciously allow our strongest drive (our passion) alone to steer us, we can become compulsive and miss much of the joy that should be the journey. Being in touch with our inner gifts also brings out our best.

We can sure confuse wants and needs. If we're not really in tune with ourselves—who we really are and what we really need—we'll go after what we think we want instead. Sometimes a desire to feel secure leads us into compulsive shopping and accumulation. Sometimes food, alcohol or drugs, promiscuous sex, talking, working, or watching television....or whatever it happens to be...can seem like a salve to ease the pain of emptiness, but what is it that we're actually after? Do we want to feel loved? Capable? Important?

The two principles work together. Self-deception in favor of our excesses is often easier than looking into a mirror, or projecting our fears onto others. On the positive side of projection, we often give others what we are actually needing for ourselves, so one way to learn how you need to be nourished is to notice how you feed others.

We'll talk more later about the Enneagram and why it's such a helpful tool. When we get very in touch with who we are at our core—our own gifts and talents, our interests, needs and passions—that's when really good stuff starts to happen! We move toward a clearer path, and that self-awareness can be the beginning of hope. It can be the beginning of healing. It can be the foundation for harmony in our lives and in the world.

**Wright**

Yeah, I've always thought that "nothing to excess" was one of the most intelligent things I'd ever heard. Eating keeps us alive, but then overeating will kill us.

**DeSanto**

Absolutely! Our strengths can even become our weaknesses if we over-use them.

**Wright**

Atomic power can keep the world running very, very smoothly and well, but it can also blow us to kingdom come.

**DeSanto**

Well, that's right. Sometimes we can get very excited about certain things—and things are good! I mean, creation is marvelous and we have to celebrate that, but we have to let go of our *attachments* to things. That's partly why I find it helpful to relate modern insights with the enduring wisdom of ancient peoples. We need the perspective of how we're connected with something much bigger than we are. Yes, something that's good can become bad. There are so many issues like that. You know, your example is very good because there are many things that are...how shall we say...analogous to atomic energy. We certainly have the power to make or break what we're given.

**Wright**

You're also writing a children's book. Could you tell our readers a little about that?

**DeSanto**

Sure. When I was diagnosed with cancer last year, I struggled with how to tell my kids. When I was growing up, the word "cancer" meant a death sentence, you know. Fortunately, today, that's not true most of the time.

**Wright**

Right.

**DeSanto**

So, that was part of the motivation. In trying to explain to my children about cancer, I wanted to somehow put it into their understanding of the natural world. Now, I'm the kind of person who avoids using chemicals—especially in my food, on my body, and for my lawn and garden – so it was hard for me to come to terms with this myself! "Well, I'm going to have surgery and I'm going to have chemotherapy and I'm going to have radiation..." How could I express that to the kids without scaring them first of all, but also without it going against what I've tried to teach them about how to live closer to nature. So the way I explained it to them was this: cancer is like poison ivy. You know poison ivy is about the only thing that I'm really willing to put chemicals on because it's so invasive, it causes so much harm, and there's no natural method that really keeps it under control or eradicates it.

**Wright**

Right.

**DeSanto**

We've all been cursed with poison ivy at one time or another, and so my kids could relate to this. It's something that does need to be pulled out by its roots, and it is one of those rare things that needs to be hit with chemicals.... otherwise it can overtake the healthy garden or the path that we walk in the woods.

Also, of course, when we have to prune a tree, it seems like a very destructive thing. Cut away live branches? I used tell my kids *not* to tear off live leaves and branches! Isn't that injuring a living thing?! A diseased limb and/or the threat of over-growth are reasons why sometimes we need, well, tree surgeons.

So, in both of those ways I realized that sometimes extraordinary circumstances require extraordinary means. This was one of those moments. As I was explaining all of this to my kids in terms of poison ivy and pruning, I realized that there was very little out there, literature-wise, for kids about cancer—that wasn't pedantic and boring, technical and dry, serious and scary, or fluffed over and sugar-coated.

I decided to write a story from the perspective of nature that would describe the treatment of cancer without using the "c" word. The story is told from the viewpoint of trees who are living in a wild orchard. A family, which is very loving to the Earth, and very much respectful of the trees, ends up having to treat the poison ivy that is fast- creeping into the orchard, as well as having to do some overdue pruning. The trees all freak out because they see those procedures as destructive, anti-life actions. In the end, though, they find that these were really life-saving, life-giving procedures.

It's how I've tried to share with my children this journey of dealing with cancer, and how I helped keep it in perspective for myself! I did everything. I did nutrition, I did exercise, and I did positive thinking, etc. but I also did the modern medical technology processes that are available...treatments that sometimes required me to hurt for awhile, but are actually protecting my health in the long-term.

**Wright**

It sounds like a great book.

**DeSanto**

Thanks, it's a pretty exciting project. It's a new arena for me, but the biggest motivation is that it's so needed right now. I think for a long time cancer was seen as an old person's disease. I've been just shocked at how many young people are now being diagnosed. Some of that, certainly, is that diagnostic procedures are getting better now, but the number of young women with breast cancer is just astonishing. You know, we don't completely understand why it's happening to so many younger women now, but I hope that I can lessen the anxiety for women with small kids (or grandkids or students) in having to explain cancer to them. I want to make the idea accessible to children without scaring them.

The word "cancer" is difficult in itself. Once I was diagnosed and began to do reading and research about it, I got to the point where I didn't even want to get within ten feet of that printed word! It's easy to get on overload with all the resources for adults that are available.

I wanted to write a good story that would stand on its own—one that kids would want to hear over again—but that could also be used to reduce stress for families in crisis.

**Wright**

Don't you think it's ironic that you found yourself with breast cancer even though you were the "health food nut" in your family?

**DeSanto**

Well, sure. We've all sort of laughed about that because of course, I'm the one who quit eating meat and sugar. I'm the one who's been eating all whole grains, taken vitamins, and been preaching and practicing natural healing all my adult life.

When I was about seven years old, my grandmother (my dad's mother) died of breast cancer. This probably planted the realization in my consciousness that breast health could be a potential issue for me. So, when I was a senior in high school, when I started learning about natural foods and natural healing, I really gravitated toward the anti-cancer diets and life style. I suppose I was led in that direction and so I've always been one to push the preventative health maintenance thing. Now I'm so grateful that I went that route because it has occurred to me that, "What if I wasn't doing all of those things right all my life?" Might the cancer have just spread like wildfire in my body? Thankfully, I'll never have the answer to that question! We can't prevent all disease, but we can always fortify our base health!

A friend of my dad's once said, "You just can't trust your ancestors, can you?" So true! Genetics do set us up, and we're only beginning to understand the field. I've really emphasized with my family, my friends, and my clients that "preventative health maintenance is always, always, ALWAYS a good investment!" If I hadn't been doing those things for the last 20 years I may not have survived so well during this health challenge! I've seen an awful lot of people have a lot harder time with all their treatments and not bounce back quickly.

**Wright**

Not to mention the fact that you probably felt better all those years....

**DeSanto**

Oh, definitely! It's really always a quality of life issue. It's not just about the years in one's life, but the life in one's years. I'm not sure, but it may have been Abraham Lincoln who said that....then again maybe it was Hagar the Horrible...or Garfield the Cat....

**Wright**

Tell me, having been on both the giving and the receiving ends of medical care, how do you now view healing?

**DeSanto**

Healing is always a partnership. We don't do medicine in isolation. When I was a massage therapist, I tried to work with my clients to help them understand that they needed to take care of themselves more than just the one hour a week (or month) that we were together. We can't continually abuse our bodies and then go to a medical person and say, "Okay, fix me" and expect to be healed. We have to work at health from the inside out, as well as the outside in. It's a both/and thing, not either/or. It's a partnership even within ourselves. It's our mind, and our body, and our soul all working together. While we can talk about them individually (like different facets on a carved diamond) they aren't actually separate things.

I also found that it was very helpful for me to enlist the help of a naturopathic physician and do my own research, as well as see my surgeon, my oncologist, and my OB/GYN. It was important to me to have deeply caring, warm individuals who I could trust, so that everyone (including me!) was working together to create a healing situation, rather than giving up responsibility and say, "Okay, someone else take care of it." There's a really important, pro-active aspect to healing that needs to happen within patients. I did try to be the best healing agent for my own clients (as I'm confident all my doctors and nurses did for me), but it's definitely a partnership. Finding a good "fit" with our medical people—both in terms of personality and philosophy—can have a huge, positive impact on health outcome.

**Wright**

Then it really does take a village.

**DeSanto**

I love it. Yes, indeed, David! It does!

**Wright**

My wife is cancer survivor.

**DeSanto**

Is that right?

**Wright**

Yes. The multitudes of friends and close relationships who have been there along the way almost make it bearable. After all...some make it and some don't. My wife is in her eighth year cancer-free, but tomorrow morning I will go to the funeral of a very, very close friend who didn't make it. So, it's really frustrating for those of us on the outside. It's almost like the whole family catches the disease.

**DeSanto**

Oh, sure. It affects absolutely everybody. What kind of cancer did your wife have?

**Wright**

Colorectal.

**DeSanto**

Oh, wow!

**Wright**

The bad stuff...and everybody thought she was going to die but her.

**DeSanto**

Well, that's the most important person to believe it!

**Wright**

That's right.

**DeSanto**

God love her! Well, a few years ago my best friend died of brain cancer. It was the worst kind that a person can get it, the very invasive and fast-growing type. She had only three months from diagnosis to death. It was so quick. It seemed sort of outrageous to pray for her recovery. Do you know what I mean—in the face of that? Although they did, of course, try everything. Everyone did everything that was possible in order to help bring that about, but the main thing we prayed for was for healing...hoping for recovery, but trusting that she would be healed in whatever way was right.

The most wonderful thing happened in the process of her treatment: she did indeed heal—emotionally and spiritually. And of course, that's what I'm thinking God is actually concerned about...that kind of healing is really the most important thing.

It was just beautiful to me to see how relationships were transformed, but also her inner struggle was healed about her own lovability. Here was a person who gave, gave, and gave...loved, loved, and loved others, but didn't feel worthy of the love herself. She found that during her treatment process that she could no longer give, and people continued to love her. People came out of the woodwork! There was just this outpouring of love, and she was so touched by that! She finally realized that "Oh, they're not loving me just because I'm giving to them."

**Wright**

Yes, that surprised me more than any thing. I just couldn't believe it! It's really hard to understand when you get all of that love from people that you know—it's almost scary. Even if you've never asked for anything in your life, it's really scary, isn't it?

**DeSanto**

It's that way so often. What beautiful opportunities those moments were. In the most difficult of circumstances, blessings can flow that may not have been able to come any other way. I'm continually awed by the gifts that are hidden inside challenges.

**Wright**

In a world where negativity seems to rule the airwaves (and everything else as far as that's concerned!), why are you so optimistic?

**DeSanto**

Well, I guess I have a very rich fantasy life! You know what? I do! I have had visions very often for a better way to be, but I've also been very privileged to be around some very wise and inspiring people in my life. People who are creating better ways to live give me hope. We must always be envisioning new ways to relate to each other, solve problems, and find some common ground between seemingly desperate views.

I believe in the evolution of consciousness. I mean, evolution is going to happen. Physical evolution can happen very slowly, but we are evolving as a species and I think that we can—with intentionality—evolve our thinking and evolve our consciousness about solutions. When I see people innovating, whether it's fuel sources and energy, or ways of farming organically, or finding new medications, or having better relationships, whatever kind of beauty that people are giving life to in this world, I have tremendous hope that if we do follow our passions, if we each take that responsibility in this world to allow our creativity to connect with other people's abilities and gifts, then really amazing and wonderful things can and will happen. We can spiral upward toward an exponentially better future. This is one of the reasons that I'm so passionate about helping people connect with each other.

**Wright**

Do you mind if I introduce some controversy into the conversation?

**DeSanto**

Sure! No, no, I mean, I don't mind!

**Wright**

OK, how did you come to be an advocate for gay marriage, even though you are solidly heterosexual?

**DeSanto**

Part of it is that I think it's necessary for non-gays like me to speak out about the validity of the nature of homosexual union, in the same way that it's important for males, not just females, to speak out for the fair treatment of women, and non-blacks to speak out for the rights of blacks re: racism. If only those who are being treated unfairly step out to say, "this isn't fair..." they sure can appear biased. So, I think that those of us who do believe passionately that this is a very important social and spiritual issue should speak up.

I see this issue as a matter of opening our minds to a new world view. I like to call it The Galileo Factor because this seems very much to me like Galileo asking the people of his day to open their minds to science, that is, to scientific evidence, that people weren't comfortable with...for a very long time. It wasn't their world view. It took 200 years before Galileo's book was dropped from the censor list, and it took the Catholic Church over 300 years to formally acknowledge that it was an injustice to label Galileo a heretic. What he revealed in his day about the nature of the Earth's relationship to the Sun is today accepted as obviously true, but when he was alive, he went through in a lot of what I see going on politically today. People said (and still say), "This isn't how we've always thought, or been taught. This isn't how we've always done things. It's against God to redefine the way we believe everything was created."

I understand that people legitimately question the changing face of the family and fear the Slippery Slope. It's as if we acknowledge that gay people's relationships could in fact be sacred unions, then somehow we're also changing the whole foundation—the building blocks of a healthy society. But in fact, homosexuality just is what it is. It's reality...and not just in the human species, but across the board in almost every species of mammal. It's science, and it's not one or two renegade biased studies, there have been decades of documentation now.

Some still say, "Oh well, that's not natural." Well, it's not natural for me, but it is natural for a gay person, and there are many gay people who want or are already in deeply holy relationships. They desire to have that relationship sanctified in the church, respected and supported by the community. Unfortunately, they are instead met with not just intolerance but outright hatred! It's incredibly ironic to me, given the core that most religious thought centers on compassion and love of neighbor, the vehemence toward homosexual people in the name of religion that I have witnessed is appalling. It seems absolutely contrary to everything that I understand Jesus Christ taught and lived. There are people who call themselves His followers who are just steeped in this hatred and this bashing.

I think it's a matter, again, of allowing our consciousness to evolve. It may take a long time, you know, but can you imagine if we were in the Galilean age...people protesting before Congress, "We're against the earth revolving around the sun! We don't believe in the solar system! It's a dangerous kind of thinking!" To me, it's on that level of reality—and in some ways we need to come out of these modern dark ages—but again, it will take time. Anger and hatred won't solve or eliminate the issue. Time might!

It's difficult for people to stop and accept some scientific evidence that things aren't the way they always thought they were. It's not easy, but it's not heresy. It's just science.

**Wright**

Sometimes things are different. It's fascinating to me, every time. I love to go to marine exhibits, like the aquarium at Gatlinburg.

**DeSanto**

Oh, yeah...

**Wright**

Almost without exception the people are fascinated the most by the beauty and the difference of the seahorses. They swim upright, you know, and they look like they were made by a committee, but they're just beautiful. But the male has the babies in that species.

**DeSanto**

Hmmm, why don't we just call him the female? Funny, isn't it?! Nature has an abundant and elegant diversity that we are learning to respect. If we're paying any attention at all, science will constantly keep us in a state of awe. As long as we have a sense of awe about creation, we will have reverence and awe about the Creator.

**Wright**

That's right!

**DeSanto**

I've also observed that how we view ourselves in relationship to the rest of creation has a major impact on health and health care practices in this country.

**Wright**

What do you mean?

**DeSanto**

We are creatures of this Earth. We're all native to this planet, and yet somehow we think that we humans are in some way exempt from the basics of nature. Hey, as you know, I'm all for the extraordinary means—high-tech procedures and medicines—when it's time to deal with extraordinary conditions, but I want to mention for a moment something that I want everyone to know:

We treat our houseplants and our pets better than we treat ourselves! What are the 5 things that all living beings need on this planet? 1) Fresh Air! 2) Clean Water! 3) Proper Nutrition! 4) Sunshine! 5) Movement! Even plants bend and stretch toward the sun and the rain. So, if a houseplant or a pet isn't feeling well, what do we do? We run down this little mental checklist. Only if making the necessary corrections doesn't perk 'em up do we call the garden guru or head for the vet.

What about us? If we're not feeling up to par, do we stop to ask the same basic questions or do we automatically reach for a pill to cover the symptoms? 1) Am I getting enough fresh air? 2) Am I drinking enough pure water? 3) Am I eating good, healthy foods and taking supplements where my diet is lacking? 4) Am I getting 10-15 minutes of sunshine a day? 5) Am I getting the movement I need? Once we have all of these minimum requirements covered, then we can begin investigating deeper health issues, but this handful of "musts" may just be the keys to keeping that from being necessary very often.

**Wright**

You've recently become certified to teach about the—and you're going to have to help me pronounce this—is it the Enneagram?

**DeSanto**

That's right. You've got it. You can say it like "Annie-a-gram" or even "(J)eannie-a-gram." I've been a casual student of these insightful and transformative principles for probably 15 years, but now I'm able to teach Kathy Hurley & Theodorre Donson's Enneagram Experience™ Workshop.

**Wright**

What is the Enneagram and why is it so important?

**DeSanto**

Well, most people do call it the "Ennea-what?!"

**Wright**

Right!

**DeSanto**

That's the general reaction that I get.

**Wright**

I hope it has nothing to do with my mother's favorite cure—the enema. You know, she used to have that to cure everything from a cold to a stomach ache. Please tell me it has nothing to do with that.

**DeSanto**

It has nothing to do with that!

**Wright**

Thank you, thank you.

**DeSanto**

The word itself comes from the Greek, ennea (meaning nine) and gram (meaning drawn). It's an intriguing and beautiful symbol. OK, imagine with me a circle with nine equi-distant points (think of a compass with nine directional markers). The points are interconnected by nine lines across the circle: three of the lines are forming an equilateral triangle in the middle, while the other six lines are connecting each of the remaining points, one to another. I do realize that as a geometric visual, this is hard to explain purely on a verbal level!

**Wright**

Can you send me a diagram of that?

**DeSanto**

Oh, sure, absolutely.

**Wright**

Oh, good. Great!

**DeSanto**

Here are some variations, if they're printable: The basic Enneagram, the numbered Enneagram, and my very own Ennea-Yin-Yang™, in which I superimpose this graceful image into another ancient symbol for Balance. It's so amazing to me, it almost makes me want to go back and take Geometry again (I said almost)!

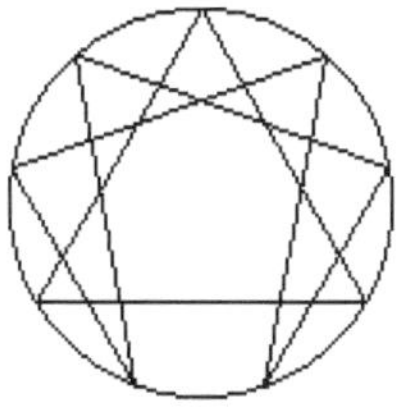

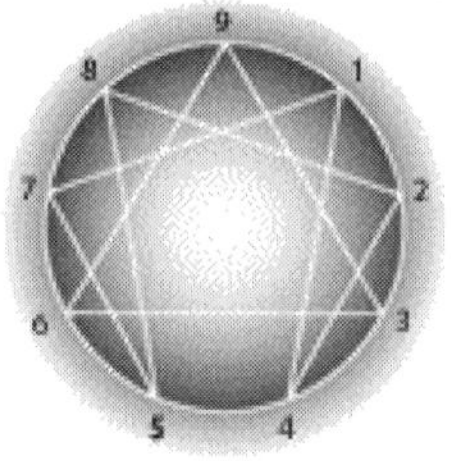

Now, why is this symbol so important? It is an ancient graphic that has been used in a number of different ways through the ages; part of its fascination is that its origins are somewhat obscure. There are connections with ancient mystical Sufis, and more recently Jesuit teachers, with sacred geometry, and Pythagoras and Plato. Variations on this symbol can be found throughout the world in many forms, so we're not likely to ever completely understand where exactly it comes from, but it has been used to illustrate natural, universal dynamics in one way or another over the millennia. I've even noticed parallels with Chi patterns as described by Feng Shui.

As it's used today, the Enneagram symbolizes a very practical set of psychological and spiritual principles that not only help us understand ourselves and others, but actually also provide a blueprint for our personal growth and transformation. So, modern psychology and spirituality are woven together, and the Enneagram comes to represent nine different personality types or core compulsions. Each person will find him or herself best described as one number, or type, and many are (as I was) startled to discover the accuracy of the insights offered in this healing tradition.

**Wright**

So you have something like a pentagram, only you have nine points on it and there are nine separate meanings for each one of the points?

**DeSanto**

That's right. Now this brings us back to the essential precept of "know thyself." So, each person, in learning about these different compulsions and personality types, can find themselves in one point on there. Now the wonderful thing about the symbol is that they're all interconnected and no number is better than any other. You know, we all have parts in common with each other and as we grow, we take on some different characteristics, but at our core each one of us has a unique set of motivations. (This is not to be confused with Dr. Stephen Reiss's 16 basic human desires as described in his great book, *Who Am I?* or with the Myers-Briggs typology. While there are naturally commonalities, this is a different system and is beautifully self-contained.)

We can more easily discern these patterns when we look at ourselves simply in terms of centers and stances. In my upcoming book, *Life's a Trip! Use Your Unique Nature to Navigate the Speed Bumps* (with my co-author Meg Scott) we explore this in more depth, as we help people work with their personality type to create more relaxed, organized, and fulfilled lives. There are also many other wonderful books just on the wisdom of the Enneagram, and I enthusiastically encourage our readers to pursue this system of sacred psychology.

For my purpose here, I'll explain the two most essential components. First, we have three centers. The head—our thinking center. The heart—our feeling and relating center. The gut—our intuitive and body center, or doing center. We use all our centers, but we naturally lead with or over-use one ("nothing to excess!") and we tend to under-use another, leaving us less balanced, developed, and actualized than our true potential.

The second triad is a basic stance. Some of us are externally motivated, that is, generally more assertive, and future-focused. Others are more internally motivated, introspective and focused on our history. A third group are motivated more by responding to others and are more focused on the immediate present.

Each combination of lead center and basic stance creates one of nine natural patterns of perceiving and reacting. These are the numbered "types" of the Enneagram. We experience and respond to the way our needs are being met (or not met) through our unique pattern. As we grow up and develop coping mechanisms, our personality (along with its compulsions) solidifies. In using the Enneagram to learn how these patterns define us, we can recognize both self-defeating behaviors and strengths that we often could never have seen before. Perspective can be everything!

I'll list the Nine Types briefly, but then encourage our readers to read a book or attend a workshop. Dozens of books are written on the subject, so I won't even begin to pretend to be exhaustive here. Different authors, researchers, and teachers have their own variations of type "names," and with new insights, the language of the Enneagram is still evolving, but these are the Nine Natures, compacted in a way that Meg and I have found both amusing and useful: 1) Ethical-Worker-Perfectionist-Reformer 2) Caring-Proud Giver-Rescuer-Helper 3) Productive Achievement-Success-Seeker 4) Creative-Imaginative Non-Conforming Individualist 5) Uninvolved-Observer Expert-Analytic-Cynic 6) Unpredictable-Cautious Questioning-Loyalist 7) Optimist-Idealist Light-Hearted Generalist 8) Strong-Protector Leader-Commander 9) Pleasant-Perceptive Passive-Peacemaker.

Why is learning our Type so beneficial? Think Apollo's temple at Delphi again (*"Gnothi se auton!")* and you've got it! The Enneagram does more than just describe, though. It shows the way for each type to heal.

We create self-fulfilling prophesies in our lives. What we believe and expect is usually what we get because our unconscious mind is quietly driving our decisions. That's fine if we believe deeply that we are lovable, important, and capable. Unfortunately, when we are out of balance, or don't "know ourselves," we can make unconscious choices (that is, compulsively) that dig us into a hole we can't see our way out of.

When we take a step back and get some insight into what we're thinking compulsively, feeling compulsively, or doing compulsively—we can create a blueprint for how to break out of that cycle of the downward spiral and really begin to grow and prosper—integrated mentally, emotionally, socially and spiritually—and create more health and harmony in our lives.

**Wright**

What about this little Aardvark? Where does he (or she!) fit in as a symbol for success?

**DeSanto**

First, I think the Aardvark is an interesting and memorable creature, but more importantly, the letters in AARD-VARK™ I found spell out for me a method for manifesting good things in your life.

Again, if you begin with knowing what you really need rather than what you think you want—or what someone else tells you that you should have—you can begin to go about getting the most out of life.

The first half of Aardvark is "AARD" which stands for the "what" affirmation of manifesting...to Abundantly Acquire what is Required and Desired. Understand that everything that you need and want in life is available and accessible to you.

The second half is how to get it. "VARK" stands for Vision, Action, Receive, and Kick-back. If we begin with a clear the Vision, (that's the first part) and then take Action steps to bring it into reality, then allow it to be Received. Finally, it's vital to Kick something back in gratitude—by tithing or contributing to a cause that's close to your heart, or passing along positive energy, wisdom, or help to another—this keeps abundance in circulation! What goes around really does come around!

**Wright**

You use the words Raw, Ripe, and Rotten. What you call the Three BananaR's™ to illustrate a non-shaming yet firm moral code with your kids. Could you tell us how that works?

**DeSanto**

Have you ever been driving along in your car and notice a police car behind you...and all of a sudden you panic because you think, "Well, maybe I'm doing something wrong!" even though you're not intentionally doing anything illegal?

**Wright**

Right.

**DeSanto**

I don't want to get in trouble for not knowing what I don't know, and there is a part of me that sometimes feels insecure about my potential ignorance of the law. I also think that there may have been times when I was a kid, for example, that I got in trouble and I didn't really know why I was in trouble. If I tried to respond, or question my supposed crime, I was told not to talk back. I'm quite sure that I'm not the only in the world who has experienced that. Parents don't consciously put their kids between a rock and a hard place, but it happens, and it feels really unfair....and can provoke anger, rebellion, even (gasp!) power struggles between parents & kids, as well as among siblings.

So with my own kids, I thought it was important to tell them in an appropriate way "why" something was wrong—and not just because I said so. Also I think it's tough for kids when they experience what sure seems like an injustice. For example, when the little tiny kid scribbles on the walls, it's cute and people laugh....but when the bigger kid scribbles on the wall, he gets in big giant heaps of trouble. Now why is that? Is it wrong or isn't it?

So, one of the things I talked to my kids about when they were younger is how kids will do something wrong or inappropriate because they just don't know better. That requires teaching and guidance. They're just RAW. Unripe. Undeveloped. We made a whole list together! Crude. Rough. Premature. Needs-work. Un-polished. Draft-stage. Un-learn-ed. Un-prepared. Incomplete. Unfinished. Immature. They aren't intentionally being "bad," they're just not-ready yet.

Other times a kid will act out an inappropriate behavior and it IS "bad." It's not that they don't know better, they DO know better. But they do it anyway.

**Wright**

So you know my 15 year old daughter...

**DeSanto**

Yes, so you know why that's when we call it ROTTEN. My kids helped me make another list. Spoiled. Over-done. Decayed. De-Composed. Contaminated. Tainted. Putrid. Stinky. Over-the-top. In-the-mud. Disgusting. Throw-it-out. Gone-too-far. Bruised.* (Yes, we acknowledge that rotten behavior often is a reaction to being hurt, and sometimes requires extra compassion.)

Well, somehow we easily recognize RIPE behavior. It's right, appropriate, and we know it when we see it. When bananas are ready, they're mature and sweet. Complete. Fully grown. Whole. Finished. Developed. Mellowed. Seasoned. Full-fledged. Primed. Keen. Consummate. Peaked. Prime.

So when child behaves in an unripe way, it doesn't mean they don't get in trouble necessarily, but the emphasis is on the opportunity for a learning experience. Consequences can be great teachers.

**Wright**

Right.

**DeSanto**

Now the consequences applied to rotten behavior might be different from raw, even if we see that the rotten spot is from a bruise, because it's important to use the opportunity to turn things around for the better. These might be more active consequences especially if there was damage done that needs to be repaired...you know, something that makes banana bread out of the bruised fruit.

We posted this in the hallway. The sign says, "Think First...is this behavior Raw? Ripe? Or Rotten? It was a very helpful tool for us, providing a process to talk about appropriate (more a-peel-ing!) behavior by not getting in trouble for something they didn't understand...yet!

**Wright**

Right! Now, before we close, what is the most important thing that you want to teach people?

**DeSanto**

Never try to install a ceiling fan in your living room while you're in the throes of PMS!

**Wright**

Thank God I don't know about that.

**DeSanto**

But you've experienced it from your side, haven't you?

**Wright**

Oh, yeah....

**DeSanto**

Well, why I say that is that so often we just press through something we're doing without stopping to consider the circumstances or wisdom of what we're choosing (or the timing). There it is again—that self-awareness!—it is at the beginning of peace and the genesis of solutions.

When we recognize our unconscious, compulsive patterns, we create opportunity for transformation—first in the individual, and then in the wider community. We've got to stop setting ourselves up for frustrations, answering violence and hatred with violence and hatred. These things can't possibly be paths to peace.

For me, the ceiling fan experience was real, but it's a good analogy for many issues. It's OK to stop, and change course...step away from the drive to keep doing what we do and in the way we always do it. We need to give ourselves permission to re-envision our lives—the way we do our chores, the way we take care of ourselves (inside and out), the way we act and react with our kids, the way we give and receive, the way we assign meaning to our lives.

The other thing is to breathe! I mean really breathe fully, deeply, consciously. Conscious breathing keeps us aware of this precious present....and it is this awareness which provides the inspiration for the growth, creativity, healing, and courage to live more fully and authentically. The word inspiration, after all, literally means "to breathe in." Do you remember that Foghorn Leghorn from the old Warner Brothers cartoons?

**Wright**

Oh yeah, I loved him!

**DeSanto**

He had to bop that cat and holler, "Breathe! You forgot to breathe again, son!" That always cracked me up. It is amazing to me how often we forget to breathe, at least fully. We are reactive very often rather than taking a moment to breathe and center and know ourselves well enough to know the best way to approach a situation. Is my instinct/intuition clear? Is it best to wait and think about it? Do I need to stop and get in touch with my feelings? Is it better to just act? When we remember to breathe, to enter into that presence of ourselves, we begin to know ourselves—what we need and what we mean.

You know, David, it's like the journey of life. We have to travel in the same mode that we want to end up. If we want to be able to create a harmonious world, we have to travel in a harmonious way. The journey becomes the destination.

**Wright**

Well, what an interesting conversation! We've covered all kinds of topics—all of which are very fascinating to me. You certainly are a remarkable woman.

Today we have been talking to Jeannie DeSanto. She was a massage therapist for many years and is now is a writer and educator. She is a breast cancer survivor and a mother of three teenagers. And she, as we have found today, has some great ideas on healthful living, both mentally, spiritually, and physically. Thank you so much, Jeannie, for being with us today on *Remarkable Women.*

**DeSanto**

Thank you, David. It's been a pleasure.

## About The Author

Jeannie DeSanto is honored to be able to share her insights and energy with audiences large and small. With years of experience creating and directing retreats & workshops, and a background including psychology, theology & philosophy, youth ministry & religious education, medical massage therapy & natural healing, music, art, and parenting, Jeannie is now a writer, teacher, and Certified Instructor for the Hurley/Donson Enneagram Experience™ and has developed a repertoire of effective and entertaining approaches to helping people create The Possible in their lives!

**Conference Topics:** Health & Wellness (Finding Balance; Humor & Healing), Personal Growth (The Enneagram; Aardvark™ Approach to Manifesting), Parenting (Empathy, Discipline & The BananaR's™), Dealing with Cancer ("But I'm the healthiest person I know!"; When there are Kids in Your Life), Communication & Relationships (Unconditional Love; "What was I thinking?!—Cautionary Tales"), Massage Therapy (Cooperative Business Practices; Couples Workshops), Color as Healing (Painting as Meditation for Emotional Wellness).

**Jeannie DeSanto**

3856 Pine Meadow Road

New Albany, Ohio 43054

Phone: 614.855.2921

Email: jdesanto@insight.rr.com

www.jeannieconnect.com

# Chapter Sixteen

## Marci Shimoff

### THE INTERVIEW

**David E. Wright (Wright)**

Today we are talking to Marci Shimoff. Marci is a woman with passion, spirit and dynamism who has touched the hearts and rekindled the spirits of millions of people throughout the world. She is one of the nation's leading motivational experts and is co-author of the #1 *New York Times* best-selling books, *Chicken Soup for the Woman's Soul I and II and Chicken Soup for the Mother's Soul I and II, as well as Chicken Soup for Every Mom's Soul,* and *Chicken Soup for the Single's Soul.* Marci's books have sold over 13 million copies and have been on *The New York Times* bestsellers list for a total of 110 weeks. *USA Today* named Marci the top female author of the year. President and co-founder of The Esteem Group, Marci is a professional speaker with a lively sense of humor and a powerful, uplifting presence. Addressing the unique issues that women face on their journey to build self-esteem and personal empowerment, Marci shares powerful techniques to establish deep and authentic happiness and joy. Over the last 18 years she has delivered seminars and keynote addresses on self-esteem, stress management, self-care, communication skills, and peak performance to numerous corporations, professional and charitable organizations, and women's organizations. Marci has been a top-rated trainer for many Fortune 500 companies. Marci earned her MBA at UCLA and is a certified stress-management consultant. She has also co-authored a highly acclaimed study of the 50 top businesswomen in America. Her latest work is the forthcoming book, *The Power of an Open Heart: A Woman's Guide to Unlocking the Joy and Love in Life*. Marci, welcome to *Remarkable Women*!

**Marci Shimoff (Shimoff)**

Thank you, David. I am so happy to be here.

**Wright**

Marci, you've been a professional speaker for the last 18 years, and you've spoken to hundreds of thousands of people. Why did you become a professional speaker?

**Shimoff**

I consider myself to be very fortunate in that I knew what I wanted to do from quite a young age. I was about 13 years old when I saw my first motivational speaker, a man many people know named Zig Ziglar. Immediately I knew that that was what I wanted to do when I grew up. Now, this idea didn't go over very well with my parents, who had never even heard of speaking as a profession. (Though my mother used to tease me that since I talked so much, I might as well get paid for it.) At the time—this was in the early 70s—I hadn't heard of any women who were professional speakers. But I knew that I wanted to spend my life inspiring people to live their highest potential, because that's what I wanted for my own life. So, when I went to college, I started taking every course and reading every book I could find on success and happiness to find out what worked. I remember sitting at my temporary job as a receptionist during summer vacation and reading all the Og Mandino books on success. I practiced the different principles I learned about, and I took what worked for me and let go of the rest. Since degrees in motivational speaking weren't offered in the halls of higher education, I did what seemed to be the next closest thing: I got an MBA in training and development. Then, after spending four years as vice president of marketing for a giftware company, I started my career as a corporate trainer and that led to my becoming a speaker. So, from the time I was 13, I would picture myself speaking in front of large audiences of women, and by the time I was 28, that's what I was doing.

**Wright**

You co-authored the women's books in the *Chicken Soup for the Soul* series. How did you get involved with writing the *Chicken Soup for the Soul* books?

**Shimoff**

During the years I was teaching corporate training programs, I decided to specialize in the field of self-esteem. I asked many people's advice about whom to study with, and the name Jack Canfield kept coming up. So, in 1989, long before the *Chicken Soup for the Soul* series was conceived, I began to study with Jack and he became my mentor. Four years later, in 1993, Jack, along with his writing partner, Mark Victor Hansen, came out with the original *Chicken Soup for the Soul* book. By then I was speaking to women's audiences on self-esteem and self-empowerment, continuing my work with Jack and frequently sharing his self-esteem principles with my audiences. I asked him if I could use some of his Chicken Soup stories in my talks, and he said, "Of course." A year later, I was on a one-week silent meditation retreat. And by the way, going into silence for a week is *not* an easy thing for someone who makes her living as a speaker!

**Wright**

I understand that.

**Shimoff**

But I did it, and on the fourth day, in the middle of one of my meditations, I had the experience of a light bulb lighting up before me. Just like in the cartoons! It really felt like that. The words "Chicken Soup for the Woman's Soul" popped into my head with a huge light around them. I immediately knew that this idea was a winner, and I felt as though it had been given to me as a gift. This was before any of the specialty *Chicken Soup* books had been conceived, and I knew it could be the start of something big. I was so excited—the hardest thing about the experience was that I had to stay in silence for another three days! As soon as those last three, very long days of silence were up, I ran to the nearest pay phone at the retreat center and I called Jack to tell him the idea. He thought it was a great idea, so he called his publisher, who also loved the idea. And that was how the specialty *Chicken Soup for the Soul* books were born. Because I specialize in speaking to women's audiences, I have co-authored the other women's books in the series, as well.

**Wright**

Had you always wanted to be a writer?

**Shimoff**

Being a writer was the farthest thing from my mind. I had never liked writing in general, but when I was teaching my corporate training programs, I had been asked to teach business writing. Well, I had always *hated* business writing. But it was the job that came my way, and I needed to do it at the time to pay the bills. So I taught business writing in top Fortune 500 companies for about eight years and got tremendous experience in editing and writing. It turned out to be the perfect training for my work in writing and compiling the *Chicken Soup for the Soul* books. This was one of the things that convinced me that there really is a divine plan for our lives!

**Wright**

The *Chicken Soup for the Soul* series became the best-selling book series of the decade, selling over 80 million books. Why do you think the books have been such a success and what have you learned or discovered from your work as a speaker and co-author of the *Chicken Soup for the Soul* books?

**Shimoff**

Many people may not have heard the story behind *Chicken Soup for the Soul*—that Jack Canfield and Mark Victor Hanson, the original co-authors, took the book to 116 publishers and 115 publishers turned them down, saying that people didn't want to read positive, uplifting stories. To this day, 115 publishers are kicking themselves for being so wrong about that. I think the books became the best-selling series of the decade because people in our society are soul-starved. We are bombarded every day with so much bad news that people want to hear something positive. These stories of hope, love and inspiration fill a void that is out there—they open people's hearts. In putting together these books, I've read over 20,000 stories that have been submitted to us, and, in doing so, I've come to have a much greater appreciation of people.

We are meant to be inspirations for each other. So many of our readers have written to me or told me that their lives have been changed by reading somebody else's story. There is tremendous power in sharing stories. We can preach and teach until we're blue in the face, and it may do nothing to inspire someone to change, but when a powerful, true story is told, it will land inside their heart. And that might fire them up to finally take action to go after whatever it is they've always wanted to pursue. People tell me, "You know, I read a story about somebody else who's living my dream, and I can do it, too!" We deeply relate to other people's stories because they touch on universal truths within ourselves.

**Wright**

Obviously you've experienced a great success in the way our society defines success. What do you think brings success? Are there certain habits that are important?

**Shimoff**

Yes, there are definitely habits that cultivate success, and certainly many books have been written on them. In fact, Jack Canfield's latest book, *The Success Principles*, cites 65 different habits for success. They are all important, but I think that perhaps the most important of all is the habit of taking responsibility for ourselves. By this I mean taking responsibility for our lives, our thoughts, our attitudes and our actions—being proactive in life, not a victim who is busy blaming others and complaining.

There's so much in life we can't control, but we can control our thoughts and make them work for us, not against us. I'm very excited about some of the latest research on the powerful effect that our thoughts and attitudes have on us, particularly the work being done by Dr. Masaru Emoto in Japan. Dr. Emoto has studied the effects that words and thoughts and even music have on water. In his book, *Messages from Water*, he describes his experiments. He put water from the same source into a number of different containers and then taped written messages onto each container. One container had the message "I love you" taped to it. Another container had the message "I hate you. You make me sick." And so forth. After leaving the water in the containers for some time, he froze drops from each of the containers and looked at them under a microscope. He found that the crystalline structures the water formed looked entirely different based on the different messages that they had been given. You can see from the photos that the water that had the message "I love you" has an exquisitely beautiful, symmetrical crystalline structure. But the structure of the water that had the message "I hate you" is distorted and chaotic; it is not beautiful at all.

Dr. Emoto then repeated the experiment with groups of people saying the various messages to the different containers of water. He also experimented with exposing the water to various kinds of music. Again, the results were astonishingly consistent: the more loving the message, and the more harmonious the music, the greater the beauty, clarity, and orderliness of the crystalline formations when the water was frozen. And remember, our bodies are almost 70% water. So, this makes it "crystal" clear that our thoughts and beliefs are having a powerful, physiological effect on us, for good or bad. And I think we see that in our lives all the time. It isn't necessarily easy to change our life-long habits of thinking, but I've seen it's definitely possible. It's important to be able to let go of the negative internal dialogue and emotions that keep us feeling stuck. One way to do this is through a releasing technique that's found in a book by Hale Dwoskin, *The Sedona Method*. I've had great success with it. It's simple, easy and it really works.

Something else that's been tremendously helpful in my life is that I've been in a women's support group, a mastermind group, for many years. We keep each other positive and lend the power of the "mastermind" or "group consciousness" to each member's goals. I encourage women to seek out like-minded women and form these groups. You can practice the habits and techniques of achieving your dreams together. It's much more doable, and a thousand times more fun!

One of the most interesting things I've learned about having material success is that, just like so many celebrities have shown us or told us, it doesn't guarantee happiness. I've gotten to know many, many successful people who feel very empty inside. So, when I think of success today, I think of it as far more than just professional or financial achievements. My goal now is to help people move beyond outer success to a deeper sense of fulfillment and joy in life.

**Wright**

Much of your speaking and writing is specifically directed towards women. What do you find is most important to women these days?

**Shimoff**

That's a great question. I have found that what women really want is a deeper sense of meaning, purpose, joy and happiness in life. The number one complaint I hear amongst women is that they feel stressed and burned out, and whether they're successful or not, they feel empty inside. What's happened is that we're so wrapped up in our activities and so busy going after what we think is important that we're not listening to what will truly make us happy or fulfilled on the inside. Did you know that one out of every five women in America is on anti-depressants? We also suffer from so many addictions that are symptomatic of trying to fill ourselves from the outside. Overeating is just one example of that. Women are feeling overwhelmed and exhausted and are complaining about a lack of energy, which is partially because we've worn ourselves out running after things that may not be all that satisfying. Our culture supports the myth that we have to have certain things to be happy. And we've been losing sight of the things that will truly fill us up.

**Wright**

What can women do to deal with the challenges they face and make their lives better?

**Shimoff**

The good news is that women have a yearning, a craving to grow and to be more fulfilled. So the first component, which is the desire to make life better, is already there.

I have always been a big proponent of taking the mind-body-spirit approach to growth in life. The most effective change happens when we address our lives on all three of those levels. I know it's not easy, but everybody knows that if you feel good in your body, it's a whole lot easier to feel happier and more fulfilled. So I'm a big believer in taking good care of your body, which, of course, includes eating well, getting enough exercise, and getting enough rest. You can do so many exotic spa treatments and healing methodologies, many of which are wonderful, but I've found the simplest, most common sense things are really the most important. For example, going to bed early. Some of the research I've read shows that every hour of sleep you get before midnight is worth two hours of sleep after midnight. So I'm big on going to bed by ten. Also, drinking lots of water is a key to clearing out toxins and feeling good throughout the day. I notice in my own life that when I drink lots of water in a day, I feel clearer and more energetic. These seem like such simple, almost ridiculously basic things to do, but these habits can have a profound influence on our overall well-being.

In terms of the mind, it's important to make sure that we are putting our attention on positive thoughts, on our life dreams, on our goals, on appreciation, and gratitude. This is why I'm so excited to see Dr. Emoto's research confirm the powerful and concrete effects of our thoughts. I am convinced that what we put our attention on in our lives is what grows. I'm always amazed to hear people putting so much of their attention on what is not working in their lives. That only creates more of what they don't want!

About 15 years ago, I had a very clear experience of how powerful my thinking was and how it was affecting my life. At the time I was in a major funk over the breakup of a relationship, and I went through the normal grieving period. However, after awhile, I just wasn't getting over it, and my life was not working. One day a good friend came to me (she later became the wife of that old boyfriend) and said, "We're all tired of hearing you complain about everything that's wrong with your life. You have so many blessings, and you are ignoring them. I'm going to give you something to do that will dramatically change your life and I want you to promise you'll do it every day for the next month. I don't want you to miss a day. Will you do it?" I told her I'd do anything at that point. She proceeded to give me a simple exercise I call "the gratitude exercise." Every night before I went to sleep I was to think of five things I was grateful for that day. At first, it was hard to come up with five, but by the end of the month, it was hard to limit it to five. But the best part of it was that my life had turned around, and I continued doing that exercise every night for the next three years. Now, when I find myself approaching "funkdom," I do the gratitude exercise and my outlook is turned around instantly. I recommend this to all of my audiences and I've gotten great feedback on the results.

This brings us to the final component—the spirit. This is so often overlooked. We need to take more time for ourselves to connect to our own heart and soul, our essence, which allows us to connect with a Higher Power, whatever we choose to call that. In all of the speaking and writing I've done, I have found that the people who are the most fulfilled in life are the people who feel most connected to a Higher Power and, as a result, feel they are living their life on purpose.

I have had many experiences of getting clear messages from inside about what to do. Sometimes I've listened and sometimes I haven't, so I've learned the hard way to pay attention to them! Whenever I have a question in my life, if I get quiet and listen to that inner voice it always steers me in the right direction. Traditionally, women are thought to be particularly gifted with powers of intuition, and I believe those powers are still there, as strong as ever. We just have to remember to turn inward and listen. We need to trust less in all the external information and directions we get, and trust more in ourselves.

**Wright**

You are considered an expert in the area of self-esteem. Why do you think self-esteem is such an important issue? And are people really able to raise their self-esteem?

**Shimoff**

Sadly, low self-esteem is an epidemic in our society. According to some of the research in this area, two out of every three people in our society suffer from low self-esteem. Again, a large part of the problem is that our society has trained us to be so externally focused. We are taught to base our self-esteem very often on our education, our accomplishments, our job status, our car, our looks. Particularly for women, that last one's an important one. And what we're missing is the internal sense of connectedness and completeness. A definition of self-esteem that I love is one by Jack Canfield: self-esteem is an internal feeling of being lovable, worthy, and capable, regardless of circumstances. People can raise their self-esteem. Absolutely. We've certainly seen people in circumstances that would logically deny them any self-esteem, and yet they've overcome that and they've learned what's important. And that is to listen to ourselves and believe in ourselves and be grateful for our own strengths. So many times people focus on their weaknesses, but it's so important to focus on our strengths. Doing so helps build our strengths even more and helps align us with our destiny or life purpose. I just heard a great quote yesterday: "Oh, God, help me believe the truth about myself, no matter how beautiful."

**Wright**

That's great! I love quotes. I don't see how people get through life without great positive things to read and positive things to say. One of my favorites is: "God loves you so much that if He had a refrigerator, your picture would be on it."

**Shimoff**

Oh! That's a great quote—I like that one.

**Wright**

You are now focusing on a new book and a new seminar you've developed called *The Power of an Open Heart: A Woman's Guide to Unlocking the Joy and Love in Life*. So what's that all about?

**Shimoff**

In the last four or five years I have been very interested in the power of the heart. I have experienced in my own life how, when my heart is open, it brings an experience of life unlike any other—it makes life "magical." I have been delving deeply into this subject and I've found that just like there are habits that cultivate success, there are specific habits that cultivate an open heart. I've identified nine habits of an open heart that I share in my book and seminars.

I'm most interested in what enhances "heart flow" and the transformation that happens when people's hearts are open and appreciative. This is what makes us feel that we're in the flow of life. Our strongest connection to our natural power is through our hearts. In our brain-focused society we've often abandoned our hearts, but the truth is that the best decisions we make are based on knowledge not from the mind, but from the heart. There's a deep intelligence we can access through our hearts.

So much of the research that's been done over the last 20 years has been on the mind and the brain, including brainwave synchrony. But the latest research is now showing that the heart is a very powerful guide in our lives. The Institute of HeartMath has done fantastic research that's shown that when you're feeling great, when you're "in the zone," your heart rhythms are more coherent. They have developed a computer program called the Freeze-Framer, where you use a finger sensor connected to a software program to monitor your "heart rate variability" and train yourself to consciously create more coherent heart rhythms. I think it's fascinating and very worthwhile.

The nine habits of an open heart I've identified help bring our heart rhythms into more coherence. Among these nine habits of an open heart are the grateful heart, the forgiving heart, and the wise heart. There are a lot of women who will say, "Oh, I live with an open heart. I fall in love with somebody every other day. And then they turn out to be a jerk." Well, I don't consider that necessarily living with an open heart. That may be living with a "needy heart." A person with a wise or discerning heart would select circumstances and people in their life that are going to serve their highest good.

**Wright**

Right.

**Shimoff**

I'm very excited about this new work on living with an open heart. When I ask people what they most want, many people say to me, "You know, I really want to know how to open my heart." So that's what this newest work is about. The stories in the *Chicken Soup for the Soul* books have helped open people's hearts—now I want to show people ways they can keep their hearts open on a consistent basis throughout the day.

**Wright**

Are there any other new projects that you are working on?

**Shimoff**

I have another new project I love that involves working with a dear friend, Catherine Oxenberg. Catherine is "a real live princess" (her grandfather was the Regent King of Yugoslavia), an actress whose credits include *Dynasty* and *I Married a Princess*, and a woman who is committed to the cause of helping women awaken to their own power. We are collaborating on a TV project and book featuring the courageous and extraordinary work of women leaders and visionaries from around the world who are actively changing the consciousness of the role of women and helping transform women's lives.

**Wright**

Based on all the speaking that you've done to audiences around the world and all the stories that you have read while co-authoring the *Chicken Soup for the Soul* books, what do you think truly makes a person remarkable?

**Shimoff**

That's another great question. I think being remarkable goes far beyond being successful. Remarkable is a term I use to honor someone who serves others, someone who's making a difference in the world, even in some small way. I was fortunate to be at a book signing yesterday with Maya Angelou, whom I consider to be a very remarkable person. She's a woman who's dealt with many challenges, yet lived a life of depth, wisdom, love and service. She has inspired so many millions of people, not just through her words, but through who she is—a woman of great strength and power that is balanced with humility. Those are two important qualities—strength and humility—and often difficult qualities to find together in the same person. Another example of a remarkable public person is Christopher Reeves. So many of us recognize that he was a hero and he lived his life, particularly after his accident, with such courage and love. He showed what "superman" really is. Again, there is power and strength balanced with great humility. There are many examples of people who aren't famous but who are remarkable just because they are living authentic lives. Lives that are guided by a higher purpose, by something bigger than themselves, and who are living with open hearts. That's what I call remarkable.

**Wright**

What is your passion? Or what is your mission in life? At the end of your life, what do you most hope that you will have accomplished?

**Shimoff**

My mission in life is to inspire and empower millions of women to live their highest and best lives. And that is my purpose for my own life as well! One of my favorite quotes of all time is the Chinese proverb that begins the very first *Chicken Soup for the Soul* book:

> If there is light in the soul, there will be beauty in the person.
> If there is beauty in the person, there will be harmony in the house.
> If there is harmony in the house, there will be order in the nation.
> And if there is order in the nation, there will be peace in the world.

My deepest purpose and hope is to inspire and empower people to find that light in their own souls, the joy, the love, the deepest truth in their hearts, and through that to help us bring more peace onto this planet of ours.

**Wright**

As I've been asking these questions, you've been answering them from the women's perspective. I've been touched by these feelings and thoughts, and as you were talking I've been thinking, "What a shame she doesn't speak to men as well."

**Shimoff**

I'm more than happy to speak to men and in fact, I do very often speak to mixed audiences. I love men! I just have a particular connection with women, being a woman, and a desire to truly help and inspire other women. But certainly I'm more than happy to have men hear this message too. It is a universal message, and I'm glad you appreciated it.

**Wright**

Thank you for the time you've taken to listen to all of these questions and answer them so clearly and openly. I learned a lot here today, and I appreciate the wonderful work you are doing in the world.

**Shimoff**

Thank you, David. And thank you for all that you do to help get positive, inspiring messages out to people. I commend you for your work.

**Wright**

Today we have been talking to Marci Shimoff. She is the president and co-founder of The Esteem Group. She's a professional speaker with, as we've found out, a dynamic personality, a lively sense of humor, great wisdom and a big heart. She earned her MBA from UCLA and an advanced certificate as a stress management consultant. She's also a #1 *New York Times* best-selling author of six of the *Chicken Soup for the Soul* books, including *Chicken Soup for the Woman's Soul* and *Chicken Soup for the Mother's Soul*. Marci, thank you so much for being with us today on *Remarkable Women*.

**Shimoff**

Thank you, David.

## About The Author

Marci Shimoff, one of the nation's leading motivational experts, speaks to thousands of people each year about the infinite possibilities life holds. Specializing in the unique struggles and opportunities that women face, Marci addresses issues of self-esteem and empowerment, sharing powerful techniques to overcome challenges and establish deep and authentic happiness and well-being. Marci is president of The Esteem Group and has been a top-rated Fortune 500 trainer and consultant for the last 20 years. She has worked frequently with Jack Canfield since 1989 and co-authored the #1 New York Times best-selling books, *Chicken Soup for the Woman's Soul 1 & 2* and *Chicken Soup for the Mother's Soul 1 & 2*, as well as *Chicken Soup for the Single's Soul* and *Chicken Soup for Every Mom's Soul*. Her books have sold over 13 million copies and have been at the top of every bestseller list in America. A lively and powerful speaker, Marci opens hearts, uplifts spirits, and transforms lives.

**Marci Shimoff**

The Esteem Group

57 Bayview Dr.

San Rafael, California 94901

Phone: 415.789.1300

Fax: 415. 789.1309

E-mail: marcishimoff@earthlink.net

www.marcishimoff.com

# *Chapter Seventeen*

## JENNIFER O'NEILL

### THE INTERVIEW

**David E. Wright (Wright)**

Today we're talking to Jennifer O'Neill. She is an internationally acclaimed actress, film and television star, successful spokeswomen, composer, author, artist, proud mother of three, and grandmother of four. Jennifer O'Neill has already accomplished enough for a life time. She began her international modeling career at the age of fifteen, after her family moved to New York from her native home of Rio de Janeiro, Brazil. Her career in the entertainment industry boasts, twenty eight feature films, including the classic *Summer of 42*, numerous television movies and three television series. In addition, Jennifer held a thirty-year position as spokeswomen for *Cover Girl Cosmetics*. Following the success of her biography, *Surviving Myself*, Jennifer adds her latest book, *From Fallen to Forgiven*, to her list of accomplishments. In addition, this month, January 2005, her latest book, *You're Not Alone*, has just come out. She has also written a novel that has been published by *Campus Crusade* titles, *Lifesavers*. She has also served on the board of *Media Fellowship International*. Jennifer, welcome to *Remarkable Women*.

**Jennifer O'Neill (O'Neill)**

Thank you so much, David, it's my pleasure to be here.

**Wright**

All of us at Insight Publishing, are excited about this project, Jennifer. To a person, all of us have been shaped by one or more remarkable women. Women such as our mother, a certain teacher, or a mentor of some sort. Although our authors won't admit it , we believe that they are remarkable women in their own right. I'm eager to explore this subject with you, but before we get down to the nitty gritty, could you tell our readers what you've been up to lately. What kinds of projects are occupying your time?

**O'Neill**

David, sometimes when you ask for God's will in your life, you better put your seat belt on. Often you find yourself doing things you never would have imagined. I have been so blessed in the last seven years or so, since I wrote my first book, to be traveling on a speaking circuit. I have been speaking to large groups with women of faith, thirty thousand at a clip. I am the National Spokesperson for *Silent No More*, an awareness campaign, which deals with the issue of abortion and healing of abortion through God's grace. The campaign is fantastic and is making such a difference in the lives of women and families, healing through the grace of God. I have also been blessed to have a platform to discuss various negative issues in my life that God has turned into positives. As it says in the Word, *"He will turn all things for good to those who love Him."* There are certain things and events that I have experienced in my life that have afforded me a platform to share some really wonderful news about Gods grace and restoration. It takes me to schools, colleges, The Senate and Congress, as well as to churches everywhere. I'm able to address the tough issues of teen suicide, abortion and sexual abuse. My daughter was sexually abused and she asked me to address that issue. I also address domestic violence, depression, and other tough issues that many people experience. Very few of us side-step hard issues in life.

The good news is that God wants us healed, whole and existing in an enlighten state and released though forgiveness and grace. It's there for all of us to have, if we ask for it. It's all in Gods word. Traveling around the country speaking to women about women's issues, I see so many women who come up after I speak, usually in a flood of tears confessing an abortion they had, or that they've been sexually abused, or they're having difficulties with depression. I kind of peel like an onion and let them know that they're not alone about certain issues. I love women. These are bright, vibrant, amazing women, that in some areas of their lives are stuck in a shameful, guilty, fearful part of their past. None of those things are of the Lord and He is well capable and willing to heal us, if we bring those issues to Him.

I have decided to do a syndicated TV series for women so that we can reach more women with this good news of what God offers us. It is titled, *Living Forever - More. Living Forever - More* is going to be a half-hour, syndicated series in a one hour Network special, and it looks as if will not only be on syndicated TV channels, but also on a new advanced channel on the web. We hope to be reaching millions of women through this project. We're going to film a women's retreat with fantastic speakers. All the women in the first retreat are leaders in their own right. Each of these women come from different denominations, are different ages, coming together to edify each other and lift each other up, share the information, listen to our speakers, have a concert, and laugh and cry. We have fun segments as well. It's not all about hard healing. It's about sharing, getting back to hospitality, and cooking. It's just going to be an absolute celebration of women. It is an encouragement to women to deal with some of those tough issues so they can be all that they can be in Christ. Since you can't give what you don't have, we want to give information they need, because God wants to help women be released from their hard issues.

**Wright**

That sounds great. Jennifer, I know movie stars grow up like the rest of us "normal" people, and you are the person you are today because of the women who loved you as a young person. Will you tell us about the remarkable women in your life and perhaps how they influenced you in your early years?

**O'Neill**

That is such a wonderful question. That's why I like this book so much. I'd love to start with my mom. I had my times, as many women do, some of the areas we want to smooth out between mom and daughter. They seem to go through various cycles. I always ask the women on my TV show this question," Is it a compliment when somebody says you're just like your mom, or is it an insult?" I have gleaned so much wonderful information and style from my mom. She is a lady to the nth degree. She was born in London. She's an extremely loyal, reliable, beautiful, elegant individual. If I have any twirl with a pen or the written word it's probably because she insisted that I develop my skills in communication. That was a great gift. I love her dearly. She and dad live with me to this day.

Then there was my Aunt Eleanor, who I must say, in many ways I was, during certain stages of my life, closer to her than to my mom because she was more playful. I kind of missed that with my mom. Ellie would play cards with me or go out and help me with my little rock garden. She seemed to embrace my love of animals, which was foreign to my parents because they didn't know it growing up. She encouraged me. She had a piano and she encouraged me to play the piano and write and be expressive. I remember as a young girl, when my parents would have a party, I would go twirling into the middle of the party dancing and leaping about. She would always applaud and encourage my behavior. I don't know how it was received by anyone else, but just pleasing my aunt was fine. She encouraged me to express myself and upon her death, she left me her piano, which I've had with me for so many years. She also was a very Godly woman. Although I didn't have any formal upbringing in the church, Ellie personified Christ that lived in her. If she had any influence, at the top of the list of the influences, I would say that she inspired me to be like her in that sense. What was it in her that was different? What was it that gave her patience that no one else seemed to have, a compassion that no one else seemed to have? She had a heart just as big as the outdoors. When I came, very late in my life, to my belief and faith in Jesus Christ, I recognized that's what she gave me. She was just a faithful, Godly, wonderful women who planted, in me, a seed of her presence and her personality and her heart that I desired and aspired to.

I remember another lady, Mrs. Leone. I still remember her name. I think she was my fifth grade teacher. Some of the events in my life were born of the fact that I felt kind of invisible and unlovable, for various reasons. Early on, I thought I needed to earn love. I didn't realize it was a free gift and unconditional. I didn't know because I didn't have my faith. I thought that if I got straight A's in school that my parents would love me and I would get their attention. It's a very basic and interesting view. If we see bruises on a child's face or they're not fed, we know they're in a SOS problem and they need help. Many times the bruises that we carry through life, through a negative impression, are on our hearts. You can't see them, but you see the result of them, the hurt. Well all that said, I was just determined to get straight A's in school, and in those days there were about fourteen marks. I had straight A's for all three-years terms, except one B in spelling. In fact, I can't spell to this day. But this lady, this wonderful teacher, gave me an A in spelling. She wrote a note to my parents and said, "It's not that I'm saying that Jennifer's spelling is up to snuff and I would give an A for her actual talent in that area, but I've never seen any person want straight A's more than Jennifer does. So I'm going to give her an A for effort." And that was wonderful because she instilled in me the idea to forge ahead. If you're not naturally gifted in a certain area but you want to conquer that area, you want to become accepted for whatever reason, keep trying, keep going. If nothing else, you will be rewarded or recognized for your effort. Never give up. That's what she taught me.

**Wright**

She would be proud today to know that you've become a well-read person and also an author.

**O'Neill**

Thank God for spell check.

**Wright**

Were there any famous women authors or public figures that influenced you as a young person or later in your life?

**O'Neill**

Yes, Margaret Meade. I was attending private school in New York, and believe it or not, she came for an assembly meeting. She was such a great anthropologist. That ignited an interest in me about the world.

I never meet Helen Keller, but she was certainly a positive influence. There are so many women if you start going through history. It's rather endless.

**Wright**

I probably should have asked this earlier in the interview, but I've saved the question until now for a specific reason. What do you think makes a women remarkable?

**O'Neill**

Women are remarkable in such a wide variety of areas because they have such an array of talents. I would say it would be their ability to accept others in an inspirational and nurturing fashion. Be it an artist, or a mother, women have a communication and caring level in them that is unique only to women. It is different than men. I think those that excel remain in touch with those parts of their femininity and are extremely effective. Those are extraordinary women to me. Remarkable women are women that have not lost the idea that they're women. They do not have to conqueror something. Here's an analogy. My ex-husband used to be a rodeo cowboy. My desire when I breed a horse and train a horse is to become a partner with that horse. It's an extraordinary match when it's right, when you're flying through the air, hopefully, with the greatest of ease. That big animal is desiring to please you, is guided by just the lightest touch of your finger or your leg. It's just wonderfully elegant. My ex-husband would want to conquer the horse. He would want to break the horse. There's a difference. So he used to laugh at me saying, "You take ten times longer to break that horse than I do." But that was my approach. What I admire about women is there is that soft touch, that incredible effectiveness, never losing their gentle touch.

**Wright**

Based on your description, which I agree with whole heartedly, many people would consider Jennifer O'Neill a remarkable women. And I know you're not looking for adulation.

**O'Neill**

I'm just trying to learn.

**Wright**

I know you to be a very humble person, but I would like to pursue some of the circumstances in your life that have caused you to stretch and to grow, to endure and to overcome. I know our readers would be encouraged; if you don't mind would you related a story or two. How have you overcome some of the challenges in your life?

**O'Neill**

Well, for a very long time I wasn't overcoming very well. I almost died three times, I was shot, and I had nine miscarriages along the way of having my three children. I was bumping into life very hard. I also broke my neck and back on the horses. But that's why I wrote my first book, *Surviving Myself*, because quite often we get in our own way. Those stumbling blocks in life, those tough ones in my case, such as being able to address my abortion as so many who had abortions, carried through my life and that negative feeling grew. On the other side was the fame and fortune, traveling the world, working in Paris at fifteen by myself, and all that a life in the public and fast lane could bring. I really had this hole in my heart. When I said earlier that God turns all things for good, he has used all those hard times for me to say experience overrides theory.

When I started to really come into my own, my life wasn't a run away train. I always had enormous drive. I like that about myself, but I realized now as I look back that it had a bit of phonetic tilt to it. I was tenacious on one hand and very shy on the other. What put it all together for me was my faith. It had to start with some very deep healing of those areas, excepting that someone, namely God, could actually love me and care about me. That He knew every hair on my head. He knew me before the creation of time and He knit me together in my mother's womb. He had a plan for me that was bigger than anything I could ever imagine. So talk about inspiration, that's a pretty exciting release. Not only did I receive eternal life, but it took me a good ten years to begin to accept what has always been a free gift from Christ—His love and His protection. The Holy Spirit isn't just a hospital, He's an army to engage. I had to accept that I could achieve anything that He set me on a path to do.

When I finally gave up "me" and realized that if I had any talents they were gifts from God, I wanted to use them for His glory. It was as if a flood gate had opened. We're all a work in progress, but I can begin to see the light at the end of the tunnel and it's not a train. I can begin to see how He's using my twenty-eight movies so I'd know how to put together this TV series to edify women and share the good news. Anything that I do I just give all the glory and honor to God because I wouldn't be here if I hadn't found Him. I had to stop looking down at all the stumbling blocks that I put in front of me or others had. At the end of the day we're all responsible for everything we think, say and do. When I finally got over myself—and that's a daily laying down of bad tendencies and just asking God to come and fill you up with the Holy Spirit and be available to Him—my life has just transformed. I am excited every day. Words come out of my mouth that are from the Word, "*This is the day that the Lord has made and I will be glad in it."* A lot of the tortures that I went through were self-inflicted. It's changing your mind about how you perceive reality.

I have had a good marriage now for eight years. My husband is a godly man. He's not perfect, I'm not perfect, but he has not been placed on the earth to make me happy. My happiness, my fulfillment, my satisfaction and my peace comes from my relationship with Jesus. I take advantage, if you will, for all his incredible offers to me, like dying on the cross for my sins. I accepted that, finally, that it's for all my sins. It's for everyone's sins. When I finally accepted that I wasn't bound to my past through regrets, shame, pain, all those secret places that we're so good at hiding and shoving under the carpet, I realized the truth really does make you free. When I accepted His grace, I started to heal. Now, I'm a better mom, I'm a better wife. I go into that relationship thinking what can I do for my husband and then I give him to God. I was a control freak because I was afraid of rejection and hurt, most of which I had invited into my life myself, through lack of discernment and not having a solid foundation. All of that is changing and it's exciting for me.

**Wright**

I can understand why it would take you ten years. When you consider grace, forgiveness, eternal life, it's almost so overwhelming that is seems too good to be true.

**O'Neill**

Exactly, but it isn't too good to be true. God is true. I'm fifty-six years old and came to my faith at thirty-eight, and it's just been in the last year or so that I've really been allowing myself to accept His grace.

**Wright**

Today's modern women must deal with countless challenges from the work place and at home. In your opinion, what are two or three of the most critical issues facing women today and what advice would you offer women regarding these issues?

**O'Neill**

In my show I call it the balancing act. Today, women's plates are so full. You just said it in the question. In the work place or at home, we're torn. There's not a better job or more important job than raising children and being a good wife and mom. Yet, we want to expand our territories and be all we can be. It's that balancing act that quite often seems to be a runaway train. And in its wake, what's left are broken relationships.

I also say in my show, "You turn around in bed and you look at your husband and say, 'Who are you and how did you get here?'" I think our relationships suffer because of the complexities of life. Also, we lose the knack with our marital relationships. I can only speak of this because I'm the worst offender. I'm finally trying to figure it out. As I said before, change me and let God do a work in my husband. Communication is the key and the fact that there're really no surprises. Married women reach a point in their marriage when they'll say I don't recognize you or how did I ever get involved with you? The fact of the matter is that most of the problems we have after the perfect dating stage was evident in the beginning. But, we just choose not to look at it or whitewash it thinking it will be fine. Then we deal with it in our relationship later. I think those are difficult areas to balance.

One thing that might be off the question but I'd like to bring up is, I think women are confused. I think men and women have become confused about their roles over the last generation. It does not bode well for solid family living. I see the desire of families to get back to that balance. We were designed a certain way. Again, I can speak of this because I was always an independent women who made a very good living and had a lot of exposure in life. Celebrity, if you will, is not about getting a table at a restaurant, but for me, it allows me to have a platform for Gods word. During those years of imbalance, I didn't choose men who were terribly dynamic. Maybe it was a protective thing on my part. So I was kind of in the driver's seat, financially and power wise. I don't say that with any kind of intent other than that's what happened. I was a very emotionally needy individual. That's not an attractive picture.

When I started to come into my faith and really understand the Word of God and the authority of His ultimate word on how He designed us to be as man and wife, I realized that's how it has to work. We need to acquiesce to our husband as a man. That's difficult for women sometimes because their men, quite often, are not acting like God describes a man (husband) should be in the Bible. There's nothing wrong to listening to a man, who according to the Bible, would lay his life down for his wife and treat her like Jesus treats the church. Men love to be there, but when we want to open our own door and make our own decisions, that strips them of that and at the same time it strips us of that wonderful feeling of being able to fall into our husbands arms and feel safe and protected and still have an identity unto ourselves. He would want us to be the best we could be. I think that's gotten very confusing. Women have confused the issues. The nth degree is the subject that I talk about all the time, abortion, where somehow society has managed to convince women that they have lost some inalienable right if they don't have the right to kill their own child. Something is terribly wrong with what one would call independence. By the way, the early feminists were all pro-life, which is so interesting to me. They were all pro-life. They just wanted the right to vote and they wanted the right to own their own property. They did not want a right to abort their children. So there's been a big mix up, I think, in the feminist movement. The roles are confused and I think it's caused a lot of problems.

**Wright**

I think it confuses men. I know I'm confused by the confusion. It doesn't take a rocket scientist to figure out that we're different. I don't understand the unisex thought that all of us should be the same.

**O'Neill**

It's so wrong and its lead the family and society down a very slippery slope. It doesn't work. I love to tell this to kids when I go to schools and talk about abstinence. Again, I'm the worst offender, but I also tell people that God is so gracious. I remind people, not tell them. I remind them that God is so gracious with us that when that negative tape, that little voice says, "You're not worthy. You're not lovable. Who are you to stand up and talk to anybody?"—I get that every morning when I get up—then I just rebuke it because God has given us example after example of people who he's used in a powerful way, who were just as imperfect as we are. Moses was a murderer and stuttered, and didn't want the job. Paul, who wrote in our Bible, called himself the worst offender, he was killing Christians and so forth. Peter denied Christ. Whenever I feel a moment that I'm infallible I just remember Peter. We need Gods grace every step of the way. I think that we can all be used in a way that we cannot even imagine if we would allow Him to work in us.

Back to your question, I was talking about the kids. I get to go to schools and talk about abstinence. I give them this illustration, David, I tell them to just think for a moment that we are Gods design and when God refers to being abstinent until marriage, do you have any idea why and what the thinking is behind that? It is because He loves us. If you believe that God created us, out of all of His creations, animals and plants and people, only people are designed, anatomically, to face each other when they make love. What would that be about? It is about intimacy and trust and looking into each others eyes. What is trust but commitment. You can't trust somebody not to leave if they are not committed. What is commitment but marriage? God designed us to be with one another in a trusting, committed fashion. Read the Song of Solomon, He designed sex, but he designed it to be enjoyed under certain circumstances that won't hurt us. Today, I see healing happening and relationships coming together again. By getting in the right relationship with God, the trickle down effect is wonderful as we're starting to heal.

**Wright**

Jennifer, you know, you're one of my favorite people. I just love to talk to you. I always want to go on and on forever. I always learn so much when I talk to you. When you were describing your mother I was thinking, she's describing herself. Because you are certainly a class act.

**O'Neill**

Then just a little bit of her wonder rubbed off on me, and I thank her.

**Wright**

Today we have been talking to Jennifer O'Neill. It's been my sincere pleasure to speak with her. She's a television and film star, but to those who know her well, she is much, much more. Jennifer, thank you so much for sharing your heart and soul with our readers today.

**O'Neill**

It's such a pleasure for me to be a part of this project. I will pray Gods blessings on it because women need to read about other wonderful women. We're all wonderful and we're all wonderfully made. It's just a super project!

## About The Author

Jennifer O'Neill is by far one of the world's most Beautiful Hollywood Film Goddesses of all time. She started her international modeling career at the age of 14. She then became a film star in some of Hollywood's most bankable films like *Rio Lobo* (with John Wayne) and the award winning classic film *The Summer of '42'* (this movie made Jennifer a household name). She is best known as the #1 Cover-Girl spokesmodel in the world. Her face & glamour made *Cover-Girl* make-up the best selling make-up for 30 years. Jennifer is also an animal activist, she races, trains, & breeds show horses, and is an advocate for charitable causes like the American Cancer Society & other women's issues. Jennifer's career has been a dream come true, but her life was a nightmare of broken marriages, near death experiences, emptiness, abuse, and even her daughter being sexually abused by one of O'Neill's husbands. She turned her life around by becoming a born-again Christian & now ministers to hurting people worldwide through seminars and her two books that she wrote herself called, *Surviving Myself* and *From Fallen to Forgiven.* The books have won critical acclaim & her seminars are packed-in by the millions (all of them long to find hope to life's toughest problems). Jennifer is an amazing lady, a mother of 3 children, a grandmother, she's a survivor, & has become a role model to all who hear her story.

**Jennifer O'Neill**

Email: jennifer@jenniferoneill.com

# Chapter Eighteen

## Jenny Nolen

### THE INTERVIEW

**David E. Wright (Wright)**

Today we are talking to Jenny Nolen. She is no stranger to the speaking arena. As a nationally known humorist and keynote presenter for over 20 years, Jenny offers a wide range of options for any conference planner including entertainment, workshops, and seminars and keynotes. Tagged as Alabama funniest lady, Jenny's presentations are full of wit, wisdom, whimsy, and wonder. She has prided herself in being someone her audience can relate to as she shares poignant stories of surviving a dysfunctional home and growing up enough to laugh about it. If it is her chemically dependent hair or her ever changing body, Jenny encourages men and women alike to celebrate the wonder of who they are. Her motto of "If you cannot lose it or hide it, decorate it" best exemplifies her commitment to live each day with joy, forgiveness, and acceptance. Jenny, welcome to *Remarkable Women*!

**Jenny Nolen (Nolen)**

Thank you for having me.

**Wright**

So you've been quoted as saying look up dysfunctional in the dictionary and you'll find a picture of our family. Can you tell me a little bit more about that?

**Nolen**

Let me first began by saying that not unlike other children of dysfunctional families, I love my family dearly, all of them. But it was Southern drama at its best. I had an absent father, a mother who suffered from a mental illness, a controlling grandmother, and a healthy dose of Baptist fundamentalism. When you mix all of those ingredients, you have a pretty dysfunctional mix for sure! I was raised in Wesson, Mississippi, in a scene right out of a William Faulkner novel; Gigantic pecan trees, the remnants of what was my Grandfather's dairy farm, and all of the wonder of the outdoors. Wesson is a town so small that: the welcome and leaving sign were on the same post, you had to go toward town to go hunting, we only had 2 pages in the yellow pages and our zip code was E-I-E-I-O! Of course in a town like this, the rumor mill ran rampant, so you learned to do whatever you needed to do to survive! Some days were wonderful, some chaotic. Not knowing which would come next was really the hardest part. So you lived on the edge with a heightened level of awareness, and anxiety. Thus is the dance of dysfunction.

**Wright**

I remember getting into a "my town was so small" discussion with a man who coached women's basketball at North Carolina State. He finally won when he said, "Well, the sign in front of my town was resume speed." So I lost.

**Nolen**

Yeah! Well, there were only 32 people in my graduating class, so that tells you how small it was. Most of them were kin to each other!

**Wright**

Music has always been important to you, so where did this love come from?

**Nolen**

I honestly cannot remember a day when I have not had music in my life in some way or another. It has proven over the years to be a healing balm for me. My big sister and I had one of those hi-fi record players that played 45's. Of course you had to put that little yellow disc on it. Remember those?

**Wright**

Oh yeah!

**Nolen**

Here is a mental picture for you..... When the Beatles came out with all of their hits, we had the mop and broom, one was a makeshift microphone the other was a guitar! Baby we would swing our heads back and forth and sing, "She loves you yeah, yeah yeah!" Manlalive, Janie could play that broom like nobody's business! I'm sure my grandmother thought we would end up in the juvenile delinquent home! Ha! Now my mother had some more sophisticated music. The kind that played on 78 records, you know the ones that are thicker than a slice of bologna and very scratchy? I did love to listen to her classical music and especially one record in particular. FAR AWAY PLACES. I loved that one. It made me day dream about all that was yet to be seen in my life!

**Wright**

Right.

**Nolen**

I loved having music around me. My Mother sang beautifully, my grandmother played hymns (Baptist of course, ha), and I too started singing at a very early age. When I was in the fifth grade my Sunday School teacher came and took me to see the movie *The Sound of Music.* I remember being riveted to my seat and totally taken with Julie Andrews. She was my role model, and I adored her! I know for a fact I saw that movie about 10 times. My mom bought the record for us not long after that and we listened to it every day. I began taking voice lessons and learning the fundamentals of music. Who knew you had a diaphragm and could breathe with it? I remember my first cousin telling me once that I had a gizzard, so I wasn't sure about believing the diaphragm existed. I did finally get it together and learned to sing with power and passion. I continued studying voice through high school and college and did aspire at some point to sing Opera professionally. I have had the opportunity to sing with the Mississippi and the Kentucky Opera Choruses, but have since decided I am far more

Opry than Opra! I still use music in my training and presentations. I know of no better way to bring people together than this universal language. You know, there's nothing that will bring cohesiveness to a group of stuffy business folk quicker than singing the theme from sitcoms of the 60s and 70s! Whoooo Hoooo!

**Wright**

I can imagine. So who did you admire most while you were growing up?

**Nolen**

Well, there were many people that stood in the gap for my sister and me, but I think, probably, I loved my grandmother the most. She was always there to care for us, particularly in periods when my mother was so ill. My grandmother, Sarah Ella Wilson Bridges was a dyed in the wool, hard core, Southern Baptist fundamentalist. She was a servant to many, yet tough as a pine knot, and unyielding on many things. I've actually seen her ask people to get out of her seat if they were sitting in her seat at church. I also remember driving up to a funeral home, walking up to the casket, and my grandmother saying, "Well, I don't reckon I know them." So we had to turn around and leave. She was a mess. She loved Dr. Billy Graham and Oral Roberts, and faithfully sent them a portion of her pension every month! Now if my sister and I misbehaved, which we hardly ever did because we were perfect children, of course, my grandmother tried very hard to take care of us by quoting scriptures. Now here's the deal. When you're eight years old, you don't realize there's not a book in the Bible called Eucalyptus. Her other book was First and Second Hesitations, and her favorite book was First and Second Magnesia. That lady loved magnesia. If you ever got scratched on your knee from chigger bites, she would say, "Hon, you just need a good old dose of Phillips." To this day I cannot walk by a bottle in Wal-Mart without breaking out in a cold sweat.

**Wright**

Right. Oh my! You believe that on some days you have to laugh to keep from crying. How did you master this?

**Nolen**

Oh my, this has been my most beneficial lesson in life! It has taken me awhile to learn it, but by George, I think I have it now! I firmly believe that you have a choice every day in your life to get up in the morning and say, "Good morning, Lord" or "Good Lord, its morning!" I am almost 50 years old, and only now owning my personal truth that MY HAPPINESS IS MY CHOICE AND BASED ON MY OWN ATTITUDE! Now let me be real clear! I don't always feel happy, but as long as I can get up and choose to be happy, choose to be positive and choose to be optimistic, I really believe the rest will fall in place. I don't know a person on the planet that hasn't had something to deal with. You know, my deal is that you can either focus on the negative part or you can focus on letting it go and getting over it. Do you know what I mean?

**Wright**

I certainly do! I do the same thing with enemas.

**Nolen**

With an enema?

**Wright**

My mother believed that was the way to solve all problems.

**Nolen**

Yeah, I've often told people I'd rather have an enema than to do something I don't want to do...but is totally not true! I hate those too. How did we gentile Southern folk start talking about enemas......good gracious!

**Wright**

Let me ask you a question. After speaking for so many years, do you think everyone has a sense of humor?

**Nolen**

AB—SO—LUTE—LY! I really do. I certainly do. But here's the way I feel about that. I believe that God gave all of us a sense of humor as standard equipment. Our challenge is whether or not we've learn how to utilize it. No matter how old we become, there's still a little kid in us that wants to have fun. Even when it seems that someone is as funny as watching grass growing, they still have a sense of humor. They're just living by very rigid standards or beliefs or behaviors. I have had several years working with Hospice in our local community, and I'll tell you, these patients have taught me a lot over the years. They've taught me that we are all terminal. And I really believe that if you get to the end of your life and you have not had fun along the way, you've missed the whole point!

My sister Jane recently sent me the following e-mail that best exemplifies my idea on living and having joy and fun......"Life should NOT be a journey to the grave with the intention of arriving safely in an attractive and well preserved body, but rather to skid in sideways, champagne in one hand - strawberries in the other, body thoroughly used up, totally worn out and screaming, "WOO HOO—what a ride!"

**Wright**

So what lessons did you learn from your past, and how do you feel that they are relevant in your life today?

**Nolen**

I can't think of a more weighted question than that one. Wow! I think I learn something new every single day. What I have discovered is that every person I meet knows something that I don't know. Learning really is for me a cradle to grave experience. But most importantly, I've learned that I am precisely where I am in life based on the decisions I have made along the way! I am responsible for my own happiness. While I did have a very bumpy beginning, as did a lot of other people, today I know I am responsible for all of my decisions.... good, bad or indifferent.

**Wright**

Did your mother ever recover from her illness?

**Nolen**

My mother...that's a very interesting question. I think that my mother did the very best with the tools that she had to work with at the time. Mental illness and mental health treatment has come a long way since the days when I was a young child. I think toward the end of her life, she did have a lot of resolution and I was very thankful for that.

**Wright**

So how do you keep negativity at bay?

**Nolen**

I'm going to tell you something. I have a low tolerance for negativity. Absolutely, whining! You know what's worse than a whining child?

**Wright**

No?

**Nolen**

A whining adult! Have you ever heard a whining adult? Oh no! Whining, ...murmuring, gossiping, pessimism—all of those self defeating behaviors. Statistics tell us that 78% of conversation every day deals with negativity. So we as human beings love to focus on what's wrong instead of what's right. The way I deal with negativity is that I try very hard, on a daily basis, to find somebody doing something right and to tell them about it. I love to do this. This week I told a lady at the checkout counter at Wal-Mart that she was doing a great job and it absolutely surprised her to death. The man at the window she served, he took out my groceries for me. I just told him thank you and how much I appreciated it, and he just stood there stunned that I would actually take the time to tell him how much I appreciated him. The very best way to deal with a negative attitude is to focus on what's right instead of what's wrong. As long as you are above ground, if you can get up and you're above ground, by George, that's a good day.

**Wright**

A good day, you're right. So what is your favorite thing to speak about?

**Nolen**

Well, I think my favorite subject is humor, of course. I love to tell funny stories about growing up. What I have found is that everybody has a story. When I tell mine, it just reminds others of what their own story is. So it's really not so much about my own personal story as taking them on a journey of remembering their own. So it's fun to be a humorous. I know when I was voted wittiest in the class if 197, my classmates never did have a clue that one day I would make a living telling stories about all of us. When I was in high school, I stayed in the principal's office days on end for talking in class. I know that's very hard for you to believe, but I did.

**Wright**

Right.

**Nolen**

When I became a professional, a member of NSA, I sent my former principal a note, and I told him, "Dear coach, people actually pay me to talk now." You gotta love it!

**Wright**

You have several signature stories. Could you share a few of them with us?

**Nolen**

Well, my favorite signature story is about my daughter, Sarah Beth, who is now 23 and starting her own path these days. I tell people Sarah is so much like me, it scares me some days. She is one of my two children that remind me every day why some animals eat their young. As a little girl, my mom gave her a Barbie doll. It was a very interesting little doll. It was a glow in the dark Barbie doll outfit. I had told Sarah Beth dressing Barbie was going to be a challenge because this little outfit, the top part was strapless and the bottom part was just a little skirt kind of thing. But it had a whole lot of accessories for it. The top part had a hook and eye on it instead of Velcro like they have now. I told Sarah Beth that I would be happy to help her put the outfit on the doll, but being true to her stubborn roots, she said she could do it by herself. She went into her bedroom and struggled and struggled and struggled to get that outfit on Barbie! And in a few minutes Barbie and Ken came through the living room in the Corvette. I looked down and saw that Ken had his hands on the steering wheel, his head was turned toward Barbie, and he was smiling. Reeeeeeeealy big! Here's the deal. Barbie had on a tiara on her head, a corsage on her arm, dangling earrings, high heel shoes, a boa, a purse, everything except guess what?

**Wright**

What?

**Nolen**

The top to her dress! I scooped up Sarah Beth in my arms and said, "Sarah Beth, Barbie does not have on a top to her dress. This isn't going to work." She put her hands on her hips, looked me square in the eyes, and said, "Mommma! Ken likes her like that!"

**Wright**

Right.

**Nolen**

So people have always known about the Barbie and Ken story. You can't write humor like that, you just have to let it happen, and be on the look out for it at all times. When People say they do not have a sense of humor, I have found that they just don't know how to recognize it when they see it! That afternoon with Sarah Beth was one of those defining moments for me.

**Wright**

Is Sarah Beth short for Sarah Elizabeth?

**Nolen**

It is.

**Wright**

That's my daughter's name.

**Nolen**

Elizabeth is a family name of ours. Sarah was my grandmother's name and Elizabeth was my sister's name. My other daughter's name is Jennifer Ashley. She is 16 and truly one of the sweetest Souls God ever placed on the earth. She goes by Ashley because I figured one "Jenny" was about all we could handle!

**Wright**

How about that! So what do you mean when you say, "live it and forgive it?"

**Nolen**

"Live it and forgive it." Boy. That is a fundamental truth right there. There's not a do-wah-diddly thing that you can do about what's happened in the past. The past keeps you in a memory and the future in a possibility. The best place to stay is "right now" and if you really think about it, there is never a time when it is not now! You know, so many of us love to nurse our wounds. I meet people every day that cannot tell me what they had on yesterday, but they can tell me what happened in 1969 because they visit that over and over and over. And they love to keep that wound fresh. Now remember, we have a choice. We can either embrace the event as a learning experience, or we can dwell on it and stay stuck in the past. Believe me; I speak from experience with this one. I have tried whining and complaining, and manipulating, but what has worked best for me is to simply ask for what I need and want instead of hoping others will read my mind! Remember your mind can only enhance what you focus on and if you focus on the negative, it will become a living and breathing thing that takes on a life of itself. Forgiveness, too, has become a key for me. Not only forgiving others, but certainly learning how to forgive myself. That has been a wonderful lesson in liberation for me! What I have found about forgiveness is that it is a gift you give yourself! It's not what you do for the other person. It's how you find peace for your own heart and Spirit. I know too, that it is a daily attitude, by that I mean it is not a one time event. I've heard people say, "Well, I have forgiven them." But you know, you have to do forgiveness every day, every day, every day. Every time that thought comes up you have to go back to that place of forgiveness again, if you understand what I'm talking about. Simply the best way to deal with negativity is to keep yourself in a place of complete gratitude for what you have, and keep an open, loving, and forgiving Spirit at all times!

**Wright**

When you talk to corporations, do they really get into the humor part of things? You know a lot of corporations that we book speakers for are looking at sales skills and this sort of thing. When you infuse humor into your presentations, what does it do for them?

**Nolen**

Well, a lot of corporations will bring me in for the afternoon because after people have had a big meal or if they've been in a conference for a couple of days and it's been kind of dreary. If they're going through mandated information, people have a tendency to loose their momentum and focus. I love this challenge because these folks are ready for some fun at this point. Laughter is such a wonderful energizer! It is the shortest distance between two people. If you can get people to laugh, it's going to reduce their stress and enhance their learning experience. Moreover they will remember the conference a lot more and retain the information they have learned! It really is a wonderful tool that brings everything together. A conference leader is going to get more for their money and their folks are going to leave feeling good about coming! That is a win-win for both of us!

**Wright**

So, when it's all said and done, what would you like for people to remember about you?

**Nolen**

It's kinda funny what turning 50 will do for you. I am not there yet, but thinking about it. I have often wondered about this...what people will remember about me when I am gone.....Hopefully that I was an Encourager, A Survivor, A Maiden of Mirth, A Wonderful Friend, A Devoted Mother, and a Catalyst for change!

When I was a young girl, I started following the music of Cynthia Clauson. I still believe to this day there is, nor ever will be, a voice comparable to hers. I have seen her in concert many times and have been moved and encouraged by her music through the years! There is a line in one of her songs that says, "O*h Lord, may the essence of my life be a song that others will want to sing.....to sing. That others will want to sing!"* That indeed is my prayer!

**Wright**

Well, I'm sure they will! I wish you the success of the century as you go around to America's corporations encouraging them to laugh a little more!

**Nolen**

Absolutely!

**Wright**

They're taking themselves too seriously, and they're going to jail because of it.

**Nolen**

Well, if you can get in touch with all of the characteristics that little children have—joy, wonder, spontaneity, creativity, enthusiasm—you're going to be able to have a place of work that's fun. A place where you can problem solve. A place where your team is growing and thriving and where people enjoy coming to work!

**Wright**

Well, you've helped me today except for the part about your grandmother. That will stick with me for a while. Thanks a lot for putting that impression in my mind!

**Nolen**

Magnesia, baby!

**Wright**

Today we have been talking to Jenny Nolen who is a speaker and humorist.

**Nolen**

I'm a humorist if you laugh. If you don't laugh, I'm a motivational speaker!

**Wright**

That's great! Actually, she's a nationally known humorist and keynote presenter, and has been doing this for over 20 years. I do love her motto, "If you cannot lose it or hide it, decorate it." When I think of my balding head, I'm going to think all day today to figure out how do I decorate that balding spot.

**Nolen**

That's very hip to have a bald head now.

**Wright**

Oh, I hope so.

**Nolen**

Put you a doo-rag up on it, if you want to decorate it.

**Wright**

Ah, there's a suggestion. Thank you so much, Jenny, for being with us today on *Remarkable Women.*

**Nolen**

You're welcome David! Thank you for having me, and remember...Keep laughing...especially at yourself.

## About The Author

Jenny Nolen, originally from Mississippi, now resides in Cullman, Alabama. She attended the University of Southern Mississippi and has a degree in social work and counseling psychology. Jenny is a member of the National Speaker's Association and past president of the Alabama Speaker's Association. She is the mother of two beautiful and talented daughters, Sarah Beth and Ashley.

**Jenny Nolen**

Amazing Adventures

P.O. Box 29

Cullman, Alabama 35056

Phone: 256.739.6800

Email: amazingadventures@msn.com

# *Chapter Nineteen*

## LISA YANKOWITZ, JD, SPHR

### THE INTERVIEW

**David E. Wright (Wright)**

Today we are talking to Lisa Yankowitz, a rare and refreshing find in the world of professional speaking and training. Lisa, an attorney is an expert in the area of employment law and employment practices. She is also a dynamic, skillful and remarkably entertaining presenter who is able to combine her exceptional communication skills and her knowledge of the law to educate people about sensitive, often controversial, issues such as sexual harassment, race discrimination, diversity, and people. Subjects that most admittedly find to be dry, dull, boring, complex, and often incomprehensible become thought provoking, interesting, easy to understand, and surprisingly enjoyable when Lisa is delivering the presentation. Audiences, time after time, share the fact that they dreaded the idea of having to sit through a session on one of these subjects, but found that they actually had a positive and very enjoyable learning experience when Lisa delivered the information. Lisa's experiences growing up in Long Island, New York, her extensive travel across the United States, along with her out of the ordinary family dynamics and situations both in and out of business are often shared during her presentations. Her stories, inspired by her passion for making a difference, quickly hit home with her audiences. Lisa helps her audiences understand the challenges that exist in the workplace, how to effectively maneuver through these challenges or intricacies, and how to play well together in the workplace. Lisa is a certified Dale Carnegie instructor, founder and training director of the Employment Law Group Training and Consulting Services, senior faculty member at Keller Graduate School of Management of DeVry University, a senior professional in Human Resources and a member of the National Speakers Association. She is a local celebrity in the St. Louis market as a regular employment law contributor for *News Channel 5 Today in St. Louis*. Lisa, welcome to *Remarkable Women*!

**Lisa Yankowitz (Yankowitz)**

Thanks, David.

**Wright**

Lisa, I would like to ask you, what does it mean to play well together in the workplace?

**Yankowitz**

To answer the question, I would like you to consider not only that question, *what* does it mean to play well together in the workplace? But also...*can* we play well together in the workplace? *How* do we play well together in the workplace?

I have to admit that I have been pondering these questions in some fashion for many years now, possibly ever since my first job. These are not easy questions. It has taken me many years and many experiences, both in and out of the workplace, to find answers. As a matter of fact, it is only quite recently, because of an unfortunate and painful situation, that my theories on this subject were put to the test, and I do believe I finally have some answers.

The long answer to all three questions involves practical as well as legal components. The short answer involves a single, key concept: in order to play well together in the workplace, people must be ***sensitive*** to the needs and wants of others. How to ensure that this takes place is the dilemma.

**Wright**

Why do you say it's a dilemma?

**Yankowitz**

Most of us would probably agree that people are complex and not easy to figure out. Paradoxically, we like to think of ourselves as congenial and easy to get along with. There is a perception, even a belief, among most people that we should automatically just *know* how to get along and *know* how to work well together. People assert, "It's just common sense." I'm sorry to say, but I no longer believe that playing well together in the workplace is just common sense. Think about it... if it was just common sense, I would not be in business, and there would be no employment-related lawsuits.

The fact of the matter is people don't just inherently know how to work well together, how to play well together, how to get along, how to communicate effectively with one another, how to handle stress and conflict, how to relate to others from different ethnic backgrounds, different cultures, different generations, different sexes. They just don't get it! Unfortunately, there is nothing automatic about sensitivity.

From the time we are able to comprehend, we are coached, educated and trained in the more basic aspects of life. We study reading, writing and arithmetic. We learn about science and music. We learn how to drive and how to cook. We practice the techniques involved in playing basketball and swimming. But think about this: how much formal education do we get in ***people***?

For the most part, we are forced to learn about people through observation, first from observing our parents, then our teachers, friends, politicians, athletes, actors, etc. These are our role models, for better or for worse. Our observations design the templates for scripts that we follow throughout our lives.

Let me tell you about my first experience discovering what people really think. (Please note that the following dialogue is written as I remember hearing it).

It was the summer before my senior year in high school, so I was 17 or 18 years old. There I was, born a New Yorker with, I have to admit, an attitude. I thought that beyond New York, everybody grew up on a farm, wore overalls and chewed hay. As the newly elected New York State President of the Future Business Leaders of America (FBLA), a student youth leadership organization, I was Cincinnati-bound to meet with 50 plus state officers from around the country. My mom helped me buy a new suit and shoes, I got a new hairdo and off I went. I was so excited to actually travel away from home on my own, and I was anxious to get to know kids from other parts of the country.

I can picture it like it was yesterday: the first morning there, I walked into the elevator. My nametag was proudly displayed on my jacket, "Lisa Yankowitz, New York." In the elevator was a girl from Arkansas, and two boys, one from Wyoming and one from North Dakota. They were busy chattering and obviously engaged in a lively discussion. When I stepped inside the elevator, they looked at me, looked at my nametag, looked at me, then again at my nametag, and, suddenly, there was absolute silence. The group took a step back and just stared. They seemed almost panic-stricken, frozen in their thoughts. We had descended a couple of floors when I started to feel a bit self-conscious. I quickly gave myself the once over to make sure everything was where it was supposed to be.

Everything seemed fine. Since I had never felt shy about talking to strangers, I asked, "O.K., what just happened? I know you were all having a good conversation before I got on this elevator." No one spoke. Finally the girl from Arkansas stated, "Y'all are from New York! Are you carrying a weapon?" I was flabbergasted. I said, "No." She continued, "Have you ever been mugged?" Without waiting for an answer, she questioned, "How many times have you been mugged?" I'll tell you, I couldn't believe this was coming out of her mouth. I said, "No, I've never been mugged." I continued, "You know, I don't know what you all are thinking, but I grew up on Long Island. It's a suburb with homes and shopping centers, schools...." They continued to stare at me. I realized that I probably was not getting through to them; I could tell that they still weren't comfortable with me. One of the boys said, "That there last name of yours, I ain't never seen a last name like that before. How do you pronounce it?" I replied, "Yank-o-witz." They tried to pronounce it. "Where's that from?" he continued. "It's Russian, and it's Romanian, a little English, a little Polish," and then I added, "and I'm Jewish." (Don't forget...this whole conversation is actually taking place during an elevator ride). I'm not exaggerating when I say that their eyes bulged out of their heads. "Y'all are Jewish?! I ain't never met a Jewish person before." "So where's that ...that beanie that you all wear? How come you don't have that beanie on your head?" It took me a moment to realize to what he was referring. He was talking about a yarmulke, a head covering that Orthodox Jewish men wear. Women do not wear it. I said, "Oh, you mean a yarmulke. Only certain men wear it." I couldn't believe what I heard next. I didn't know whether to laugh or cry at this next remark: "Well, if you don't wear it, where do you hide your horns?" "My horns," I repeated, stunned. "What horns?" They persisted with their comments. "Well, we heard y'all wear those beanies on your head to hide your horns."

At this point the elevator doors opened. Luckily, I was closest to the door. Instinctively I hit the close button and pushed the button on the panel that would take us back to my floor. I told them that there was no way that I was going to let them walk around the conference for a week thinking that the girl from New York was walking around carrying weapons and hiding horns. We missed breakfast and the first part of the general session, but we spent the next few hours talking, breaking down barriers and dispelling misconceptions that we had picked up from our parents, schools, houses of worship and, of course, television. We learned a lot of fascinating things about each other. I realized that just as they had stereotyped me, so had I stereotyped them. I guess I was successful in my efforts to better understand and appreciate others, as we were inseparable for the rest of the conference. As a matter of fact, we kept in touch for years. Looking back, I realize that this was for me Sensitivity Training 101 for sure.

Think about what would have been if I had not said anything to them or if they had not been such a confident group of people, assertive enough to ask questions. Had they not had the confidence to even make that initial comment, they would have gotten off the elevator and run over to the other kids saying, "Wow! Guess who was just in the elevator with us...."

And so it was that after this experience I really began to think about issues like group dynamics, how people think, what influences those thoughts and how to make people from diverse backgrounds feel comfortable and better able to communicate with one another. I have been on a quest ever since to help people realize that working with people from different races, cultures, genders, generations, personalities and life-styles is really not that difficult. Yes, it is a challenge. But with true sensitivity we can successfully address and embrace diversity in the workplace. We can figure it out.

**Wright**

Do you believe it will be difficult for organizations to figure it out?

**Yankowitz**

Well, let's face the facts. How many of us have ever taken a course entitled, *Interacting with Others 101* or *Valuing Diversity 202*? Not many. You know, even with the knowledge of the existence of Title VII of The Civil Rights Act of 1964 (the law that prohibits discrimination in the workplace based on race, color, religion, sex and national origin) and the obligations it imposes, even after the Clarence Thomas/Anita Hill hearings, even with the knowledge of the explosive and potentially debilitating results of an employment lawsuit, it is still so typical for me to go into an organization to conduct training on diversity and/or appropriate workplace behavior and hear most employees share that this is their first time taking such a class. Some of them have been working for the same organization for five, ten, perhaps even fifteen years, and yet this is the first time their organization has brought them together to discuss these types of issues.

**Wright**

Why do you think this happens?

**Yankowitz**

I believe that most organizations have adopted the philosophy that if there isn't an apparent problem why address it. As an example, several years ago, my training and speaking company decided to select a specific market, car dealers in the area, to make it aware of the employment laws specifically dealing with harassment and discrimination. It amazed me when I heard negative responses from either the CEO or CFO to questions like: do you have a policy in place or have you trained your managers and your employees on what harassment is and how to avoid it? And when I explained why such training was so essential, indeed beneficial...in most cases they listened. But they really did not hear nor care. This was obvious when the response typically was, "Well, we don't have any problems here, so we don't need any help." Several months later in the newspaper, I read about one particular organization with which I had spoken and that had stated in no uncertain terms that they had no need for my services. The article was titled "Car Dealer Hit with Sexual Harassment Lawsuit."

**Wright**

So, can you pinpoint what you see as the root of the problem?

**Yankowitz**

Organizations spend so much time, money and energy on the technical aspects of their operations, such as state-of-the-art equipment, and the physical plant. Most possess clearly written vision and mission statements in addition to pages and pages of description on their product line and/or services offered. They may even have some human resources-related written policies in place. The emphasis, however, is on the "bottom line." And the most important, influential ingredient, **the people in the organization,** is not being given comparable consideration. It is because of this disconnect that problems arise.

And there *are* problems. In fact, surveys consistently reveal that over half of all employees hate their jobs. Think about that: they don't simply *dislike* their job, they *hate* it. Hate the act of getting out of bed. Hate the idea of sitting through another mandatory, disorganized, unnecessary meeting. Hate feeling ineffectual and insignificant within the workplace. They don't like their boss or their co-workers. They don't like seeing the favoritism and inconsistencies that go on each and every day. They don't like working for bullies, who in the simplest of terms, are a unique breed who have a devastating effect on the workplace. Whether they make employees feel like they've done something wrong, they belittle employees directly, or they simply make employees feel like lesser people, organizations need to make decisions about such individuals for the betterment of the whole. It's sad, but this hate list goes on and on....

In many instances, the workplace is just a place to go to earn a living, a series of cubicles filled with people punching a time clock, automatically answering "yes" to their supervisor's questions that often require a "no" response. It is often a climate quite devoid of genuine concern for people. As long as everyone follows the rules, doesn't ask questions, goes along with the crowd and, of course, looks and acts alike, with the same socio-economic background, same skin color and same religious beliefs, there **appears** to be peaceful coexistence. So the question is the following: does the organization really know what is brewing within? The answer: no, organizations really don't seem to see it.

I know at this point some of you reading this may be saying to yourself, "this doesn't sound like my organization." "We have good people. People who respect each other, care about each other and understand each other. People who try to continually improve how they work and play together within the organization." If this is the case, if you really believe this is the case, then good for you. That is terrific. And I have to say that some of the organizations with which I work *are* doing a great job. Keep in mind, however, that over half of employees are miserable at work. These people are in *all* of our workplaces. Many are feeling this way right under our noses. It is a sorry state of affairs.

**Wright**

What do you mean it is a sorry state of affairs? Can you elaborate on this?

**Yankowitz**

You know, when you walk into an office space, you can tell from the first person you meet if there is "life", if those you meet possess that spirit that springs from a supportive, creative, truly collaborative work environment. It is this "life," in part, that helps to shape and define an organization's culture. Of course, we can toss around the term "culture" and profess that an employee's zest for her job stems from a creative culture, but the issue goes far beyond culture: the workplace must become a home away from home, a place where employees truly feel engaged invested and empowered. Unfortunately, many organizations don't live this, and they pay the price with human currency. Take for example a well-known real-estate company that at one point in its history, at least on the local level, had a phenomenally strong leader who not only talked about establishing a strong culture, he lived it, developed it and encouraged it. One day, it was a great company with a great leader, great people, and great culture. The next day, the son took over and was the antithesis of his father. He didn't value the culture, didn't value his people, and so they left.

My mother always says that the workplace is like a marriage: it thrives on mutual trust and respect. If one of those two components is absent, the workplace falters. It is these two components that foster a healthy work environment. For example, many organizations will tell you that they care about their people. That they value their people. That they foster teamwork and support diversity. They will even tell their employees that they come first over their customers. In some organizations, employees know this and feel it. But, from my experience and from informally polling thousands of participants from my training classes and speaking engagements over the years, most employees don't really feel the actual impact of the organization's assertions. They see it as lip service: sounds good but doesn't take place in reality. And so they lose trust, and many, unfortunately, lose faith. In fact, these are the employees that are likely to become the well-known "disgruntled employee." These are the employees that will keep records, document every incident and will mostly likely, at some point in time when they feel the time is right, haul their employer into court on some violation of the employment laws.

**Wright**

Lisa, give me an example to illustrate this point?

**Yankowitz**

For example, let's say that an organization hasn't really taken care of a particular employee, and now that employee is fired or transferred because the organization is "downsizing." Most likely, the reasons for taking this action were not properly explained to him. And, according to the employee's last three performance reviews, he has been a model employee. The employer, under this scenario, may have created an incredible amount of vulnerability for itself. Here's why: if that employee happens to fall into one of the protected classes- they're of a particular race, color, sex, religion, national origin, age, disability, sexual orientation, and so on and has not been given any valid reasons for the termination or transfer- he will *believe* he was fired or transferred because he falls into one of the protected classes. He was given no other reason to believe otherwise. Thus, he may have a strong legal claim against his employer.

It is for this very reason that when I am asked, "Why can't I just fire my employees, aren't we 'At-Will Employers,'" my answer is emphatic: "You have to act as if 'At-Will Employment' no longer exists." Briefly, let me explain: it is true that there is a doctrine in existence called "At-Will Employment," which means, in theory, that an employer can fire anyone for any reason, no reason, a good reason or even a bad reason. This is true. However, there are so many exceptions to the rule that these exceptions have effectively "swallowed up" the rule. In essence, "At-Will Employment" no longer really exists. I can't emphasize this point enough, and it is my hope that you will seriously consider the implications involved in denying this reality.

**Wright**

So, I'm wondering if it is possible to "just get along" ... as the saying goes?

**Yankowitz**

Well, stop and think about the state of the workplace today. Organizations are focused on quantity. Deadlines. Making money. Streamlining processes and people. Leaning up. Downsizing. Doing more with less. At the same time, most will say they are concerned about safety and ethics, quality and morale. Preventing harassment and discrimination. Establishing and maintaining diversity. But it is my experience that many organizations don't know how to blend these key elements together. Some try, but in most cases there is no real organizational initiative, follow up, or follow through to make sure that everyone is "on board," working hard to make it happen. The organization may sermonize that it is not just concerned with the product or service and that it does care about its people, but actions have proven this to be invalid. For example, some organizations believe that distributing and having employees sign off on a sexual harassment and discrimination company-wide policy in writing is enough. It's not. They think that a policy written in legalese will equate to a true understanding of and appreciation for what sexual harassment really is. It doesn't. We have all heard the rhetorical question, "Why can't we all just get along?" The need for training has a great deal to do with this. Diversity education and sensitivity training for all employees and managers, and *not* just on sexual harassment, is essential and shows a willingness and desire to invest in people and is what is needed to make the difference.

**Wright**

Based on what you're saying, I can see how training is crucial, but is such training being offered?

**Yankowitz**

Not really. Organizations spend money on products and services. Processes and procedures. Product knowledge and sales training. State-of-the-art, cutting-edge technology. Automated systems. However, most organizations spend close to nothing on the growth and development of their people. On interpersonal skills. Conflict resolution. Team building. Problem solving. Understanding others. Sensitivity training. **People training**. In short, they don't spend money on developing the most important influence on the organization's success: its people.

Let's be real, nobody is questioning that business success is about the bottom line, but organizations too often view the bottom line in a vacuum. What they fail to realize—and this ends up costing them in both dollars and human currency—is that they will make more money if they take care of, or better care of, their people. Organizations can be shortsighted. They need to look beyond the short-term objectives and instead think about how to achieve and sustain their long-term goals through better use of their people. For example, jumping into major projects without appropriate setup when combined with the associated pressures inherent in these projects can cause some employees to hit a wall and their performance to decline. However, an organization that does the appropriate set-up takes the time to really make sure its people have a good understanding of and appreciation for one another, ensures that all employees comprehend the project's objective, makes certain people know that they really can bring value to the table—such an organization will ultimately meet with the most success. For the first few quarters, it might not outperform the organization that jumped immediately into work, but in the long term, its productivity after the group dynamics kick in will be greater. A well thought out plan will allow time for those who need it to stop, refocus if necessary and refuel. This helps prevent people from becoming frustrated, burning out and feeling trapped. It keeps productivity high and morale up, especially helpful in avoiding the creation of an unhealthy workplace environment that can set the stage for the disgruntled employee and potential legal issues.

Take a look at your own workplace. The make-up of the workforce, for the most part, is probably diverse. You may not think so, but it is. The reality is that within your workforce there are people from different religions. Different cultures. Different educational levels. There are men and women of all ages. There are different races. Different personalities. Different learning styles. It is important to note that we all do recognize this on an intellectual level. In fact, we often comment that, "We are all so different." Yet, we don't spend much time really internalizing what that means. We must begin to appreciate how these differences impact our relationships in the workplace. Lack of education and training to gain awareness and insight into how to make these differences work for us will have a tremendous negative impact on both the morale of the people as well as on the bottom line. Organizations need to understand it, accept it and most important, they need to act on it.

Let's look at why organizations have such difficulties with their people. It's safe to say that training dollars allocated to Human Resources (HR) and utilized for what is known as 'soft skills' training, such as how to communicate effectively, how to problem solve or how to resolve conflict, are typically the first dollars cut within organizations when they tighten their belts. Unfortunately, an HR specialist who should be overseeing people development is not always trained to do his job nor is he given the appropriate tools to help develop people. To illustrate the point, let me share with you a not-so-uncommon fact: in many organizations HR is handled by the Chief Financial Officer (CFO). Does this really make sense? A numbers person handling people issues? Rarely have I seen it work. And, most will tell you that they don't like handling the HR issues, they have enough to keep up with in their own area of expertise.

In other organizations and in many instances, even where there are dedicated Human Resources professionals, these people most often are not adept and knowledgeable enough in this area to be considered help. They may have come from another department as a lateral move with no real HR experience. All too often out of necessity they spend most of their workday handling benefits and payroll and the related administrative tasks. They do the paperwork around a hiring or firing, and they try to put out fires. Not a very proactive approach, I might add. In most instances, the HR professionals do not have the time to keep up with the ever-changing world of employment law, therefore keeping the organization current. Who, then, is there to make sure that all employees are trained and educated on such important areas as diversity awareness, preventing harassment and discrimination and the gamut of employment laws that have to be strictly implemented and followed in the workplace? Organizations must redefine how they view and utilize Human Resources. It is, or should be, a strategic component of the organization's success strategy as they are, or should be, the organization's major source of strength.

**Wright**

What should employers do?

**Yankowitz**

Employers need a new mindset, for many, a complete paradigm shift. They have to make a commitment to educate themselves and their employees about the people-related aspects of the business before they move on to things like new idea generation and how to make the company more money. Establish trust, respect and comfort among employees, and you will make money. Build an appreciation for diversity, and you will make more money. You will make money because your employees will feel that they are important. There will be more "buy in." Your goals will become their goals; your success will become their success.

Take, for example, Southwest Airlines. They get it. This organization works very hard at making sure that it hires good people who care about what they're doing and can still be themselves, which I think is to be commended these days. It doesn't stop at just bringing good people on board. The organization works hard to make sure that their people have a voice, have "life" and feel at one with the company; that they enjoy coming to work everyday

Unfortunately, most organizations don't get it like Southwest Airlines does. In fact, I think that people in general don't inherently get it. Most people don't truly understand all the dynamics at play when people work together. There has to be a company-wide initiative in order to help people get it. The organization has to make a commitment to its employees that every member of that organization will live the basic guiding principles, guiding principles that should be in place to help people be sensitive to the needs of others. The basic guiding principles are honesty, trust and respect.

The workplace is becoming a more challenging, complex environment in which to play. Employees, now more than they ever have been before, are aware of their legal rights. It is much easier for employees to get access to information. Five, ten, fifteen years ago, if an employee believed that her manager or supervisor was not treating her appropriately, legally or otherwise, it was very difficult to determine if that really was the case. So people suffered, but they walked away from these situations much more quietly than they do today. Now people are more aware of and confident in their rights (and keeping lengthy written records, too), and they're more willing to pursue these rights. They know of Title VII (the law that prohibits discrimination based on race, color, religion, sex and national origin). They know of the ADA (the law that prohibits discrimination based on disability, both mental and physical). They make it their business to know the employment laws, and they know what their employers are doing and should not be doing. It is important for employers to realize this and to be just as aware, if not more so, than their employees. It is only through this realization that organizations can avoid problems and legal actions that may have started off simply as poor management.

When you read and hear about employment practice violation cases out there, you wonder, "How is it possible that the organization didn't see it, that the organization let it go so far?" So many things in the workplace start out as possibly an inappropriate comment, miscommunication, poor leadership, etc. For example, an inappropriate comment repeated two or three times could be written off as poor leadership or poor communication. However, the same comment repeated over three to six weeks can be perceived as no longer an offhanded remark and could escalate to the level of what the courts would consider offensive, even potentially harassing or discriminatory behavior—not a situation in which any employer wants to be.

**Wright**

Can you give me a scenario?

**Yankowitz**

Here's the scenario...you start a new job, and within the first couple of months your boss says something that you don't feel is the most appropriate comment, but you let it go. No big deal. Then a few weeks go by, and he sends you an email that you have to read once or twice just to make sure he really wrote what you think you just read. "Did he really say that?" goes through your mind. But again, you are new to the company, so you chalk it up to a poor communicator and a poor leader: simply an inappropriate comment. Now, a few months pass. The comments and emails have continued, and you can no longer write them off as offhanded as they have now established a pattern of behavior. You receive an email just like the ones you had been receiving. But now at some point, not only do you read the email three times, just to make sure you are reading it correctly, but you call a co-worker over and ask her, "Are you reading what I'm reading? Do you see anything wrong with this e-mail?" And so what you once wrote off as just a stupid, offhanded comment you are now questioning to determine if your boss is crossing the line. Did a mere isolated, inappropriate remark now escalate to something more? You start to become more aware of other inappropriate behaviors and begin to realize that your workplace is an environment seeded with harassing and discriminatory behavior. Situations like this happen all the time.

It appears that an organization that works hard to insure that this does not happen to them is the Ritz Carlton. This organization invests a lot of time from start to finish in the employment relationship. The organization looks for high-quality people, people that are good at their core, people who appreciate diversity, people who have a certain level of professionalism, work ethic and respect. It works hard to bring those people into the workplace and continually develop them to their full potential. They continuously train and educate their workforce. I think this is where other organizations miss it. Many organizations will say, "We care about our people." "People are our most important asset." "Our people come first." Yet when a budget needs to be cut, again, the first thing to go is training dollars. Organizations generally do not see the necessity of spending money on respect and diversity training, on learning how to appreciate the differences between people, specifically, on how the sexes communicate differently, on the different religious influences at work, on understanding different personalities at play, on how to communicate more effectively, on how to negotiate more effectively, on how to be a better leader. Yet these are the skills that allow employees to truly excel in the workplace. These are the skills that one must have in place before one can truly maximize sales performance or managerial acuity. In short, these are the skills that organizations should want to invest in developing within employees first, and they are precisely the things that we have to really work hard at convincing employers to do. A few years ago, I had breakfast with one of my clients, a CEO of a Fortune 500 company to discuss training initiatives. I had been doing customer service training, and sales training, and negotiations skills training, among other things, for his organization for several years. I suggested that they do anti-harassment training, in the near future, to protect themselves. They had, in at least one division that I worked, a lot of young people who not only worked together but also played together and I wanted them to make sure that everyone was aware of the issues and what to do if they believed someone was crossing the line. He told me, very boldly, that anti-harassment training was at the bottom of his priority list. He had other things to worry about and he would take his chances.

Employers think they are doing a much better job than they really are, but employees don't believe employers are coming close. When jurors are questioned, after a case, about why they ruled in favor of the employee, what you hear more often than not is that they didn't rule in favor of the employee as much as they ruled *against* the employer. They are very, very skeptical of employers. The message is clear: organizations need to act and act now.

Unless significant changes are made in some organizations, there will be problems. There already *are* problems. Take a look at all the downsizing-taking place. Bankruptcies. Ethics violations. In the early stages, organizations don't see these problems on the horizon; they can run on autopilot for a certain length of time. For example, I'm working with one organization right now that became very, very successful because it did a great job of hiring great people, and it assembled all the right players in all the right positions. For years that organization picked up momentum, and morale grew. There was great energy. People had fun. Employees loved the work environment. Over the course of the past one to two years, however, the organization has been slowly losing some of these key players. As you see time and time again, with the loss of those players, you lose productivity, you lose quality, and you lose efficiency. You lose some of the passion in that original workplace, some of the buy-in, some of the role models and some of the fun. What's worse, in some cases, you lose some of the "insulators," those individuals who help disguise or shield employees from the injustices taking place under the surface. And unless the organization decides to do something about the situation, such as bringing new people on to fill the voids, inspire, educate, train and/or re-train the people it wants to retain, and/or fire those people who exhibit characteristics that are detrimental to the organization's goals, values and culture, that organization is going to start losing speed, if it hasn't already. The lesson to be learned, which is a lesson so difficult to teach in theory, is that you can have the best systems in place, you can have the best software programs in place, and you can have the best product, but it's the people that make the difference.

One of the most difficult, and yet the most necessary tasks is for an organization to honestly and effectively evaluate its staff, especially its management and supervisory personnel. As tough as this sounds, organizations must make difficult decisions regarding its people. There are many managers who don't know how to be managers, some have been "home-grown" by an organization and have risen through the ranks, having never received any formal managerial training, the idea being that they performed their jobs extremely well so they must be good leaders. So what is an organization to do? They have to be willing to start off right. Organizations need to be willing to get rid of the individuals causing disharmony or those individuals who are not team players, regardless of individual productivity. This task is truly difficult for it takes time for organizations to see past an individual's contributions to the bottom line and to truly understand the individuals' effect on others and thus overall productivity.

**Wright**

There appears to be so many issues, can employers work through them?

**Yankowitz**

One of the challenges that we have is that we don't know what we don't know. Unless things surface inadvertently or we go fishing for them, we'll never realize and appreciate all of our differences and how they impact us in the workplace. In order to build such appreciation, each organization has to tackle the problem in its own unique way. I've worked with many different organizations as both an employee and a consultant. I've worked with union and non-union employers. I've worked with private employers and public employers, with large and small employers, with restaurants, car dealers, within white-collar environments, etc. They're all very, very different, from the people to the situations with which they deal. Because of that and all of the different dynamics at play each organization's game plan needs to be a bit different. (Of course, this presupposes that each organization is working off of a game plan to begin with.)

Each organization must ask itself the following questions: 1) What is our main objective? 2) What are we here for? 3) How do we make the best of everything that we have working for us and for our people as well? 4) What are the challenges that we have in the organization as regards our people? 5) What are our strengths? 6) What are our weaknesses? 7) Do our people respect and like us as an organization? 8) Do we have the right people on board? How do we know? Have we evaluated our people since we hired them? 9) Do we have good people? 10) Do we have people who are passionate about their work? 11) Do people understand what is expected of them? 12) Do we expect the right things from our people? 13) Do we truly have a diverse workforce? 14) Are we taking advantage of the opportunities that a diverse workforce provides? 15) Do we know how to work in a diverse workplace? 16) What have we done to develop our people? 17) Have we provided training and continual education for our people? 18) Are our managers "living" our policies and procedures?

With those answers in hand, organizations must then ask, now what are we going to do to work through our challenges and our weaknesses in order to focus on our strengths so that we can move forward, always keeping in mind those guiding principles, honesty, trust and respect. Be sensitive. Realize that people with whom you communicate are different than you. Be reflective. Understand that financial compensation alone is not enough for most people. Organizations need to find out how to motivate and manage each individual individually. They need to listen to each other more, care about each other more and smile more. They need to give others the benefit of the doubt. They need to solicit help from advisors who can provide objective observations and suggestions. This is what they all need, but every organization is unique and will get to where they are going differently. *They need to just start.*

**Wright**

Are employers the only ones with responsibility in building a better workplace?

**Yankowitz**

Employers are not the only ones who have responsibility for building a positive culture and making sure that sensitivity is alive and well within the workplace. Employees also play a significant role; they must also be reflective. Here are some questions employees should ask themselves: 1) Am I happy where I am? 2) Do I like my job? 3) Do the people here care about me? 4) Am I being challenged? 5) Am I being stifled? 6) Am I being allowed to grow? 7) Is the environment comfortable for me? 8) Do I feel like I can voice my opinions without fear? 9) Does my job allow me to come alive? 10) Is this job really worth everything I invest in it if I feel I have to be someone other than who I am?

Assuming that both the employer and the employees have worked themselves through this process, or at least a similar one, organizations will benefit from the fruits of their labor. Some will see changes and improvements overnight. For the most part, though, this is a lengthy process. Changing the core of organizations takes effort, commitment and time, yet over time, they will see results. The key is to stay on course and not give up.

**Wright**

Well, what an interesting conversation. I think I've learned a lot here this afternoon.

As a final thought, what advice do you have for employers?

**Yankowitz**

After all that has been written here, you may still be asking yourself is playing well together in the workplace *really* possible?

Absolutely. It *is* possible for us to learn how to play well together in the workplace. But, to do so, organizations need to have the awareness of, appreciation for and willingness to work through and deal with people-related and employment law-related issues on a much greater scale than they do now. Again, it will definitely take time, consistency and continuous effort. It will take a sincere desire and a true commitment on both the part of the organization and the employees, always mindful of the fact that most people, who are the basis of every organization, don't just inherently **get it**.

It is important for me to mention that there are some organizations out there that I do believe are doing a good job and are trying. They are investing in training and education of their people. They may not always be doing it in what I would consider to be an ideal fashion, but they are doing it. And you can see and feel the difference, so kudos to them. When organizations educate themselves and their employees on people skills and employment law-related issues, "playing well with others" will be more than just a phrase recognizable to kids on a playground.

I would also like to give a huge thanks to my mom, Sandy Yankowitz for all of her support, insights, and love during the writing of this chapter. She has been an integral part of my life and this chapter, and I owe my success to her and her endless, selfless efforts to help me achieve my goals. And, to Laura Lotz, a good friend and excellent teacher, for her assistance with helping us pull this chapter together.

## About The Author

Lisa Yankowitz brings a unique mix of enthusiasm, knowledge, humor and professionalism when presenting workshops, seminars and making public appearances on an array of employment law issues and employment practices. Her presentations have been described as "dynamic, " "fabulous" and "fun," words not often associated with an area of the law that is so serious and volatile. Lisa is a Dale Carnegie Certified Instructor, Senior Faculty at Keller Graduate School of Management of DeVry University, where she teaches the Employment Law and Negotiations Skills courses and is a Member of the National Speakers Association. She is a Senior Professional in Human Resources (SPHR) and is a member of both the Florida Bar and Missouri Bar.

**Lisa Yankowitz, JD, SPHR**

Phone: 314.607.9915

Email: lisay@elgtraining.com

# *Chapter Twenty*

## MEGAN ZUCARO

### THE INTERVIEW

**David E. Wright (Wright)**

Today we are talking to Megan Zucaro. Megan is a Financial Advisor with over 6 years experience. Leading, managing and building personal financial plans, developing and coaching other financial advisors with their businesses. She speaks to thousands of people a year on these topics; she is an expert on visioneering; how to visualize and live your own reality as a family or a couple and how to get the maximum potential out of a relationship. Her goal is to make each and every couple, a powerful couple. This unique presentation on stage with her and her husband is something to experience. Megan, welcome to *Remarkable Women.*

**Megan Zucaro (Zucaro)**

Thank you so much.

**Wright**

So being from an entrepreneur family how did that influence your life?

**Zucaro**

I am blessed to come from a great family. My dad had a CPA firm in Minneapolis, and it never ceased to amaze me, how whatever event I was participating in my father would be there. He'd probably be the only man in a suit, but he would always show up. I was on the starting basketball team, and in one of games I looked up in the stands, I saw my father and one of his clients. I thought boy, isn't that interesting that my dad brought a client to my game. After the game, I said to my dad, "Why did you have a client at the game?" " Well, I told him, that my daughter had a game and if he wanted to speak to me, I'd be there and he had come along." So at that point I realized the benefit of the flexibility and control of your life to take care of what's important in your life. So my parents really influenced that for me.

**Wright**

So when did your entrepreneur career begin?

**Zucaro**

Initially, I went to college to be a news anchor, and I was in the news business directly after college, which I really enjoyed and had a great time doing. However, I realized being able to control your schedule and control your destiny was the ultimate goal. For me, being able to bring a product to the public always excited me. I got out of the news business to work with a girlfriend of mine who had a hair care, skincare cosmetic company. She asked me to be the marketing director and she wanted to get her products into Wal-Mart. After we accomplished our goals and made the company successful I realized it still was not my own. However, I realized how much I enjoyed creating and making a company successful. After a trip to Spain I decided to start a swimwear, Resort Wear Company. We manufactured swimwear and resort wear. I started very young having that entrepreneurial drive, and I feel like that was what really continued to drive me being able to create companies and ideas. With the financial planning business that my husband and I are currently in, I feel like it gives me an opportunity to help people create their personal financial goals. I get a lot of personal satisfaction from the financial planning aspects and helping people achieve their financial goals.

**Wright**

I remember several years ago when I learned the rules of '72, I almost turned a back flip. Why in the world didn't somebody tell me this when I was twenty years old.

**Zucaro**

Exactly, and its interesting for me I'm really selling peoples their dreams and selling the fact that they can achieve these goals, but more than anything, like you said the rule of '72, a light goes off in their head and you can see it click they go, "Wow"!, I can retire. You know, only ten percent of people retire at age sixty five and are actually successful. When I say financial successful, that's something different for everybody. Some people might say they want $10,000 a month, and some people might need $20,000 and some might need $5000, but the fact is no matter what, only ten percent of society actually achieves financial success, which is unfortunate.

**Wright**

Tell me what makes you such a great leader and mentor?

**Zucaro**

I'm a huge believer in lead by example, and my mother taught me to have balance. Moral and values are very important, and what you find as you progress in life is that you have a lot of choices and the choices that you make no matter what position you have, you always have to think of yourself as if you are in the spotlight. So I'm a firm believer in lead by example. It's ok to make mistakes as long as you actually admit that you're making a mistake. It's ok if you don't know absolutely every business aspect; however, you must surround yourself with very successful good people who can get the answer for you very quickly. I think the number one thing along with leading by example and having balance in your life is having the respect of the people that work for you. Without the respect of the people that work for you, you don't have a chance. I'm very blessed to have a great group of financial advisors that work for me.

It was interesting a couple months ago, I found out I was having our third child in three years, I felt guilty about the fact that I usually try to get out of the office by 5:15 so that I can be home to make dinner for my family and have a normal family life during the evening. So I said to my agents, I should just step down from the management position so that I can give them somebody that will actually be able to be here until later at night and do those types of managerial jobs versus leave at 5:15. I was amazed because when I told them that they looked at me like "are you crazy," we don't care a bit if you leave at 5:15 because you do more for us than most people do between 9 and 5, and we prefer to have you be here than not to be here as much, because of what you do. At that point it really made me realize that people respect you for leading by example, and for having true balance in your life, because we all talk about balance.

But when you are a truly driven individual who wants to be successful and always be the best in the company that you're working for or the best in the industry that you're working at. Its tempting to say, "I'll just get home at eight tonight," but if you do that over and over and over again, then the people that your leading, start to go well, if she believes so much about balance then why is she here till eight every night? So I would say that balance and the respect of the people that work for you is what makes people a great leader.

**Wright**

Why are personal finances so important in people's lives?

**Zucaro**

One of the most stressful things that people deal with is finances. When people don't have money trouble it seems like the stress in their life goes away. Maybe I feel so strongly about that because I meet with people all day long and I see their stress of finances. Once people have a budget set up, I always tell people it doesn't matter if you make a $1000 or $10,000 a month, you have to have some type of budget to work from, because if you don't $100 becomes $1000 and $1000 becomes $10,000. For some people spending a $100 is a significant amount of money. For some $1000 is nothing and for other people $10,000 is like a hundred dollar bill. It's all perception. But with every single income bracket, every single income family, if there's not enough it causes serious financial stress and marital stress in their life. It's not the only thing obviously; but when you get peoples finances under control it gives them a sense of security with their budget, they have a happier life in general because their not worrying about how to pay their bills at the end of the month. No matter what their situation is financially, you have two people in a relationship and sometimes some people are very frugal and the other isn't. So you almost end up being a financial counselor in a sense that you can help marriages or relationships feel comfortable with each others spending habits.

I just met with a gentleman today, who is twenty four years old, no debt, about $40,000 in investments, owns a home. He was saying to me that he wanted to buy a car and I said, "That's great." He said, "Well, you know, I would pay cash for it."

I asked him, "What makes you so disciplined, (he already is saving $900 a month of his pay of his pay into his investments), at twenty four years old, who taught you this?" He looked at me very serious and said, "I don't know why I'm like this." I thought to myself, there you have it, because some people are so disciplined and understand how much interest, time, value and money and other people don't realize it until thirty or forty. It's just amazing to me! It has nothing to do with age. I used to think it was your education or how you were bought up, but it seems that doesn't make that big of a difference either.

**Wright**

Some people just get it.

**Zucaro**

Yeah, some people are just disciplined on having money and no debt.

**Wright**

I think my son is that way.

**Zucaro**

That's great!

**Wright**

He just owns all kinds of things like houses and new automobiles, and his friends who are the same age are still borrowing money before next Friday's payday.

**Zucaro**

You must have done something along the line to help him out there.

**Wright**

Hopefully! Why do you feel finance visualization and balance are so important?

**Zucaro**

I feel finance is important to help give people ease in their relationship. Visioneering I feel is very important. I'm amazed at how many people when you sit down with them and you say (again this is a huge part of what we do) what do you ultimately want to accomplish? Where do you want to be at fifty? Where do you want to be at fifty-five? A lot of people when you ask them that question will say, "I never thought of it." I guess its something that you progress in life and as you become more mature you start thinking about what you want to accomplish. I found that it's extremely powerful when you sit down at whatever age you are today and say in five years, in ten years, in fifteen years, in twenty years, this is what I want to do and this is what I want to accomplish, you can actually accomplish those goals. It continues to build on everything that you start to visualize because in your subconscious mind you start thinking about what you ultimately want to be able to accomplish.

**Wright**

So what are you currently working on?

**Zucaro**

Currently we're working on the visioneering; Engineering a platform for people to achieve visionary goals. It's such a powerful thing for people when they sit down and identify the vision they want to achieve. I have an office of about thirty five people and I sit down on a yearly basis with the assistants and talk about what they want to achieve each year? Generally ninety percent of those assistants will say to me, "I've never thought about my goals or what I want to accomplish." After the first year of doing that, I had one of the assistants outside my door and she said, "Can I please come in and talk to you Megan?" She said, "You're never going to believe this and probably never going to remember it, but do you remember a year ago and we sat down and wrote out my goals?" I said, "Absolutely." She said, "You were right, every single goal I wrote down I accomplished in one year." She was so excited. I said, "That's what it is all about. If you write it down its going to happen." She said, "Can we write next years goals down?" I believe so strongly in helping people achieve what they ultimately want to achieve. It can be anything from business to personal to family to spiritual. When you have the end result of what you want you can get there once you have a plan and once you're able to engineer that plan to live into your future. There are people that have dreams and there are people that proceed with their dreams. Not everyone can do both; the key is to help people put into place the actions to act on their dreams.

**Wright**

So how can you help others do this?

**Zucaro**

My husband and I speak together, through our personal story, to help people see how they can achieve their dreams and goals. Visioneering will be our next book. It's being able to help engineer peoples ultimate goals and visions.

**Wright**

You and your husband speak weekly. Why are you so busy?

**Zucaro**

Well, you know, we're really fortunate that we are able to speak on a weekly basis. We're fortunate because we have been very successful being able to speak to a large group of people on financial planning. When you have good results speaking to a large group of people it seems like it blossoms and more people want you to speak weekly.

**Wright**

I have been booking speakers now for about fifteen years and there are not many husband/wife speaking teams. Why did you choose to speak together?

**Zucaro**

People talk about soul mates, my husband and I, we really complete each other. We are very good when we speak on our own, but when we're together, I've found the energy between the two of us really projects to the audience. When people meet us together they say, "Wow! What a great couple." So, we really like to be able to speak together because of that energy that we give to each other and the audience.

**Wright**

So how do you and Zeke work together, live together, laugh together, all the time? What's your secret?

**Zucaro**

Having fun. We were just in Los Cabaos for the last four days. I was laughing and told my husband, I'm glad you don't get sick of me, we are together 24/7, and I never get sick of you. The bottom line is being able to have respect for each other in order to work together. When you have a way of life and when you enjoy what your doing, its not necessarily like work. We do what we like to do on a daily basis, its not a job, its helping us to achieve our life goals for the next twenty or thirty years.

**Wright**

So, to what do you attribute your success?

**Zucaro**

God and Faith number one! We've been very blessed throughout our life.

**Wright**

So it is not only a union of a partnership, its also spiritual?

**Wright**

The One above with the higher plan is definitely the One in control of our lives. We pray on daily basis for that guidance and direction to get us to where we should be. A lot of times what we think is for the best is not the best and what ends up coming to you and in your place ends up being a better plan than you could have ever imagined. So I would say that is the number one thing I attribute success.

**Wright**

So as you look down the road what's in your future?

**Zucaro**

Zeke and I are having our third child. We have an eighteen month old, a five month old and third on the way.

**Wright**

Is your name in the dictionary under prolific?

**Zucaro**

Yeah! Everybody says, "When you guys put your mind to it, it really happens." It was visioneered! We said three years ago we're going to have three children in three years. Everybody said, "Yeah, you're crazy. After the first one you won't." Well, when they found out that we were going to have our third they said, "You guys definitely do what you say you're going to do."

**Wright**

That's great.

**Zucaro**

We are very involved in Real Estate on a personal level, and ultimately, we will speak full time on visioneering. Being able to be with your children, help your children, being able to be at those events as my parents were at those events when I was growing up is very important to the two of us. Ultimately, when we're fifty, fifty five years old we envision floating around in a yacht and seeing our children and our grandchildren as much as they allow us to.

**Wright**

That's nice. Well what an interesting conversation. I really appreciate the time that you spent with me here today answering all of my questions. I wish you both the best of luck, but I don't think your going to need my wishing. I think you guys are goal setters.

**Zucaro**

We can always use everybody's wishes. Thank you, David.

**Wright**

Today we have been talking to Megan Zucaro, who is a Financial Advisor with years of experience, leading, managing, building personal financial plans and developing and coaching other financial advisors with their business. They do unique presentations together and as we have found out today they're talking about some really interesting things and think that will make your life much simpler. Thank you so much, Megan, for being with us today on *Remarkable Women.*

## About The Author

Megan Zucaro and her Husband Zeke are experts on Visoneering your life to achieve the goals you want personally and professionally. Visoneering helps everyone have the opportunity to achieve all of your life goals whether it be a year from now or 25 years from now. With the Zucaro's visoneering concepts and philosophies the sky is the limit as long as you can develop and see your ultimate goals and aspirations. Megan and Zeke are Financial Planners and real-estate investors residing in Belton, Texas with their two children.

**Megan Zucaro**

Phone: 254.534.1953

Email: megazee@direcway.com

# *Chapter Twenty-One*

## COLLEEN CASSIDY-WOLFE

## THE INTERVIEW

**David E. Wright (Wright)**

Today we are talking to Colleen Cassidy-Wolfe. Colleen is the mother of three children, wife, active community leader, and business executive. Her last business assignment was as vice president of sales operations. Colleen has led many multi-faceted organizations while managing a family and home. She has discovered a successful model for balancing home and work. Not only has she discovered the balance between home and career, but she has also identified this unique balance missing in corporations today. Through coaching and investing in individuals, she assists them in creating lasting life changes that reveal their individual desires, values and goals. She leads individuals through self-discovery, empowering their beliefs that will enable them to rewrite the software of their minds in order to change the maps of their future. Through her own personal discoveries and successes, Colleen has developed a coaching philosophy that assists individuals striving for their desired balance. She believes that the best way to construct a desired outcome is to provoke self-discovery. Colleen provides leadership and coaching to executives, managers, entrepreneurs and individuals, helping them unlock and access underlying beliefs and attitudes in order to enable new sustained desires, values and goals. Colleen, welcome to *Remarkable Women*!

**Colleen Cassidy Wolfe (Wolfe)**

Thank you very much for including me in your book. I am very excited about this opportunity to share stories along with other women.

**Wright**

You have ordered your life's responsibilities from caring for your children to your work responsibilities. What led you to know that your priorities were imbalanced?

**Wolfe**

My journey was and continues to be an amazing discovery of my authentic self. To be perfectly honest, it was a long process of discoveries, experimentation and setting into action small desired outcomes.

I had intended to get my life re-prioritized and balanced. I began looking at my current realities and realized that the what, when and how questions provided the opportunities to access my own wisdom, enabling myself to create more positive circumstance in my life. I found and continue to find that replacing why questions with what, when and how questions, can powerfully access ones own wisdom.

I found myself focusing on the limitations of my life. I desired a shift in my values to align with the changes that were occurring. Discovery was critical. I needed to set time to discover what was important in my life. I was in search of a way to sort out where I was coming from, where I was in the present and where I wanted to go next.

Initially, small goals were set and prioritized with the intention to realign my values and beliefs systems with desired changes. I began by realigning and focusing on intended outcomes I desired for my future. I established and set small, easy and desirable intentions so that I could experiment with outcomes that could occur in my life. Simple experiments, yet important outcomes.

One of the most difficult experiments for me was the reworking of my embedded vocabulary. I discovered I was stuck in the way that I problem solved. I was result-oriented; it seemed natural to ask "why" questions to get to the real issue. "Why did we not meet our numbers?" "Why is production down?" "Why is so and so not on board with us?" "Why won't the children eat when I put dinner on the table?" etc.

Remarkably, changing the why questions to action-oriented questions was the most radical and deliberate intention I set for myself.

Discovering and experimenting with new ways of accessing answers allowed me to stop searching for the answers, and assisted in seeking the answers with ease and resolve. Through gathering evidence from my past, I learned that why questions held me back in the past and sought to explain rather than to move forward. This was so intriguing and powerful for me. This discovery was a transitional point where I knew I was moving from fixing problems from a child's perspective to resolving a situation from an adult's perspective. Moving from my past to my future and setting my intentions for desired outcomes felt much more authentic and positive.

**Wright**

How did you realize you had the controls to empower yourself to create your desired future?

**Wolfe**

When I began listening to the messages and signals around me, my desired changes no longer seemed monumental in scope. I was realizing that I was making decisions and acting in accordance to rituals and limiting beliefs that were learned and carried forward from my youth. It had never occurred to me that there were defining beliefs from my childhood that I could release. I finally began to realize that I was not responsible for holding on to belief systems that no longer served my desired purposes. I was discouraged with my current set of defining beliefs. I believed that I was not equipped to manage the multiple areas of my life with grace and contentment. I was searching for others' belief systems inside of help books. I had been looking in the wrong places to define my desired future. I was in search of a solution and had at this point not realized that I had the inner wisdom to access my own values and apply them to my desired outcomes. I soon would learn, however, how to calm my inner- critic (defining belief systems) from my youth. I desired not to wander without purpose. I wanted to put a voice with my desires and evolve into what I was meant to be.

A significant process for me was setting aside time to discover order in my life: where I was coming from, where I was in the present, and where I wanted to go. In this process I began documenting and journaling what held me back from achieving what I valued and wanted most out of life. As I focused on defining my desires I found myself realizing that I had spent the majority of my life listing all the reasons **WHY** I was being held back from achieving my desired balance. I learned that I spent much time paying attention to what did not feel right, particularity focusing on behaviors, relationships and routines, which no longer served my higher intentions in life. I identified the areas I was negatively repeating: the *"stuck places,"* where I was at this particular time. I was able to utilize learned coaching structure allowing myself to "flirt" with experiments to view new ways of answering questions and redirecting my desired outcomes.

I had developed stop places (triggers) that I could now recognize and work through my resistance to change. I was learning how to push beyond the uncomfortable feelings with assistance from my coaches I had in my life. We would work toward uncovering how I could move beyond and what was making me feel uncomfortable. My coaches kept me accountable to access my own wisdom to overcome the obstacles (inner critic) that held me back from my authentic self and desires.

**Wright**

You speak about accessing inner wisdom to unleash a world of possibilities. You also speak of approaching situations from a place of curiosity, an open heart and the desire to listen to what is so. How were you able transition to desired expanding beliefs, when you had such a deep-rooted belief system that was contrary to what you desired in career and family?

**Wolfe**

While deepening the accessibilities of my own personal coaching skills I began experimenting with these tools in my career. I began *gathering evidence* that the skills I was sharpening could be effective for visionary leaders. It was another experiment for me to gather data that the tools I was learning were effective in many aspects of my life. I began trusting that I could use them to develop my own set of belief systems that would ultimately map out consistent values and accountabilities. As in my personal life, I began *discovering* my *"stuck places"* in my career and experimenting with alternative ways of assessing my current reality and solving problems, by creating forward actions and accountabilities. It became very exciting to see tools I applied personally to work effectively in business. I knew I was taking action that honored my set of belief systems as I began following through on family and business goals. I was definitely becoming a person who was a much better coach, manager, leader, mother and wife. I was elated to discover I could apply my authentic self to family and career and align one set of values to guide me through decision making in all areas of my life. It took determination and commitment to replace the limiting beliefs with positive expanding beliefs.

**Wright**

It seems you may have had many moments where you could have chosen actions that could either move you forward or ones that would hold you back from accessing successes. What significant choices did you make to empower yours to move forward?

**Wolfe**

While I was focused on desired actions, I began asking myself how satisfied I was with who I am and how I aligned my perception with what I desired most. Redefining what kinds of new things I wanted to emphasize more in my life and creating specific intentions became a necessary value to me. These defining beliefs were critical, truly the key to moving forward and out of the "stuck place" I felt I was in. For example, I held a belief system that life is something that should be attacked as hard and arduous. My life had always been controlled and self-contained with few moments of heart. I was ignoring what was extraordinary about myself; I was a person of heart and emotion. This specific belief created such a struggle for me in my career and parenting. To be a leader without allowing myself to communicate with emotion and heart was ignoring the core of who I was. Therefore, I could not have been giving my all. I knew that companies I supported were not receiving the full value of what I could provide in leadership effectiveness. Parenting by way of modeling without emotion was gut wrenching. I was making choices with defined belief systems and ignoring my desired ways of being. I decided to expand my defining belief systems to align with my desired future.

**Wright**

Defining beliefs seem to limit individuals in achieving an extraordinary life. Do you agree and how did this show up in your life?

**Wolfe**

Yes, defining beliefs can be negative, while trying to move out of a place you no longer desire. Defining beliefs can hold back an individual to imagine successes and achieving a desired outcome. There are fears and assumptions about yourself or outcomes that hold you back from a willingness to integrate new desires into your life. Everyone gets stuck sometime in his or her life. It is the desire to move beyond and the willingness to "flirt" with new possibilities that keeps each of us positive and motivated to achieve extraordinary lives.

I realized that the balance of the essentials of work, the gratitude of family and love for the gifts of life needed to be discovered. Powerful questions would become part of my desired future.

**Wright**

Did you ever feel discouraged in your process?

**Wolfe**

YES, YES. That is the best part of my experience! I no longer embraced discouragement as a roadblock. The experience of discouragement had become a signal for me that something is about to change and to wake up and pay attention to what is pulling at me.

I did struggle to learn to trust myself to make necessary transitions, to move when my intuition told me to move, and to find confidence in a plan. There were so many obstacles to overcome, most obstacles created by my inner critic. The inner critic holds belief systems that can hold one back from achieving a desired intention. I would find myself relying on old belief systems and would find comfort in my stuck places. I would revert back to asking myself non-action oriented questions. At the time, I could not see that simplifying my life was in my control. In hindsight, I could have made a change, in any area of my life, easily and without much commotion. I had to set the intention in order to influence the experience I desired. However, I held very tightly to a belief system that any action I would take would create such a void that it was easier to take no action. This belief system mirrored my experiences in youth.

As I look back and assess my journey, I find it remarkable that I found myself entering into my own coaching successes through my own classroom experiences with Learning Journeys International Center of Coaching. I was preparing for actions and successes that were led by my intention to live life with purpose, action and aligned values. By doing so I could feel confident that my future would not be limited by any change I would make.

In a moment of clarity I realized I owned my future with the skills I already possessed. I had the controls. I could control the chaos. I was currently leading groups of individuals to achieve growth and improvements each day in business. I could simply apply my newly refined coaching skills along with basic goals (intentions) to myself. Simple strategic leadership skills aligned for myself could be as effective for any desired change. It became clear to me that with a successful plan of committed intentions and self-accountabilities, I would create a structured life map for my future self. I would start to align my agreements and actions with my values. It was time to act on my own beliefs and to direct my own future. How else could I truly be a successful role model for my children? I needed to hold myself accountable for my desired outcomes. At last, I had defined what balance had meant to me!!!

This balance was what I desired and it honored my authentic self. To balance my life was not a sacrifice of one part of my life over another. It was not creating one set of values and beliefs for each aspect of my life. Balance was defined by aligning a set of values to be applied to all aspects of my life. I discovered I had been making my life difficult; I was segmenting and creating different rules for each role I took on in my day. Simply said, I had created a set of defined values and beliefs for each role I supported: business, friendships, motherhood, sisterhood and marriage.

**Wright**

Where in your process was a wake-up call to hold yourself accountable for your own desired happiness?

**Wolfe**

I believe it was in the process of integration, applying of all that I had learned through experimentation of my desired expanded beliefs. I knew it was time to take my life back and invoke my inner wisdom to define what I authentically desired from myself. I realized I wanted to orchestrate my change and not allow anyone else to direct my life without consulting with me. I had accomplished so much. It was very exciting to me to actually see that I was beginning to quiet my inner-critic. I was listening and responding to my highest calling. I become a warrior to myself. So many doors have opened with my integration, which brought me to your book, speaking and coaching.

The most exciting part of this whole discovery process is that I have healed so many areas in my life and let go of so many beliefs and values that no longer serve my higher purpose and were taking up too much space and energy needed to be used for forwarding actions.

**Wright**

So when and how did you achieve your priorities?

**Wolfe**

This was an amazing process for me. I know I started many years ago, before I knew I consciously was seeking a more secure model for my authentic self. This journey was done in several segments and sometimes with long gaps of time in between successes. However, when I began the work I described earlier, I knew I achieved my priorities when I committed to a very intense discovery process. The process conjured up ugly things I had put away hoping never to have to relive or redefine for my future. An unstable childhood, the long sickness and eventual death of my parents, secrets and unresolved conversations with family and friends were among some of them. I began looking at these areas of my life very differently. I discovered that something had changed in the way I held onto these experiences. But I was not sure exactly what the change was. I was searching and found an incredible reality of my current self. I had created my life within a set of values and belief systems I had fought against my entire life.

Before my committed way of being, I was repeating a cycle that was unfulfilling and not what I desired for my desired purpose in life. I found myself getting up each day and filling in the hours.

It was time to rearrange what I thought was most important and desired most from life. I had a belief system that self and family came behind everything else. This belief system is what I despised most about my values that I carried forward from my youth. I desired to honor the values of family and self. I knew it would be rewarding and my children would feel so confident towards their future self and the world. Additionally, I knew balance was needed when I recognized that I was missing out on the small giggles around the kitchen table with my family and my company was making changes without needing my advice.

Once I discovered that my current reality was a cluster of old belief systems that no longer served a positive purpose, I changed what was no longer desirable. Eventually, a big wake-up call was when I began getting physically sick, as I would continue to delay making my desired changes. I knew I needed to do something; I could no longer sustain my current reality. I couldn't change and/or stop being accountable to my family. This, of course, was the highest value in my life. I looked at my work environment; this I knew I could change and wanted to change. In fact, it was creating chaos in its current state, and I no longer was willing to negotiate my life around it. I knew that I was just in a survival mode with my current career, as it no longer was feeding me. It made sense at this time to take a break from that part of my life in order to achieve my desired sustainable future.

I wanted to be accountable for myself, and I needed to easily identify my beliefs in a committed contract with myself. I released an important part of my life that I believed defined me. It was a loss. Yet I have never looked back with regret, but only with optimism that I can recreate my life at any time. I am now prepared with life tools that will guide me toward answers and desired outcomes.

**Wright**

Your discovery that corporate is missing the opportunity to assist in supporting the necessary connection between career and family life has made a profound impact to your life's mission. Can you tell our readers more about this?

**Wolfe**

First of all, I find it interesting to know that there are so many women with similar experiences as myself. I am discovering that most women who start out in a productive career and add family, new friends and responsibilities of home feel the conflict for desired balance. Balance is difficult to achieve with many different roles to manage each day. It is necessary for women to take time to assess and align intentions of their complete self in comparison to their desired values and belief systems. An understood agreement must be struck with self, family and employer in order to feed your authentic self and desired values. The agreement must be made by a clear prioritization of values and belief systems aligned with each aspect of their life: one set of values and beliefs to lead each role.

I desire each woman to know her authentic self and to find power and satisfaction in the gift of achieving balance necessary to unleash endless possibilities in her life. We are all created for more than just instant and personal achievements in life. We are created for unlimited experiences and extraordinary happiness.

When I discuss that corporate business models are missing opportunities, I believe it to be a lack of prioritizing a value system that honors and understands the individual employees' values and defining belief systems. The necessity to understand what motivates employees, to contribute fully, is vital for companies. Companies should expect their leaders to source their employees' full potential through visionary coaching skills. Visionary coaching creates environments in which individuals are driven by goals of the company aligned by empowering their employees to align their desired outcomes within corporate goals. Happiness is more than just short-term gratification moments; it is more than just the ability to obtain wants in life. The company must create the environment that individuals' basic needs are met each day to enable employees to meet their fullest potential. A safe, creative and empowering work philosophy is the anchor that is needed for the employee to trust, and experience happiness.

I believe the most powerful companies want to find out what employees are longing for and help them see that there are areas in their lives that are close to what they desire. Companies must understand that they have responsibility to champion powerful living with their employees and ensure that the employees' desired outcomes are aligned with the company's vision/goal. If a company is not aware and does not align with the employees' desires, they will not meet their own goals. Part of this formula is clarifying the various elements the employee has provided to the coach who must give feedback to the employer in a simple manner. Clarifying the objectives and desired outcome of the employee serves the company to understand, as well as put the pieces together for the purpose of meeting both employee and company's desired outcome. I believe that companies who are open to setting aside time for their employees to experiment and trust in their employees to meet their personal needs will be successful

It is vital that a company understands their employees' motivational styles as it feeds the successes of the employee, creating a solid, successful relationship. However, in striving for this relationship, it is vital for the company to understand where each employee is right now. The employee may be between what she has learned up to this point and how her motivation has evolved to shape who she is and how she plays a role inside the company. Listening to feedback from employees is perhaps the most critical skill of an extraordinary leader/coach. Listening sets into action a freeing of all other distractions of the mind and requires purposeful attentiveness to the employees' current reality of what they feel is so.

Each employee has distinct responsibilities that contribute towards meeting the companies' goals. I have learned to look at achieving these goals with a beginner's mind, setting aside preconceived notions of successes or failures. I have personally experienced and witnessed the successes when a business group is allowed to freely brainstorm, exploring new possibilities, while using my experience of coaching techniques to move the group forward. My desired outcome when coaching is to allow teams to put their own personal attitudes and expression into the results. This is a key element I see that is missing.

A simple model is used in coaching and it can be applied in any business model. First, the leader/coach must *create a ritual* with their teams by clearing and setting standards. Creating a diverse team to tackle a deliverable can do this, as well as creating rules within the team, timelines and basic business etiquette rules. Layering the next level of coaching enables the team to move into ***Discovery**, which* can be brainstorming in a free form and safe environment about what is the current reality here and now. What is the current reality? This is where the coaching process begins in transformation of the current reality to set intentions/goals of a desired outcome. All along, the coach/manager is *benchmarking and giving acknowledgement* to team members for their valued beliefs and contributions. Lastly, *action* is desired. Applying what has been learned from the discovery, transformation can then be formulated into an action plan and integrated into company for actions. This simple model, executed and led by a well-trained visionary coach, is effective and open to possibilities.

Simple coaching tools to be used consistently to assess individual's performance, desires and intentions would position a company to know easily and quickly which teams and individuals to utilize in the many areas of their business model. In this way, they are understanding and effectively using their human assets. Aligning the individuals' intentions with the company's goals and needs is critical. I believe this to be the primary responsibility of the leaders in the organizations.

I believe that companies who deliver results by applying successful coaching models in business/life is where the relationship between coach and individual shapes the direction of the relationship and desired outcomes. Many possibilities emerge when leaders/coaches apply coaching process tools, techniques and methodologies. The exciting part of my experience is that each person possesses the inner wisdom of coaching and mentoring by simply taking time to understand what the desired outcome is and allowing each person to explore experiments. Visionary leaders/coaches free their teams from the prejudices of the past and open their team's minds to new possibilities.

Understanding clients, employees, and companies' motivating desires is vital to the outcome that a visionary leader desires. One key in the process is to honor, wherever the individuals are at the present time, and explore their current realities. As a coach/leader, listening to employees' responses provides a bridge into how to shape the action needed to achieve the intended goals. Listening is the most critical skill of a coach/leader. However, key to the success of coaching is listening without an agenda and accepting what is being conveyed as their reality. Successful leadership is asking powerful questions at the appropriate times so that the individual can reflect and arrive at her own answers.

The best tip I received from my mentor in coaching was to ask questions that will result in reflection. Think of questions that are oriented toward solutions, assume resources are available, and see situations as lessons to be learned. I believe if leaders adopted these simple philosophies, they would find themselves surrounded by happy individuals who were more productive than they could imagine. First and foremost, laugh with your teams. Find joy in the small successes and benchmark the successes through celebration. Furthermore, leaders/coach should not be afraid to get personal with their employees.

**Wright**

Who are the individuals that are seeking your services? Are there commonalities to their backgrounds or professional achievements or anything that strikes you as watch signals?

**Wolfe**

A coaching relationship moves the individual to desired goals. An individual can expect that a coaching relationship will empower them to move forward to a desired outcome that they may not have been able to see as possible by themselves.

Here are a few examples of people whom I can build a relationship with: Companies that cannot consistently meet production requirements and have high employee churn; and companies with increased employee sicknesses and lack of employee commitments. Individuals who are seeking a change but do not know where to start will benefit from a coaching relationship as well.

**Wright**

Where do you start with executives and leaders to realign their predetermined values, goals, and/or beliefs?

**Wolfe**

Actually there are so many places to start. I allow the individual to lead in identifying her individual starting place. Together, we explore the current reality ("Where do you want to go from here?" "What would it look like if you could make the change?"). I immediately establish an agreement that is based on trust and commitment between us. I commit to the following: being present, being honorable and being respectful of what is being created. I commit to always speak the truth while listening from that place of curiosity. A successful coaching relationship will help the individual to see that there are areas in her life that are close to what she dreams about. I want those individuals to begin to look for evidence in their life that tells them they can have what they desire in life.

I spend much time in inquiry processes and tools. Some may call it reflection, prayer, or quiet time. In a coaching relationship, inquiry is a process where questions are designed to provoke multiple perspectives, exploration of options, introspection and reflection. I ask the individuals to think about the questions for some time. I want them to take the time to notice the feelings and emotions and look at various perspectives. These inquiries lead themselves to know what needs to be changed and prioritize these changes and be aware of the effects the changes will have on their lives.

I listen to conversations, and I am honored to be a part of their process. I believe people's stories unlock so many possibilities, and stories are waiting to be told to enable the unlocking of desired futures.

**Wright**

How do you determine where a person is today and where they would like to be tomorrow?

**Wolfe**

Where a person is today is just where they are. Their current reality is where we start. We determine together what our steps are to be by setting new intentions and asking powerful questions of ourselves. I ask them to set an intention on when they will take the action. They define what the evidence will look like, or how it will show up in their lives today, so that we both know that it was accomplished. Holding the individuals accountable for their own actions empowers them to trust themselves. They may be short-term intentions, as building blocks to the larger desired change and/or transition. But, through personally defining where they would like to be tomorrow by asking the powerful question: "Who are you today?" is a gift to themselves to create the ability to self-coach through desired changes and/or transitions. I desire that each person knows that desired changes can occur today and that we each hold the truths within ourselves. It is through a successful coaching relationship that individuals can get assistance to begin their journeys.

**Wright**

So if I wanted to get the most from my employees that I have invested both time and experience in, how do I keep my corporation from neglecting the balance of home and work?

**Wolfe**

I would have the company define their current reality of the situation. This is a great way to understand where the commonalities are and where the realities are dissimilar in a company setting. In a sense, what is being created is a clearing, setting aside anything that they need to before starting the process defines the desired changes. Companies need to develop an environment where the individuals are led in self-sustained frameworks to achieve the individual and company goals. Establishing agreements between company and employees is the foundation of a successful working environment. Setting standards that include the values of the company allows employees to be encouraged to access their own experience and knowledge, which enables them to create more positive circumstances within their business. With a foundation based on aligned values, companies can set accountabilities and make requests of the employees. Additionally, leaders who enable individuals to experiment with ideas create additional ways to gather evidence and feedback to the company. Progress stops being achieved when individuals and the company are not integrated with a clean, congruent vision and value system. When companies do not empower their employees to put their own personal beliefs and experience into the workplace, companies may not experience a sustained employee base and predictable production.

Understanding and aligning intentions with employees influence their experiences and they begin to focus their attention on what is created together as "our" intentions. The intention is designed to call forth the attention to shape the outcomes. The intention is not the goal or result. The intention is allowing the possibilities (brainstorming) that are designed to guide the action to the desired results. I have failed in the past when I have not felt safe in my environment to be myself or when my values and beliefs were not recognized or valued. I was not able to balance the priorities of my life. Extra energy and time was spent in the business day chasing intentions that did not have a desired outcome. When my creative expression became stifled, my leadership competencies did not show up with ease in any areas of my life.

**Wright**

What is the upside of following your lead? And then what is the downside of not following your lead?

**Wolfe**

Really the upside is that the impact we can each make to the world begins right in the place that we are all at. When we set intentions we honor our authentic selves and our inner wisdoms. By honoring these aspects of ourselves, we each can contribute without limit to the world. In addition, our competencies show up with ease, conscious of them or not. We experience energy set into motion that will see no limits. We each have the ability to transform many times in our lives. We should all be delighted in change and others' desire for change. The environment must be created to foster transformation. Additional upside is that we will continue to have confidence in our outcomes. We will continue to have positive results, and we will continue to get feedback and wisdom from others and ourselves.

**Wright**

It's strange that you haven't mentioned in that question anything about happiness.

**Wolfe**

I haven't? I believe the desire for any change is the pursuit of happiness. Balance is just another way we capture the essence of happiness. I have a mission in my life that happiness just.... happens. The relationships that I choose to build honor the essence of who I am and the values I believe in. When individuals follow their inner wisdoms, it does something. It creates happiness and it creates self-fulfillment. I think the desire for it is innate in each of us. I believe happiness allows you to extend the learning and forward the action, and that's the opportunity that a business should feel honored to extend to their employees, as well as friend to friend.

**Wright**

So let me ask this question. Since the title of this book is *Remarkable Women*, what defines remarkable women to you?

**Wolfe**

I think a remarkable woman has an infinite amount of descriptions. My mother was remarkable as are her children, my siblings. I am grateful for the strength of the women in my life and I am always drawn to women who want more than they have achieved today.

Remarkable women understand their worth and they value themselves and others. Remarkable women listen to each other; they have extraordinary conversations that enable understanding. They know they're part of a whole, and they work as part of a whole. Remarkable women dream high dreams and they have extraordinary wishes. Their achievements are very action oriented, and they move themselves and others forward. They pay attention to what has heart and meaning. And I think above all, remarkable women have stories and they share those stories. They share them because they know stories are the essence of who they are and it depicts their contribution to the world. Remarkable women ask powerful questions. Remarkable women support each other and they encourage others to achieve their own desires.

**Wright**

One of the great things about having the job that I have is that I get to talk to famous people all the time and get to interview folks of all walks of life. And it's odd how the larger percentage of them, not all, but the larger percentage of them when I ask the question about who influenced you the most, they talk about their mothers. And they talk about them as if they were sitting in the seat next to them. In some cases they have died years and years before, and that the remarkable qualities still...you know still live on. I know in my case, my mother, I think, was a remarkable woman, and all three of her children also went kind of the top of everything they did. I mean even if they were going to go dig a hole, it was the deepest hole, the one that had the sharpest corners. In almost everything that all three of her children did or have done, they did it well and were really beacons in the industries that they chose. And so that goes on and on and on. It sounds like that's what your mother did for you and it sounds like that's what you're doing for your children.

**Wolfe**

Oh yes. I believe the essence of a remarkable woman is a product of many generations of women before them that passed on their inner wisdom. I can remember my mother talking about my grandmother and great aunts. I never really knew them, but I could relay the stories as if I had lived the stories, myself. The essence of these women that my mother admired was in each of her stories. I am positive that when I tell my stories to my children of their grandmother, I will relay the essence of a remarkable woman. I like to think that as the color of our eyes is inherited, so is our strength as a woman.

**Wright**

I think you're on to something with that inheritance thing. My mother was 84 when she died, so I got to keep her for a long, long time. But throughout my entire life she spoke of her mother in such great and glowing words. Even though her mother died when she was 13, she spent the rest of her life talking about how her mother had influenced her and how strong she was. Well, this has certainly been a great conversation, and I really appreciate all this time you've taken to answer these questions. I have learned a lot and I'm sure our readers will. I just appreciate you taking this much time with me.

**Wolfe**

Oh, it's been a pleasure. Thank you very much for having me and including me in this remarkable book.

**Wright**

Today we have been talking to Colleen Cassidy Wolfe. Colleen provides coaching to executives, managers, and entrepreneurs that unlock and access underlying beliefs and attitudes to enable a new sustained value, goal, and/or belief. Colleen, thank you so much for being with us today on *Remarkable Women.*

## About The Author

Colleen is the mother of three children, wife, active community leader, and business executive. Her last business assignment was as vice president of sales operations. Colleen has led many multi-faceted organizations while managing a family and home. She has discovered the key in balancing home and work. Not only has she discovered the balance between home and work, she has sensed this unique balance missing in many Corporations of today. Through coaching and investing in individuals, she assists in creating lasting life changes that align individuals' desires, values and goals. She leads individuals through self discovery, empowering beliefs that will enable them to rewrite the software of their minds in order to change the maps of their future. Through her own personal discoveries and subsequent successes, Colleen has developed a coaching philosophy that assists individuals striving for their desired balance. She believes that the best way to predict a desired outcome is to provoke self discovery. Colleen provides leadership and coaching to executives, managers, and entrepreneurs, helping them unlock and access underlying beliefs and attitudes to enable sustained desires, values and goals.

**Colleen Cassidy-Wolfe**

Phone: 952-250-6669

Email: colleenwolfe@mn.rr.com

# Chapter Twenty-Two

## DEVONA E. G. WILLIAMS, PH.D.

### THE INTERVIEW

**David E. Wright (Wright)**

Today we are talking to Devona Williams. Devona has always been a person with multiple interests and talents and who pursued a career path that reflects her uniqueness. Highlights of her public career include her appointment as Presidential Management Intern in the Reagan administration and as a Legislative Fellow in the Delaware House of Representatives. With an eye to business as a young child, she found her way clear to start her own successful full time consulting and training business in 1993, Goeins Williams Associates, Inc., by taking advantage of a corporate downsizing opportunity from the DuPont Corporation. Devona has had her equal share of obstacles in her nearly 30-year career and personal challenges that she has overcome including sexual assault she endured during her college days and a divorce. For most people, these obstacles and challenges would have ended a career and certainly a business, but Devona has a unique philosophy, strength, and faith that have allowed her to persevere and continue to prosper and grow. As president and CEO of the company she founded, Goeins-Williams Associates, Inc., Devona has contributed her talents to helping more than 20,000 individuals in a myriad of organizations improve performance and increase effectiveness. Devona, welcome to *Remarkable Women*!

**Devona Williams (Williams)**

Thank you.

**Wright**

So, how did your childhood and your upbringing prepare you for success in life?

**Williams**

I was blessed with two parents who loved me and who were strong influences with a clear set of values and standards. My mother was the greatest influence in my life. I grew up in Philadelphia, Pennsylvania, during the 1950's and 1960s, the fourth of five children. Although I was the fourth child, I was the middle child of the last three children because there was a nine-year gap between the second and third child. So I functioned like a classic "middle child." My parents nurtured and supported my independent, creative and adventurous nature and I was allowed to pursue many different hobbies and interests. I liked art and participated in the Saturday Art Leagues from the time I was in the fourth grade until I graduated high school. I liked music and dance and took lessons in organ, classical piano and voice. I won a scholarship to the Germantown Settlement Music School for piano. I learned to sew and knit. I attended Sunday school and participated regularly in church activities. My two older siblings played a major role in my upbringing. My brother, the oldest, encouraged me in science and mathematics and nurtured my curiosity. He also encouraged and supported my budding entrepreneurial interests. My oldest sister was a mentor and role model who encouraged me academically. She blazed the trail by attending a highly touted school for girls—the Philadelphia High School for Girls and earned her Master's Degree at age 24. Because of her I enrolled in that same high school which provided a challenging academic structure and enhanced my personal development. I was raised in an area of Philadelphia called Mount Airy, which was at that time one of the first areas in the City of Philadelphia to be racially integrated. As an African-American, growing up at that time—we were colored and then black—and I never really experienced open or overt racial conflicts but more subtle forms of exclusion. The way my parents handled racial animosity contributed a great deal to how

I dealt with barriers and obstacles during various periods throughout my life. We never openly acknowledged racial discrimination in our family and when instances did occur that might seem like they could be attributed to prejudice, I was taught that it was never my fault and it was because of the ignorance of other people. My mother was orphaned as a young child and assumed the responsibility of raising her younger siblings and supporting herself and those siblings as a teenager. As children, we knew about our mother's struggles and were taught to be appreciative and thankful for life's blessings and to make the best of whatever hand life dealt. My mother was a superb homemaker who had strength and courage. She was a graceful and elegant lady who was an active learner. My father was the leader of our household and always worked three jobs to more adequately provide for our family. He worked a combination of entrepreneurial jobs, like insurance sales, to security and driving a school bus. My dad had several businesses and part time ventures that I was included in, such as a water ice truck, which he operated with a partner. At the age of eight, I was my dad's helper on the truck, allowed to scoop water ice and serve pretzels with mustard to eager children, collect their sticky coins and put it in the change belt I wore with pride! I was fortunate to learn about hard work, responsibility, business, and respect at a young age.

**Wright**

So how did your academic experience contribute to your success?

**Williams**

The Philadelphia High School for Girls was an academically accelerated school with high standards. This all girls school with selective admission citywide gave me the unique opportunity to excel in and exhibit leadership skills in athletics, student government, the arts and academics in a multicultural environment. I was a solid B student throughout high school. I took advantage of the three academic shift schedules and elected to take extra majors, including art and four years of German. The all girls' environment encouraged me to step out and take risks and challenges academically, creatively and socially. I was part of the first group of young women leaders to ask to share academic equity with our partner school, the all boys academic equivalent, Central High School, located just across the street. I was a hard worker and also worked part time throughout my high school years to pay for my personal needs and save for college. I went out for gymnastics, varsity cheerleading, dance and a host of other sports. I was captain of our varsity cheerleading and gymnastics team and lettered in both these sports. I was a part of the first girls cheerleading squad to cheerlead at Central High School for Boys. In high school, I learned about leadership and taking risks in uncharted waters, and balancing priorities. Success was gained by planning, taking calculated risks and performance.

I applied to eleven colleges around the country and selected the University of Delaware, in Newark, Delaware, taking advantage of a full academic scholarship for my first year. It was also a chance to be nearby home and my high school sweetheart who received a Presidential appointment to the US Naval Academy in Annapolis. And that's what brought me to the State of Delaware! I took my independent spirit, entrepreneurial nature, attitude toward hard work and confidence into my college career. My financial resources for college were almost completely limited to my academic scholarship, so I was a working student throughout my college days. Like my father, I usually worked two or three part time jobs, from washing dishes in the dining hall, to teaching art, music and cheerleading classes with the City's recreation program, and working in a dress shop at a nearby mall. I progressed in food service and recreation programs. I became the youngest and first full time student manager to work for the University Department of Food Service. By my junior year, I worked 30 hours a week as the weekend dining hall, coffee house and building manager. The City of Newark, offered me choice assignments and by the time I graduated, I was directing several summer programs—these jobs and relationships lasted nearly 10 years beyond college. I was a 17-year-old college freshman and majored in commercial art initially. With the financial demands of this major, even with my scholarship, I became an art education major my sophomore year. I married at the age of 19 during winter break of my junior year to a college boyfriend, not my high school sweetheart—more about that later. In many ways, this helped to relieve some of the financial pressures of college expenses. I was able to declare myself as an independent student and became in-state student as a result. I became eligible for academic scholarships that were not previously available because of my sound academic performance and residency status. I graduated with a degree in art education, certified to teach art in grades Kindergarten through twelfth grade. But I found that when I graduated, a lot of the teaching positions that were previously available were just simply not there. In 1976 when I graduated,

Delaware's northern school districts were undergoing court ordered racial desegregation, and teaching jobs were not plentiful, particularly for people who were teaching minor subjects. Because I was a working student with four years of solid employment experience while in undergraduate school, I had no trouble being offered employment upon graduation. I was offered a full time food service management position at the University of Delaware and also a position with New Castle County's recreation programs administering a bicentennial program celebrating America's 200 years. I decided to move into a government career, taking my first professional position with the New Castle County Department of Parks and Recreation. Government work, service to others, entrepreneurial pursuits and business would become the basis for my career path and ultimately my business and the work that I perform today. I was excited about working in government and I was intrigued by planning, budgeting and program administration.

After my second position, I knew that it was time to pursue advanced education. I was selected as a New Castle County Fellow to attend a masters degree program; this fellowship enabled me to complete a master's in public administration at the University of Delaware on a stipend for two years. I completed that program and landed a position as an Executive Director of a new nonprofit housing corporation, which led to many other successes. In only a few short years, I was appointed a Presidential Management Intern in the Reagan Administration in Washington, DC. I worked in a number of key assignments in several Federal agencies. One assignment in particular, exposed me to the world of management consulting— and I knew I had found my next career. I made a decision, while in Washington, DC that I would need to continue on to earn further education to fulfill my career ambitions. Once back in Delaware, I applied to the doctoral program in urban affairs and public policy at the University of Delaware. Once again, I was honored to receive full fellowships, (including a Legislative Fellowship to Delaware's House of Representatives) and stipends to complete my doctorate over a six year period! I have been truly blessed to have such stellar academic opportunities and professors/mentors who challenged and supported me. I have maintained my affiliation with the University by serving as an adjunct faculty member, mentoring other students and volunteering.

**Wright**

So what are some of the positive life changing experiences that you've had that you know are responsible for who you are today?

**Williams**

I've been fortunate to have been exposed to successful entrepreneurs as a young child through family members, my father's interests, attitudes towards life from my mother (she believed the world was our oyster and we could do anything we put our minds to), and through mentors that I've had throughout my life. In high school I had a teacher who made a difference in my life. One teacher encouraged me in my art talent and helped me understand that being able to express oneself creatively was just as important as academic success. Her sponsorship led to my first successful professional art experience. I was hired to paint a portrait for a school. I had a college professor and mentor during my undergraduate career who was someone I wanted to emulate professionally and personally. This professor was the only black female Ph.D. on faculty at the University of Delaware. Attractive and articulate, she supported my choice as an art education major and encouraged me to complete the program that I was enrolled in. She also, however, showed me that there were numerous options, academically and professionally, that I had the intelligence and wherewithal to pursue. I learned from her that I should seek excellence and initiate change when it makes sense. I had a business mentor from my days with the DuPont Corporation — he is the person who actually recruited me to work for DuPont, who was just a wonderful mentor who taught me the "corporate ropes" and made sure I had opportunities for assignments that would showcase my talents. He always provided open and honest feedback that gave me what I needed to make the necessary changes to develop professionally and personally. I credit him with helping me develop corporate savvy and confidence to succeed in that system. DuPont recruited me just before I completed my dissertation work for my doctorate. He gave me the support to complete the doctorate while working in a new, full time executive position in corporate life while balancing motherhood and duties as a wife. He took the time to get to know my family and provided the needed moral support when my mother died. He shared his investment strategies with me, and wisely counseled me by stating, "The person who has financial resources always has options." And now I have a mentor who was a client through my business, a client friend turned mentor, and she's now a very active part of my life. I think having people in your life at different times allows you to grow and be made aware of the things that can challenge you as well as point out things that you need to do to become a better person. When I think I of the positive changes in my life, a mentor was very influential in helping me to process these changes and see problems as opportunities.

**Wright**

So what personal tragedies have you had to overcome and how have the experiences helped you in your life?

**Williams**

As I mentioned earlier, my boyfriend from high school attended the US Naval Academy while I was a coed at the University of Delaware. I did not get to visit him often, but when I did it was for very special occasions. Weekend car pooling trips were carefully planned and coordinated with other campus coeds who also had Midshipmen boyfriends. At that time, visiting conditions were quite restrictive for girlfriends who were required to stay in chaperoned drag houses that were prearranged by the plebes (Midshipmen freshmen). On one particular homecoming weekend during my freshman year, a planned weekend, there were no rooms available as a result of some kind of mix up with the arrangements made by my boyfriend. In the time that we had before curfew, we looked for other rooms where I could stay. We were not able to find a room before my boyfriend's curfew. Reluctantly, we decided that I would take a cab to a nearby motel that did have rooms available. The cab driver drove me to the motel on the edge on town and during the ride, he commented about the rarity of black Midshipmen and naval officers. He inquired about my status and I naively shared that I was a coed at the University of Delaware with aspirations of someday marrying my Midshipman boyfriend who I adored. I must have struck a nerve with the cab driver that might have become jealous or envious. After dropping me off to my motel, he doubled back to my motel room, and knocked at the door under the pretext that I left a bag. With the door cracked and the chain on, he forcibly pushed his way into my room. I had just turned 18 years old and I was still a virgin. My boyfriend whom I loved dearly had never been intimate with me. I wanted to be a virgin when we married. The cab driver violently attached me, and during our struggle he yelled racial and sexual obscenities, letting me know that he intended to rape me. He punched me in my eye and nearly knocked me unconscious. Then he ripped off my underwear, and discovered I was on my period. At this point, I called out to God to intervene because I thought he was going to kill me. I got a burst of strength and was able to hit him in the head with a lamp. I scratched his face, ripping skin off with my long nails and drew blood. He got up in a rage and cursed me as he ran from the room. He did not rape me, but he attempted to. I was able to get away, locked my door, became hysterical and found myself wandering the street to find another place to stay. I could not contact my boyfriend or the other girls in the drag houses. It never occurred to me to call my parents. I was picked up by a police cruiser who took me to the police station where I spent the night. The unsympathetic police officers chastised me for traveling alone and told me that I should expect what happened to me because I was attractive and young. I was able to describe my attacker and provide the cab number, but the police refused to look for the assailant or allow me to press charges because of my age. They informed me that unless I contacted my parents they would not take any action. Because of the police officers' initial comments, I blamed myself and I was too ashamed to tell my parents. I never told them! This was 1974, and even now it's hard for me to talk about. In the morning, the police dropped me off at the Naval Academy where I met my boyfriend in our previously planned meeting spot. When he saw me he could tell by my face that something terrible had happened. I burst into tears and tried to explain what happened. We eventually found a drag house that belonged to a couple who allowed us to be together in one of the rooms un-chaperoned where we had a chance to talk and cry. He blamed himself for over 30 years.

When I went back to campus I never revealed to anyone what had happened to me. I never revealed it to my parents or my friends. But I was deeply ashamed and somehow I internalized what had occurred. Subsequent to that life changing event, perhaps six or eight months later I was on a college trip to get my mind off of things and to try and mentally escape what had happened. The adult chaperone coerced and locked me in a room, turned up the television and raped me. He told me that no one would hear my screams, even though the other students were sitting outside the door and he dared me to tell. He said that he would deny that it ever happened. I now understand that because of the sexual assault that occurred only a short time before, that contributed to my silence. I never told. I never told. I was never able to tell. I believed I was somehow a person that was destined to be picked for sexual abuse, that I must have looked like someone who deserved this kind of treatment. This led to a sort of perpetual depression. I thought about quitting college. I went home frequently to Philadelphia, to be near my family, but I was unable to tell my mother or my sisters about the assault and now the rape. I was so ashamed! My grades suffered and I thought of transferring schools, I continued to work. I could not face my Annapolis boyfriend and tell him what had happened for the second time. I blamed myself. I did not get the kind of help that people have available to them today, and I had to work through it on my own. I felt that with the kind of upbringing that I had that saying that I was a victim of sexual assault and then rape, to my parents, would never be acceptable. It took a whole lot of inner strength to be able to overcome these personal tragedies. I lost my virginity, my dignity and the love of my life because I could not face him. I was a working student throughout my college years. I had to continue to work and deal with the shame and anguish privately and not being able to tell my parents. It was largely because of what the police had said to me initially that I internalized the worst of this experience. I blamed myself for years; inwardly I felt it was something about me that attracted these men, and I had brought this on. I continued to battle a belief that even as some wonderful things happened to me somehow I wasn't deserving. I've learned, of course, that it wasn't me and that some people are just bad people. And when bad things happen to good people, everyone's not always in a position where they are able to overcome. Most draw upon inner strength and continue to persevere. What I learned in my college years I was able to use over and over again. If I could get through that, I could get through a lot of other tough challenges and obstacles. I learned valuable lessons that I have used throughout my life such as the importance of self-forgiveness, faith and the pursuit of excellence. And it's really only in recent years that I've been able to fully deal with the events of those times and how those experiences were manifested in other relationships.

**Wright**

Goodness! What do you consider your greatest accomplishments?

**Williams**

Well, I would say first and foremost motherhood. I have one son whose family I am very proud of. I'm now a new grandmother of twin boys. I believe I raised a very good child who is now contributing to society as a third grade teacher, coach and role model. He's independent, a loving, responsible person and a great family guy. I'm also very proud of the fact of what I've been able to accomplish in my own life coming from fairly modest home and being able to achieve in the way I have academically, and in my career. I am proud of my business and the opportunities I've had to help so many other people through what I've learned. If I can think of a theme song, what comes to mind is a Frank Sinatra song, "I did it my way." That was also one of my mom's favorite songs. With God's blessings and the support I've had from others and through the use of my God given talents and strengths, I have forged a successful career, creating a business niche for myself where I am able to help and support other people in an effective way.

**Wright**

So being a young mother, balancing career and family in the 1970s, you must have learned some real lessons.

**Williams**

Well, sure. I got married at 19 to my best friend in college, who was there for me after those events we discussed earlier. At the time I thought I was pretty young, but I was mature for my age. My financial circumstances and my view of the world contributed to my decision to marry so young. With what had happened to me I thought, 'Well, you know this is safe. I can do this.' And so I got married young. I found out that I was pregnant a month before my college graduation and I became a new mother at the age of 21. I soon discovered that in order to accomplish the things that I wanted for my family, and ultimately myself, a team effort was going to be required. I had to be a part of a working team, and that was not really the picture of what I had in mind before I got married. You see I grew up in a home where my mother was a homemaker and that was her career. By the age of 24, I had been married 5 years; we owned a home and two cars, and my spouse was working on his Master's degree. I was the director of a senior citizen program that was part of county government and I supervised a staff of five people. Because I grew up watching my dad work three jobs, I knew how to work hard. I worked hard in high school and college and I was also a multi-tasker. Not only was I a hard worker, I looked for ways to grow career wise, took on extra course work, went back to school, but also did all those things required to make a nice home. I believe I was a very good wife and mother. I was frugal, maintained and managed the home, was involved with my son throughout his childhood and in all aspects of his life. It was a difficult balancing act because I was living a life when expectations were changing about the roles of men and professional working women. It was an era before microwaves and adequate child day care, cell phones or flex time at work. Many employers were intolerant of working women. I was laid off from a professional job when I was eight months pregnant because some of the elderly people in the building where I worked thought I looked disgusting to be that far along in my pregnancy and working. At the same time, it was hard to get unemployment because I 'wasn't able to work'. Once I had my baby and I began to interview for jobs, I was told in one interview by the man that interviewed me, that mothers who worked with infants were terrible people. Although he felt I was the most qualified person for the job, he would offer it to a man who was a Viet Nam veteran who he felt needed a job to take care of his family. The first few years I worked with a small child were the most challenging because there were no allowances for children being sick or even being late for work because of family issues. When my son was hospitalized as a baby my female boss, who believed that I should not work with a young child, chastised me. She docked me routinely for being less than five minutes late to work. Another time, when my son was knocked unconscious while participating in a school sports activity, my female boss refused to give me time off to go to the hospital. I should have quit. Throughout my marriage, my child and family always came first. I genuinely believed that most of my career changes and continued education-were for the betterment of my family.

**Wright**

Oh, yeah.

**Williams**

To hear that, it reminds me a little of "caveman days," but I think I did a good job balancing family and work responsibilities. One of the things I definitely remember is that in the '80s it was the era of the superwoman. You wanted to have this beautiful home and try to have a great career, and try to be a good wife. And what I've learned is you really can't do all of it well. You can't do it all well without some sacrifice and you never want to sacrifice your children. And in my case, we chose and I chose, because I felt I did have a choice, that I would not have more than one child. And that way I felt able to pursue academic and career goals without seriously affecting all of the responsibilities that I had or would have in my home. But it was tough because I think for at least in my situation, the majority of the household duties, including the financial management and childcare responsibilities, still fell on my shoulders. Balancing work and family—yes, it can be done. Here are the lessons I've learned about balancing work and family. Everybody in the family has to multitask and I think you have to set priorities in a family about what is going to be most important, and if it's time, then it's time spending with each other and having family dinners and doing those things where the children of the home are nurtured. And I think my former spouse and I did a good job in nurturing our only son. But that's what I would say is the most important. We did not do as good a job nurturing each other. My spouse was often in competition with my career and me. I was the one who usually compromised my career to his benefit and for what I thought benefited the family as a whole. I tell younger women now who ask me, "Well, how did you do it?" I tell them, "Well, you have to decide up front. Maybe there are some things that you can do before you get married and have children. And maybe there are other things once you decide to have a family and a household that you just say, 'I don't have to do all these things.' Or, 'I don't have to hold myself to this really high standard as far as keeping my home as neat as a pin.'" There are shared responsibilities about housework and chores and financial management of the home that spouses share equally and it has to be agreed to before getting married. Also children should have a contributing role in the family, chores and responsibilities. When the home doesn't function right, people have resentments. So that's some of what I have learned from that era.

**Wright**

It's interesting that your marriage lasted for 27 years. So you know in this day and time, that's a long, long time, and what impact has your divorce made on your career?

**Williams**

The divorce has had an impact on my entire life, not just my career and it is truly difficult to separate the two. What I have learned is that when people go through divorce, the marriage is over long before a divorce. So it's the two years, three, four years before that, where there was impact to my life and now things are good. So the impact is less severe now. I have found that the divorce has had an impact on almost all of my family and close relationships in ways that

I could have never predicted; it has changed my perspective on life, faith and business. I never planned for divorce and I had no frame of reference as to what I should have expected. I am happier as a person now, and much more ambitious in my business. I am able to be a risk taker in my business, which I was precluded from doing earlier with my more conservative former spouse. During the period of separation and divorce, I launched our first company product, and expanded my business significantly to the western region of the US. Personally speaking, I am more realistic in my expectations of other people, probably less judgmental and certainly more compassionate and empathetic. I'm one of those individuals that are able to work even harder through personal tragedy. I learned how to do that as a result of my ordeal during my college years. I have endured the death of both parents. While going through my divorce and dispute over our financial estate, my only brother died under somewhat controversial circumstances and I was the one who carried out his last wishes. What you learn is that you can work through these challenges that are indeed tragedies; tragedy is a part of the human existence. Because I had been through those experiences that I could work through and continue to work through my divorce during the period of my marital separation. I had to work very hard at not blaming myself, but marriages do break up and they break up for a number of reasons.

**Wright**

I can imagine.

**Williams**

My attitude has been impacted by the divorce. I feel good about myself and I'm not angry with my former spouse. I'm just disappointed that we were not able to work through it. My message to other women having gone through it is that it doesn't mean that you're a bad person or the other person is a bad person. It just means that the relationship didn't work. It's no longer meeting the needs of the couple and the people who are involved in it. Everyone has perhaps five or six core needs that if they are not met, make a marital relationship extremely difficult.

**Wright**

So through all of your accomplishments and all your tragedies, what can other women learn from you?

**Williams**

I think that number one is the ability to persevere. No matter what you have to be able to move forward. Ideally, it's more helpful if you can move forward in a positive way and continue to do things that help you get through those down times. I'm the type of individual who is able to continue to be productive in spite of things that have gone wrong. I find meaning in my work when I am able to help others and have faith. I have faith in God. I have the belief that I know that I can persevere, that I have strength and courage. I can overcome, and that my attitude really did determine how I got through it. The experience of having gone through other days of sorrow and getting through them is a frame of reference. Power comes from getting through it and coming out victorious. I've had other times when things weren't ideal and I've been able to persevere, by having a plan, and focusing on where I'm going, not where I've been, enabling me to move forward. And that would be my message for others that regardless of those challenges, life's challenges, you can move ahead and be productive and still be successful. Some of the biggest impacts in my business since going through my divorce are that I have no ceilings, imagined or actual, of what I can do. I have expanded the business to Colorado from Delaware. I've added two new products, the first products that we've sponsored, created, and developed on our own, and done other things in the business that I didn't do during the time that I was married because I just didn't think I could do them. So in some ways, having something bad happen is a way to rethink and reshape and reorient oneself into saying, "Well, okay. What can I do now to make things better for myself? And how do I keep moving ahead?"

**Wright**

You said something about faith giving you the impetus to get through all of the trials that you've had. During your marriage, was...did you have shared faith?

**Williams**

No, we didn't. We were on two different tracks. We never shared each other's faiths. We were in the same basic value system, but we never...we were not strong believers together. We did not share our faith together. And I think that was a significant deficiency of our marriage when I look back on it. I have become more committed in practicing my faith and openly acknowledging it. I have been reacquainted with my boyfriend from high school who was the same person I spoke of that was at the Naval Academy. We were fortunate enough to be reunited in this last year. I've learned that sometimes by exercising your faith in God a lot of things can happen. I've spent a whole lot of time soul searching in the last couple of years, and by activating my faith—maybe that's a good word, a way to describe it—I've found that there's tremendous power in that, *tremendous* power in that. But I also believe and know for a fact that in times where I have had these personal challenges that God has been on my side. So I was always a believer. It was just in my first marriage we didn't...I don't think we shared it. We never really openly communicated and talked about our shared faith the way we should have. And I think that's important in anything that I do going forward. A few years ago, I had major surgery, having a hysterectomy and a major fibroid removed the size of a large pumpkin. I nearly lost my life and at one point asked for a chaplain to stay with me. In a moment when I thought I would take my last breath, I asked God to let my old boyfriend, the love of my life know how much I truly loved him. My relationship has grown with him and it is by a miracle of God that he was placed back into my life. He came to me at a time when I needed him most, and I him. It was God's way of protecting me from the hurt of an unfaithful husband. With God's grace, I am now married to the love of my life.

**Wright**

What is your personal philosophy about success?

**Williams**

Well, I believe that success is planned. Success is truly planned and people who plan their lives have multiple plans. It's not just one plan because you know as I've indicated things sometimes don't always go the way we think. But if you have an overall vision for your own personal success, and then you have multiple approaches or multiple plans, most of them written down or at least in a framework, when things happen and all of a sudden you're not in a position to follow that initial path, you're able to move into something else that's still going to eventually get you there. Obstacles that come along the way should be viewed as just those kinds of challenges that are temporary, that can be overcome with just re-orchestrating a plan and finding out another way to get around them. Learn from them. Use what was either painful or a key learning to continue to reach your vision. I really believe that planning is the key to success and having those multiple plans and a personal vision really makes a difference. Using the resources around you, recognizing opportunities, and taking feedback from trusted mentors can help keep you on target. Having the support of family and true friends is equally important.

**Wright**

Well, what an interesting conversation. I really appreciate you taking this much time today, Devona, to discuss these tough questions with me, and I'm sure that our readers are going to be inspired by the obstacles that you've overcome.

**Williams**

Well, thank you very much. It's been a pleasure to talk with you today.

**Wright**

Today we've been talking to Devona Williams. She is President and CEO of a consulting and training company she founded. She has contributed her talents to helping thousands of people, individuals, and organizations increase their effectiveness. And as we have found out today, she's a woman to be reckoned with and one that's been there, done that. Devona, again, thank you so much for being with us on *Remarkable Women*.

## About The Author

Devona Williams is an accomplished inspirational speaker, trainer and consultant with nearly thirty years experience in the fields of public policy, planning and public relations with the corporate, government, and non profit sectors. Devona has had her equal share of obstacles in her career and personal challenges that she has overcome including a sexual assault and divorce after a lengthy marriage. For most people, these obstacles and challenges would have ended a career and certainly a business. Devona has a unique personal philosophy, strength and faith that have allowed her to persevere and continue to prosper and grow. As President and CEO of her company, she has contributed her talents to helping more than 20000 individuals and organizations increase their own effectiveness. Devona can inspire and motivate your organization by sharing her secrets of success!

**Devona E. G. Williams, Ph.D.**

President/CEO Goeins-Williams Associates, Inc.

Consulting, Training & Speaking

Phone: 302.655.4404

Phone: 1.877.3DEVOGO

www.goeinswilliams.com

# *Chapter 23*

## CYNTHIA M. CUEVAS, CLC, CPM

### THE INTERVIEW

**David E. Wright (Wright)**

Today, we are talking to Cynthia M. Cuevas. Cynthia is a professional living life on the offensive. A public speaker for many years she has used every experience personal and professional to gain wisdom and success using them to their optimum. She is a motivational speaker with a message for everyone. Some of her mottos are "Uncertainty can be certain when realized, " and "The sting of surprise's remedy is preparation." Her personal life has been marked by a physical death comeback that is genuine and triumphant. Crisis can make a difference. It can be for the good depending upon vision and skills, practiced to minimize the sting of error, disappointment and the unexpected. Her career has been successful, being the only woman in a predominately male team. She has methodically designed a program to capture the essence of realism to life's challenges. Communication in uncertain times is a topic for today's individual, whether youth to senior, helping you to make critical choices, and realize confidence in ever changing times. Cynthia is a woman of faith a mother of five, professional project manager for E-911 technologies, and lives in Orange County, California. Cynthia, welcome to *Remarkable Women!*

**Cynthia M. Cuevas (Cuevas)**

Thank you very much David.

**Wright**

What makes you a remarkable woman?

**Cuevas**

That's a great question. Going back fifteen years ago, I was a successful Director of Marketing for a computer company. I was married and a mother of five. I never expected that on the morning of November 16th , 1989 after dropping off my children to school I came home to my husband, at that time, who just psyched out and he strangled me with an electrical extension cord and he left me for dead. So in the process of having a physical death then coming back to life, I really learned to live my life according to the word of my faith, we are more than conquerors through Him who loved us. Struggling, I was left with no money, five children, and had lost my job at the time due to some absences in the hospital and living in a shelter for my protection. I had to work three jobs to feed my children. As a result of that, and what took place in that one year, in an uncertain time, in a uncertain place that I developed, "How to have certainty in an uncertain time."

**Wright**

Define certainty for us, in a world filled with uncertainties.

**Cuevas**

I define certainty by first defining my vision statements. The first one is, "Uncertainty can be certain when realized, and second "The sting of surprise's remedy is preparation. The kinds of experiences we go through can cause a tailspin if we're not prepared. For example, how do we prepare for life's experience getting laid off, stress on the job, divorce, life as a single parent, being a grandparent and raising a grandchild because of a death of a loved one and so on. Preparation is mandatory, training of the mind is essential, and change of a pity party/blame game attitude, critical. Example being, how does anyone get a job except by preparation and interview and presentation? How do we as people who have experienced the horror of 9/11 prepare against another attack? How do we prepare for an earthquake? Certainty is having a system of how to think, seek out resources, and take action that gives you confidence in confusing times.

**Wright**

Could you explain how we can have certainty and confidence in confusing times?

**Cuevas**

More than ever, as you can tell, we live in these turbulent confusing times. We see it everywhere. Technology has made our society move faster than any other era. In the fifties, sixties, seventies to the present and we see vast amounts of money being spent on government programs, although we fortunately see the economy coming on the rise, these changes have caused us to live as fast as we can, hoping not to lose out on anything. Some have the attitude of mind that we are just barely living to get by, but I really believe not so, certainly because, certainty is the highest valued commodity in life. So I have designed a system whereby attitude becomes vision, situation yields the plan, the preparation begets conquests. When you define your highest valued commodity, life is lived to the fullest. A highest valued commodity is, an advantage or benefit. It can be used or traded away. It requires skills to keep it. When you identify what is your personal highest valued commodity, your family's highest valued commodity and apply it to real life experiences like your job, relationships, quality of life, you can then create certainty in your life.

**Wright**

What about when life seems to be a crisis at home or on the job?

**Cuevas**

Well, if you stop and think about life, its living experiences moment to moment isn't it? I have lived through many crises, but I bet you have too, right David?

**Wright**

Right.

**Cuevas**

For example, what would you have said about my crisis? Some would say poor thing, that's so sad, unbelievable, and you'd be right. But we have a great gift to acquire, which is the highest valued commodity and that's "CHOICE." I used to ask myself, what made the difference between myself and the women living in the shelter? Some still live in shelters and I don't. Why? Because I know with certainty that one of my highest valued commodities is living life and the choice to live it.

**Wright**

Who and when can we have certainty?

**Cuevas**

Everyone can have and live in certainty when they define their highest valued commodities, and systematically train their attitude, developing vision, evaluating situations, creating the plan and preparing to succeed to conquest. Another highest valued commodity, for example is communication through which confidence is gained.

**Wright**

Could you tell our readers a little more about your principles for communication in uncertain times?

**Cuevas**

One of the principles I believe in, is empathy. It's the ability with practice to put you inside a persons experiences. There are many ways to get there. It could be with asking questions, and you know many people don't really know how to ask questions. Like how can I support you? Do you need me to problem solve? Can I be a team partner for you? Another principle is honesty. Communicating the truth with simplicity can never be negated. It is necessary for yourself more so than the other person you're speaking to because it alleviates tension, and creates confidence within you. A third principle is confrontation. I can't tell you, David, how many people who I've spoken with, who say these words to me, "I don't do well with confrontation" and completely cut off communication. There are times when there must be confrontation. Learning how to confront in a diplomatic way affords you to take control and yet act as an ambassador to solving the problem.

**Wright**

Could you explain the skills learned to bring stability to life situations?

**Cuevas**

Assessment is one skill learned. It means taking into consideration whether this is your problem or someone else's. Often times we get involved in situations that are not our concern. One of the questions that needs to be asked is "How does this impact me?" My attitude, vision, plan and preparation to get what I want. If it has no impact to get your conquest, then it was a waste of time and entangles you weaving a web of complications. Another skill is offensive action. My, *"Offensive Activities Training"* is a strategy. This strategy works great when learning how to create, avoid or change a situation. It's the difference between becoming competitive or being left behind. It's the puzzle piece that is the plan to your conquest. Another skill that I really love, and this is my favorite, is "Sshhh". Sounds rather odd, right? "*Sshhh Training*" is learning the skills, of how to find balance, perspective and peace, by taking time out. A Shalom greeting means health, wealth, peace and prosperity. This is probably one of the most important skills you'll ever learn; it's what I call the, "Golden Nugget."

**Wright**

Who can use these skills? What age people?

**Cuevas**

Well, everyone can. Let me explain how I use these skills on my children and how they really learned some valuable things. My children would get into these fights as kids usually get into, right? And you know the kinds of fights like sharing a room. One of them was messy and the other was meticulous. The one who was meticulous woke up looking at the other's mess. The messy one woke up to complete order. I taught them that they were to accept each other's gripes and they were to look at each other, each eye to eye speaking to the other their own gripe, and the only thing they could respond was, "Thank you very much for letting me know how you feel." The other took their turn, then each was to ask for each other's forgiveness, with each taking turns to acknowledge, yes, I forgive you. Then they were to hug and kiss. Neither could bring up the issue again, and I can tell you for years our household's highest valued commodity was peace. Each child gained confidence. They could say what they meant with ease and attention. Also, they learned how to communicate honestly. They learned how to assess the consequences that I as a parent could have enforced, and I can tell you that by the time they hit thirteen years old, all I had to say was, "Do I need to have you both communicate." I remember to this day seeing two teens automatically taking action.

**Wright**

I've got a fifteen year old daughter who will be sixteen Monday, I may try that myself. How does learning and using these skills benefit others and us?

**Cuevas**

The benefit of acquiring the new skills is that it could be applied when communicating, with your mother, your father, your in-laws, (sometimes that may be very difficult), your boss, and the list goes on David. Learning my system and going through my "*Destiny Driven Planning,*" training will bring increased self-esteem, confidence and bring more satisfaction to living life.

**Wright**

What value does communication in uncertain times offer?

**Cuevas**

It's time that people identify what is of value. What are the values to themselves and their relationships to society? If you were the only person on this earth, it might be stated that you might be lonely, right?

So, why is it that people are always thinking companionship and then only retreating from each other when situations arise that are uncomfortable? The value offered here is a systematic training to get what you want, by assessing what you think you want, defining what you think you want and then creating an offensive plan to achieve getting what you want and ultimately living life as a conquest.

**Wright**

When will our quality of life be realized?

**Cuevas**

When you are acutely aware of who you are, that is the highest valued commodity. In the training sessions you'll learn about the Pewter Attitudes, The Bronze Vision and The Silver Plan, preparing you for the Golden Conquest. Every time you achieve identifying a highest valued commodity, you win. Doesn't that sound great David?

**Wright**

Sounds great! So, what is the most important certainty that you want others to know?

**Cuevas**

Well, the most important certainty that I want you to know and everyone else is that we were destined to be a conqueror.

**Wright**

Well, what an interesting conversation. There is so much more that I would like to learn from you, like what in the world did you do after your husband tried to strangle you, my goodness, then raising that many children, that must have been something.

**Cuevas**

It was definitely a challenge and I'll tell you that's what spurred me on to developing this because, as I said earlier with regards to what's the difference between myself and that woman who's in the shelter, it's all about understanding what it is that you want and what you need to do in an uncertain time and just having the confidence to be able to move forward. It was just really a very unfortunate situation at the same time it was very fortunate for me because I have an opportunity to be able to share that with other people.

**Wright**

Before the tragedy on November 16, 1989, were you the same kind of person that you are now?

**Cuevas**

Oh, no! I was a very aggressive woman. I'm sure there were people who thought I was pushy, bold and rude. You know, we women tend to, if we don't get our way, have two things that we do. We either cry on demand or we aggressively try to beat down the door, and I found that I tried to make my life one that I could have control over and yet when the situation happened I found obviously that there are some things that you just don't have control over. There are those uncertain times that come up that we need to just really turn over our life and have faith and understanding that God cares about our life and through faith, He said that we're more than conquerors because He loves us.

**Wright**

Well, speaking from a man's point of view we can handle it when you knock down the doors aggressively, but the crying is just not fair. We can't handle the crying.

**Cuevas**

Well, as you can tell being a only woman of a twelve man team and working in a demanding field of technology and my being the project manager over these projects its important really as a woman to know how to communicate effectively with a man and how to help men understand what the objective is and how to get it accomplished as well.

**Wright**

You reminded me when my first two children who are now forty-three and forty-one as they were growing up, I taught them transactaul analysis as a great communication tool and it has lasted until this very day as a matter of fact, and I get a lot of straight talk out of both of them and we communicate very well together. So since that time, how have the children come out? Have they handled the problem that you had on the $16^{th}$ fairly well?

**Cuevas**

Yes, absolutely! They benefited by what I have implemented in our family such as, realizing what is the highest valued commodity, and at that time was peace. Because you know in a chaotic situation, especially in a crisis you can often times get into a tailspin. How that's been translated now is that the three daughters that were home at the time, they're now married. They have their own children. They're professional women, their very successful. They are demure women, which means that they are not aggressive. They have extremely well social skills, and they can communicate effectively.

**Wright**

Well, that's great.

**Cuevas**

And they also have identified what are their highest valued commodities in their own family system.

**Wright**

Well, that is wonderful! What an interesting conversation. I really appreciate you taking all of this time with me this afternoon to answer all of these questions, and I have certainly learned a lot. I'm going to think a lot about what you said.

**Cuevas**

Great David, I'm so happy, because one of the things of my interest particularly is for men. The fact is that you men have to live with us women. And more than ever before we have to just really be in partnership because, I really believe that the husband is the leader of the household and if a man wants to live a life of integrity, it would probably benefit him to understand the language of what is the highest valued commodity in their personal life, their work life and how they communicate with their family as well.

**Wright**

Well, I think it would be so nice if the two genders did understand each other, and some things are unfortunate. I'm going to ask God when I get there, after I die, why in the world would he give you guys all of the intuition in the world and me none. You know that's just not fair. Anyway, today we have been talking to Cynthia M. Cuevas, she is a professional, living life on the offensive as we have found out today. Moving from tragedy to triumph it sounds like to me. Her career has been successful, as she has said being the only woman on a predominately male team, she has methodically designed a program to capture the essence of realism to life's challenges. And Cynthia, thank you so much for making us aware of these principles and being so up front about it. Thank you so much for being with us today on *Remarkable Women.*

**Cuevas**

It's been my pleasure, and I really look forward to speaking with you in the future and speaking to anyone else who really would like to find out and define what their highest valued commodity in life is, because I truly believe, with all the certainty within me, that you and everyone else were born to be conquerors.

## About The Author

Refreshing and inspirational woman, Cynthia is ahead of life's challenges. By her testimony of death to life experience, you will be influenced to overcome your own barriers of the mind.

Her "Highest Valued Commodities and Strategies" are powerful and respected throughout the professional and spiritual circuit. This is a message that can be understood by all ages and gender.

Cynthia and her husband live in the Orange County area where they both enjoy the fruits of their experiences team speaking and consulting.

Cynthia's other topics include: Be His Bride Before Your Anyone Else's and I Danced With The Groom, and Youth Making Critical Choices.

**Cynthia M. Cuevas, CLC, CPM**

Phone: 888.446.1343

Email: cctrains@adelphia.net